Milligan's Meaning of Life

Milligan's Meaning of Life

An Autobiography of Sorts

SPIKE MILLIGAN
Edited by Norma Farnes

VIKING
an imprint of
PENGUIN BOOKS

VIKING

Published by the Penguin Group

Penguin Books Ltd, 80 Strand, London WC2R 0RL, England

Penguin Group (USA) Inc., 375 Hudson Street, New York, New York 10014, USA

Penguin Group (Canada), 90 Eglinton Avenue East, Suite 700, Toronto, Ontario, Canada M4P 2Y3
(a division of Pearson Penguin Canada Inc.)

Penguin Ireland, 25 St Stephen's Green, Dublin 2, Ireland (a division of Penguin Books Ltd)

Penguin Group (Australia), 250 Camberwell Road, Camberwell, Victoria 3124, Australia
(a division of Pearson Australia Group Pty Ltd)

Penguin Books India Pvt Ltd, 11 Community Centre, Panchsheel Park, New Delhi – 110 017, India

Penguin Group (NZ), 67 Apollo Drive, Rosedale, Auckland 0632, New Zealand
(a division of Pearson New Zealand Ltd)

Penguin Books (South Africa) (Pty) Ltd, 24 Sturdee Avenue, Rosebank,
Johannesburg 2196, South Africa

Penguin Books Ltd, Registered Offices: 80 Strand, London WC2R 0RL, England

www.penguin.com

First published 2011

1

Set in Minion Pro 12/14.75 pt
Typeset by Palimpsest Book Production Limited, Falkirk, Stirlingshire
Printed in Great Britain by Clays Ltd, St Ives plc

A CIP catalogue record for this book is available from the British Library

HARDBACK ISBN: 978-0-670-92076-1
TRADE PAPERBACK ISBN: 978-0-670-92077-8

www.greenpenguin.co.uk

This book is dedicated to
Bill Kenwright,
a piece of gold in showbusiness*

* Borrowed from Spike

Contents

Acknowledgements

I wish to thank Will Hammond, my editor, aka Billy Liar, for his tremendous help and advice and that wonderful sense of humour. (Spike would have liked him.)

Eric Sykes for his support.

Niki Charlton, who believes in me and thinks I can do no wrong.

Mary (from the dairy) Kalemkarian for all her encouragement.

Jack Clarke, my old man, who puts up with me.

Lastly, that very special lady Janet Spearman, who organizes my life, for her undying loyalty.

Introduction

'A sort of autobiography.' Yes, Spike would have liked that. I can hear him saying, 'Yes, well, I suppose I've had a sort of life.' The concept of this book was to tell Spike's life story through his writings, using extracts not just from his many memoirs, scripts, sketches and works of fiction but incorporating letters that he wrote to the world, complaining or campaigning about his many causes, and his poetry, which in many cases shows a different side of the man. His many followers will, no doubt, find gaps, but it wasn't my intention to give a complete account – rather, an impressionistic journey. I did my best, but as Spike used to say to me: 'That's what worries me.'

Spike was born into a loving, wonderfully eccentric family. His grandfather, Sergeant Trumpeter Kettleband, fought in the Boer War and was awarded the South African medal with Johannesburg Orange Free State Cape Colony clasp as well as a long service medal. Spike was proud of his military background and told anybody who would listen that he came from a long line of 'military men'.

His father, Leo Alphonso, was an original, extremely talented Irish romantic. His parents had chosen the name Percy Marmaduke for him, but just before the baptism at Sligo Cathedral the priest said, 'Why not name him after the dear Pope?' And so it was. His mother, equally talented, was a strong-willed, powerful woman. The first time I met Grandma Milligan I remarked to Spike, 'If you had a vision of one woman that built the British Empire it would be your mother.'

Spike inherited their talent and more. Author of over eighty books, a musician who played four instruments professionally, a scriptwriter of twelve television series and, memorably, of radio's *The Goon Show*. An artist of many paintings, he had his own exhibition at the Whitechapel Gallery. One of his paintings was hung in a summer exhibition at the Royal Academy. Illustrator – well, not really. A cartoonist – not really! A quirky drawer? Yes! His drawings have been turned into greetings cards that have sold over one and a quarter million, calendars and also a line of stationery.

The man with all this talent was a very complex character; mean, generous, lovable, hateful, kind, hurtful, calm, mercurial, and all on the same day. He was anti-violence, yet he shot a boy in his garden. An explanation? Vandals had damaged his garden quite considerably on several occasions. Each time, Spike telephoned the police to make a complaint and have it logged. Finally the vandals did unspeakable things in his daughter Jane's Wendy house. That was it. According to Spike the police did nothing, so he decided he would catch the offenders. He did, and with his air rifle shot the boy in the shoulder. This from a man who was anti-violence. The case went to court. I offered to get him a good barrister. 'No thank you, I'll defend myself.' I thought, 'God help us all.' But the magistrate at Highgate Crown Court lived in the area, was aware of the vandalism and Spike was given a twelve-month conditional discharge. The luck of the Irish!

Spike had been in court before. It was 1937. He was desperate for money to buy a new trumpet. He was working for the Spiers & Pond tobacco company in the stockroom, packing cigarettes for delivery to local shops. He figured no one would miss a few packs, so he loaded them into his overcoat pockets. Now the new trumpet was in sight, but what was also in sight was the senior stockman, Mr Ripler, and his sidekick, Mr Leighy, who caught Spike in the act. Another trip to the local court, but this time he was to be defended by a romantic, theatrical Irishman who had kissed the Blarney Stone. His father!

Leo spent several days rehearsing at home the defence he would deliver for his unfortunate son. 'Look at him, a young lad. His crime was his love of music. He needed the money to buy a violin and study classical music, but he was so poor he could never – you hear, N-E-V-E-R – afford one. His only way was to pilfer stockroom goods and sell them. This has afforded him a second-hand violin, which even now he is learning to play. Have pity on this boy because, as a result of this action, he could become a virtuoso!' He did, on the trumpet, playing in the Harlem Club Band in Lewisham, and the case was dismissed. Yet again, the luck of the Irish!

Like father like son. Spike was amoral. He would tell you a story you knew wasn't the truth, and when you questioned him he would say, 'There, but it made you laugh, didn't it?' This all stems from the first lie his father told him, when Spike was eight years old. His father was relating a story to him of how he had shot a tiger. Spike said to him, 'Father, that's a lie,' to which his father replied, 'Now, son, would you rather have an exciting lie or the boring truth?' And so it was for the rest of Spike's life. By the way, he repeated that story all his life.

The 1970s and 1980s was Spike's prolific period: his television shows and his books; a tireless campaigner to save the planet and for animal rights. But it was in the early 1970s that he also fell in love with pantomime. Up until this time he had only performed *Treasure Island*, as a pantomime at the Mermaid Theatre. He had a ball. He turned his dressing room into a cave and filled it with 'treasure', including hundreds of gold coin chocolates. He invited children backstage to 'enter the treasure cave'. He loved it. The rest of the cast thought it was a nightmare, dozens of little horrors running around backstage. And so it was 'Get me a pantomime for next year!' for many, many years.

Then, suddenly, 'I'm not doing any more pantos. I *can't* do thirteen performances a week. What do you think I am? You are killing me!' So for a couple of years I stopped killing him – until . . . 'Everyone is working at Christmas. You never get me a pantomime. You are keeping me unemployed!' And so the killing game started once more, and continued until 1989, when he appeared in *Snow White* at the Assembly Hall, Tunbridge Wells, an hour's drive from his home in Rye. (His love of panto didn't stop his 'conditions', and one condition was, 'If I'm going to do thirteen performances a week, I need to get home every night and sleep in my own bed.')

In the early 1990s Spike's health started to deteriorate. I had already completed negotiations for the 1990 pantomime, posters had been printed, contracts signed and exchanged, but he became ill, and it had to be cancelled. This was a severe 'black dog'. His mother had died on 3 July 1990. It left him devastated. He had been depressed before her death; not getting out of bed, totally lacklustre in his voice. It was as though all the emotion had been sucked out of him, and for the first time in about twenty years he asked for ECT (electro-convulsive therapy). I begged him not to have it. 'Please, Spike, it's not good for you. It fries your brain.' He wouldn't listen. He became obsessed with having it, and in October 1990 he went into the Godden Green Clinic and had ECT for the last time. Later he confessed to me that he knew it was damaging but it was the only thing that got him out of the depths that he was in. 'Norm,' he said, 'it's terrible to be your own murderer.' I've never forgotten that despairing look in his eyes as he said it.

In 1993 he had a triple heart bypass that didn't go according to plan. Twelve hours after the operation a valve failed and he had to have a second operation. Two doses of anaesthetic left him very weak and his recuperation took many months. He was getting low – not depressed but low because the recuperation wasn't quick enough for him. I was desperate for him to continue his writing and encouraged him to write some poetry. He wasn't having any of it and became quite grumpy, and I told him so. Then what a put-down: 'I'm not grumpy, I'm going to rewrite the Bible.'

'Of course you are, Spike, just get on with it.' I thought it was a joke.

But that year saw the publication of *The Bible According to Spike Milligan*, and several classics followed which became the 'According to' series. Even so, 1993 was a depressing time for him. In November that year his two great friends Jack Hobbs and Alan Clare died within a week of each other.

The next year, 1994, was a better one for him, and as it drew to a close the spark was ignited again when he was given a Lifetime Achievement Award at the British Comedy Awards. Over the years different versions have been recounted of what happened that night. I was there, so let me put the record straight. Prince

Charles had sent a tribute to be read out at the ceremony. It did go on a bit, and Spike became impatient. He interrupted the reading with 'The grovelling little bastard.' The whole room erupted with laughter.

The next day Spike and I were laughing about it when he said, 'I'll send him a telegram.' It read: 'I suppose now a knighthood is out of the question.' Prince Charles's equerry rang that afternoon to say they had been watching it together and it was one of the funniest things they had seen. The true version, folks.

That same year, I got a call from a dear friend of mine, Malcolm Morris, who was a producer and director of *This Is Your Life* for over twenty-five years. He rang me to arrange a dinner. 'It's part business, but please bring Jack [my partner], and we'll have food, wine, nostalgia and a few laughs along the way.' Jack and Malcolm had worked together for many years at Tyne Tees Television. Of course, it was to tell me he wanted to do a second *This Is Your Life* on Spike. He had already done one in 1973, and he thought Milligan warranted another. I was delighted and promised to give him all the help he needed, but there was one condition: he must invite Toni Pontani from Rome to be on the show.

I told him the story of Spike and Toni, whom he had met and fallen in love with in Italy in 1944, so it was Malcolm's turn to be delighted. When Toni appeared I don't think I'd ever seen Spike so stunned and lost for words. Did I really write that? Spike Milligan lost for words! Well, he was when, on 24 January 1995, Michael Aspel announced 'Toni Pontani'.

Several years later, in 1999, I went down to Rye, where Spike was living, to show him the cover of *Spike Milligan: The Family Album*. We were discussing some of the photographs he had chosen for the book. He stopped talking, looked up from a photograph and said, 'Toni was the love of my life.' She hadn't been mentioned. We hadn't even been talking about the army or Italy. It came from his soul unaided.

The Eurostar was a bonus for Spike. Although Toni lived in Rome, her daughter lived in Paris. Until two years before he died he would take the Eurostar to Paris to have lunch with Toni, whenever she was visiting. I don't know why but it always made me smile when he told me he was having lunch with her in Paris. I'm smiling now as I write this.

For me 1998 was possibly the last year that he had that wonderful sparkle. After nagging 'Can we have a poetry book?' for months, he rang me to say he had finished it. He hadn't bothered to tell me he had started one in the first place! It was *A Mad Medley of Milligan*. 'Why didn't you tell me you had started a poetry book?' I asked. He said, 'You like to nag, so I thought I'd let you get on with it.' Spike at his best.

Spike loved to tell everyone he was Irish. He wasn't and had never lived there, but he loved the Irish and wanted to be one of them. So to him he was Irish. So when I suggested to him it was time he returned to Dublin with his one-man show, it was the best idea I'd ever had! When I suggested the Gaiety Theatre: 'You really are my sunshine girl.'

On 14 June 1998 he performed at the Gaiety to a sell-out. He pulled out all the stops; he was at his best. The standing ovation lasted for what seemed forever, and they wouldn't let him leave the stage. He knew he had 'gone okay' – his comment when he had been a great success. I had arranged dinner after the show. Everyone was in high spirits – although only Champagne and wine were consumed. Jack said he had never seen Spike so happy. Spike's reply: 'Oh Jack, it's because I've come home!'

I thought his performance there was worthy of a night at the London Palladium and arranged one for 20 December 1998, but a very different Spike appeared at the theatre. He looked tired, but I wasn't too concerned because, after years of experience, I knew when he went on stage the tiredness would disappear and he would deliver. He did – but it wasn't the anarchic, cheeky, mischievous Milligan. I stood in the wings and watched. A sadness came over me. I knew it was the beginning of the end of his one-man shows.

He did, in fact, perform again – at Hull and Chichester – reading his poetry and telling anecdotes. But his timing had gone. On reflection I should never have arranged these performances. He persuaded me he could do it. I shouldn't have listened.

Again he turned to his writing. The result: *A Children's Treasury of Milligan*, a compilation of his wonderful poetry for children and one of his most successful poetry books.

I forgot to mention, in 1999 he was voted funniest person of the millennium in a BBC News online survey. And in 2000 his poem 'On the Ning Nang Nong' was voted the Nation's Favourite Poem. In September 2000 the BBC released Volume 19 of the *Goon Shows* on CD, and still the same reaction from Spike: 'When I die they'll say, "He wrote the *Goon Shows* and died!"' How many times did I hear that. (To date the BBC have released nine more volumes. Currently I'm working on Volume 29 and the fifth compilation.)

But that month Spike was admitted to the Conquest Hospital in Hastings. He had developed septicaemia after some injections, and went in as an emergency patient. Jack and I visited him on 23 September. He looked frail and tired, but as Jack I were leaving he got hold of my hand and said, 'Norm, remember, life is one long hell. I know you won't, but don't let the bastards grind you down.' Jack looked at me and said, 'His fighting spirit is still there,' and I was happy to leave him knowing Jack was right. As I kissed him goodbye he said very quietly, 'Norm, look after Eric. He's very special.' I thought it must have occurred to him he was not going to see Eric Sykes again. A friendship that had lasted nearly sixty years.

A sad year for Spike was 2001. 'My mate' Harry Secombe died, and it broke his heart. He was too ill to attend the memorial service for Harry, which took place on 26 October 2001 in Westminster Abbey. He sent his tribute: 'Harry was the sweetness of Wales.'

Four months later, on 26 February 2002, he joined his mates Pete and Harry. I remember Eric writing, 'On 26 February 2002 one of the jewels fell from the comedy crown. It was the day Spike Milligan, with whom I'd shared an office for over fifty years, passed away. I use the phrase "passed away", for that is exactly what he did. Spike will never die in the hearts of millions of us who were uplifted by his works. For me and Norma, his manager, he still prowls the building in unguarded moments. He will always be welcome. As

Hattie was my sister, so he was my brother. Rest in peace, Spike, and say hello to Peter and Harry.'

I wonder if they are causing havoc up there, with Pete, as always, asking Spike to write another *Goon Show* 'just so we can have some laughs'.

I would like to think so.

Norma Farnes
May 2011

I am the pen,
  without me this paper
  cannot live.

– Open Heart University

'It's a small world,' he said.
  'Yes, I nearly fell off.'

– 'Spike on Spike', *Memories of Milligan*

1
Beginnings

My father had a profound influence on me – he was a lunatic.

– 'Spike on Spike', *Memories of Milligan*

Spike's mother, Florence Mary Winifred Kettleband, was born in Woolwich in 1893. Her father, Alfred, had been born in Agra, India, and enlisted as a boy soldier in the Royal Artillery. Her mother, Margaret, had been born at Gosport, England, the daughter of a Regimental Sergeant Major in the Royal Artillery. The family were interested in music, theatre and music hall, so it followed that they visited Woolwich Empire to see Alfred's favourite acts, G. H. Elliott, Eugene Stratton and Dan Leno. At the end of the Boer War, Alfred was sent to a military depot in Ahmednagar, India, where Florence and Margaret joined him. In 1903 they moved to Alfred's new posting in Kirkee.

Spike's father, Leo Alphonso, was born in Sligo, Ireland, in 1890. Leo's father William was also in the Royal Artillery. In 1896 the family moved to Poplar, London. William was captivated by the theatre and got an evening job as a stage hand at the Poplar Hippodrome, which led to his appearing as an extra, eventually taking on major roles at the Queen's Theatre in Poplar. He enrolled Leo into the Steadman School of Dancing and encouraged him to play the trumpet. He then forced him to join the army as a boy soldier in 1904, enlisting him in the Royal Artillery at Shrapnel Barracks, Woolwich. In 1906, Leo was promoted to trumpeter and took part in army concerts, dancing and singing, and became a champion at the soft-shoe shuffle. He adopted the stage name Leo Gann after he had won several talent contests. On 14 December 1911 he sailed on the SS *Plassey*, having been posted to India. He arrived in Bombay and travelled to Kirkee.

So Kirkee became the meeting point for Spike's parents. There Florence and Leo fell in love, eloped and were married by registrar in Room 13 of the Poona Hotel. Florence's family were appalled, and when Leo returned from Mesopotamia a year later they insisted on a church wedding at St Patrick's Church in Poona. This took place on 19 August 1915. By then Florence had become an accomplished organist and trained contralto. Leo was appearing in army concerts and together they formed a duo entertaining the troops.

In 1917 Leo was posted to Ahmednagar, and there, on 16 April 1918, Florence gave birth to Terence Alan Milligan.

Spike looked back on his boyhood in India with great fondness: 'It was an ideal childhood. I loved the lakes, the beautiful colours and the gentle people.'

It was here, too, that Spike got his taste for the military. Spike loved the army life, as he would, as the fourth generation of Royal Artillery soldiers.

In 1924 Leo Milligan was posted to Rangoon in Burma, and the following year, on 3 December, Spike's brother, Desmond Patrick, was born.

In 1926 Leo gave Spike a birthday present of his first gun-belt, and in 1930, at the age of twelve, Spike started his own 'army'. It consisted of five soldiers: himself, his brother Desmond, Sergeant Taylor's son, the Havaldar's son and their servant's son, whose name, truly, was Hari Krishna. Spike named his army the 'Lamanian Army' and wrote an anthem, 'Fun in the Sun'.

That same year he joined the 14th Machine Gun Company. According to his brother, Spike could dismantle a Vickers .303 machine gun and reassemble it. After practising it a hundred times he drove everybody mad, so to take his mind off the gun his father bought him a banjo, which he practised a hundred times, driving everybody mad. It was the beginning of his love of music.

His 'ideal childhood' continued. Leo gave Spike and Desmond a pair of old muskets, with which they pretended to shoot birds, cats, dogs, lions and tigers. In fact, the whole family were interested in guns: the boys had their muskets, Leo had three or four pistols and Florence had her .44 Winchester rifle. As late as 1967, when Spike visited his parents in Woy Woy, Australia, one of the highlights of his visit was to spend time with his father in his gun room.

from The Bible According to Spike Milligan

The Creation According to the Trade Unions

In the beginning God created the heaven and the earth.
2. And darkness was upon the face of the deep; this was due to a malfunction at Lots Road Power Station.
3. And God said, Let there be light; and there was light, but Eastern Electricity Board said He would have to wait until Thursday to be connected.
4. And God saw the light and it was good; He saw the quarterly bill and that was not good.
5. And God called the light Day, and the darkness He called Night, and so passed His GCSE.
6. And God said, Let there be a firmament and God called the firmament heaven, Freephone 999.
7. And God said, Let the waters be gathered together unto one place, and let the dry land appear, and in London it went on the market at six hundred pounds a square foot.
8. And God said, Let the earth bring forth grass, and the earth brought forth grass and the Rastafarians smoked it.
9. And God said, Let there be lights in heaven to give light to the earth, and it was so, except over England where there was heavy cloud and snow on high ground.
10. And God said, Let the seas bring forth that that hath life, flooding the market with fish fingers, fishburgers and grade-three salmon.

11. And God blessed them, saying, Be fruitful, multiply, and fill the sea, and let fowl multiply on earth where Prince Charles and Prince Philip would shoot them.
12. And God said, Let the earth bring forth cattle and creeping things, and there came cows, and the BBC Board of Governors.
13. And God said, Let us make man in our own image, but woe many came out like *Spitting Image.*
14. And He said, Let man have dominion over fish, fowl, cattle and every creepy thing that creepeth upon the earth.
15. And God said, Behold, I have given you the first of free yielding seed, to you this shall be meat, but to the EC it will be a Beef Mountain.

⌒

from It Ends with Magic

Bombardier Leo Sparrow was a very smart soldier in the Royal Regiment of Artillery. He was also a talented amateur stage performer; he could do the American Negro 'buck and wing' dance, and would black up to do coon songs like 'Lily of Laguna'. He was a good comic and clown and he had a pleasant singing voice. He had joined the Artillery when the family moved from Holborn Street, Sligo, in Ireland, at the time his father Sergeant William Sparrow was posted to Woolwich. Leo wrote in his journal:

My early recollections are of life in London. We settled into a flat in Grosvenor Buildings, 426 Manisty Street, Poplar, overlooking the Blackwall Tunnel, which was just being started. From our second-storey window, we watched the workmen in the street below cooking their eggs and bacon for breakfast on shovels over coke braziers and, from time to time, we would see a man who worked in compressed air conditions being carried on a stretcher from the tunnel to the Poplar Hospital.

By day my father was a gunnery wheelwright instructor at the RA Barracks. He obtained weekend employment as a janitor on the maintenance staff of the Grosvenor Buildings; he also worked part time, hauling up scenery in the flies of the Queen's Palace of Varieties in High Street, Poplar. The stage door was in Manisty Street and we youngsters were intrigued watching the artists arrive and depart in horse-drawn carriages. Such performers as Kate Carney, Marie Lloyd and Esta Stella were favourites, as also were Alec Hurley, Eugene Stratton, Chirgwin the White-eyed Kaffir, Pat Rafferty, Tom Leamore, Bob Hutt and numerous others of that day.

It seems only yesterday that we went to Wade Street School run by headmaster McGynty and, in the evenings, we became lamplighters and galloped up and down the stairs of Grosvenor Buildings with a perforated brass lamplighter igniting the gas jets, as Dad Sparrow turned on the gas in the basement. We used to delight in this job and would race a bloke named Mickey who did the other half. There was a friendly rivalry between us as to who could finish first. We never got paid for this job; I can't remember ever getting a penny.

Despite his extra janitor's wage it was hard going trying to support a family of four unruly Irish boys and their sister; so, Leo, the eldest, now fourteen, was forced by his father to join the Royal Artillery. He was heart-broken, for he had set his heart on being a variety performer. The back door to the Sparrows' family home was dead opposite the stage door of the Queen's Palace of Varieties. At night, arriving in their carriages, young Leo watched the performers adoringly, yearning to be like them. He had a moment of glory when the theatre manager sought out local boys to play the part of 'supers' in some of the visiting acts.

I remember too, our various jobs as supers: one bloke I remember used to sing 'Playing the Game of Soldiers' as we all marched round with our paper hats and toy guns. Then there was Arthur Bright with his 'Susie's Band' when we played the Star Music Hall in Bermondsey, or some such place. We all played old brass instruments. I remember also Kate Carney when we were among her costermongers in 'Liza Johnson, You Are My Donah'. I can also remember playing the lame kid with a crutch with Loonar Mortimer in 'Paying the Penalty'.

But alas, no further; one chill winter's day in 1881 his father took him to the RA enlisting office at Shrapnel Barracks, Number One Depot, Woolwich.

*

Everything was done to a trumpet call. You were awakened by the trumpeter sounding the reveille which was followed by the quarter, and then the five minutes and finally the fall-in. There was the warning for parade ('boots and saddles' as it was called) sounded by the trumpeter half an hour before. There was even a trumpet call to bring up the urine tubs at 0900 hrs.

Despite his yearning for the stage, he became a very good soldier. He passed his Third-Class Certificate of Education, was promoted trumpeter and, though initially frightened of horses, became a first-class horseman specializing in dressage; but all the while he organized entertainment for his comrades and their families. He even got leave from his commanding officer, Major Sheppard, to appear in an amateur talent concert at the Imperial Palace, Canning Town, which he won! On the strength of this he was offered a week's contract to appear for the incredible sum of £5.00. For this he was again given permission by his Officer Commanding. For his appearance on the bill he called himself Leo Gann. 'Sparrow looks too silly,' he said.

From then on, as is usual with the British Army, he was posted to various parts of the British Isles. In time he was promoted to Bombardier, all the while keeping up his troop entertainments. It was in the course of these postings that he arrived at Fermoy in Ulster; there he put on a show at the New Barracks. For one of his song presentations he needed a lady to help, he put up a notice to this effect. It was answered by a Miss Florence Kettleband. Kettleband? What a funny name, he thought. She turned out to be the daughter of Trumpet-Sergeant-Major Alfred Kettleband, who brought his daughter along.

CHILD SONGS

There is a song in man
There is a song in woman
And that is the child's song
When that song comes
There will be no words
Do not ask where they are
Just listen to the song
Listen to it –
Learn it –
It is the greatest song of all.

London
12 April 1973
0200 hours

– from *Open Heart University*

from It Ends with Magic

Now wedding bells! Ex-Trumpet-Sergeant-Major Alfred Kettleband announced that his daughter, Florence Winifred, was to be married to Bombardier Leo Alphonso Sparrow at St John's Church, New Road, Woolwich.* It was a real Artillery wedding with members from Bombardier Sparrow's 76th Battery and from Alfred Kettleband's regiment, 18th Royal Field Artillery. The groom arrived in full dress-uniform, riding on a spit and polished gun-carriage; he stood nervously adjusting his blue Melton jacket with its polished brass buttons and his gold chevron stripes. His best man was his brother, Trooper William Sparrow of the North Irish Horse. Alas, Leo's father Sergeant William Sparrow couldn't attend as he and his battery were stationed in South Africa because the colony was still unsettled, so Leo's mother Elizabeth attended, so they hid all the bottles.

St John's Church (built by Pugin) was packed with relatives, all in their best Sunday clothes – the ladies wearing big, wide-brimmed hats with ostrich feathers and spotted lace veils. Bombardier Sparrow and his best man sat in the front pew nervously awaiting the arrival of the bride; there were hushed whispers and giggles from young girls as the verger lit the long, yellow candles on the main altar. Suddenly, at a signal from Father Rudden, the organist, Miss Eileen Breech, started to pedal the pump organ furiously and play 'The Wedding March'. All the congregation stood up as Florence, on her father's arm, came slowly down the aisle. She was in a stunning white satin and silk gown, and he wasn't; over her head was a white veil held in place by a crown of small, embroidered wild flowers. Her father was in his service dress, complete with his gold trumpet-major badges, his gold service stripes, along with his medals from the Indian Mutiny; on one was an oak leaf which meant he had been

* The names Leo Alphonso were inflicted on him by the idiot priest who baptized him. His parents had been going to inflict a worse name – Percy Marmaduke – but the idiot priest insisted he be named after the 'dear Pope'.

mentioned in despatches for gallantry.† Bombardier Sparrow arose and took his place beside his bride at the Caen stone altar. They sneaked each other a glance, he smiled, she giggled, putting her hand over her mouth; the Reverend Father Rudden called them forward and commenced the ceremony; in a castrated-adenoidal voice the priest droned on, and the couple made their replies.

'If any man see why they should not be joined in holy matrimony will he now speak or for ever hold his peace.' Whoever it was, didn't speak up and for ever held his peace. The ring: the best man handed it over, the bridegroom dropped it, it bounced across the floor down a heating grille. There followed the small ceremony of lifting up half a ton of iron grille and rupture; lots of giggling accompanied the efforts. Finally, the ring in place, and 'I pronounce you and the heating system man and wife,' Leo kissed his wife through her veil, bringing it back on his teeth.

The reception was held in the Sergeants' Mess at Woolwich Garrison Headquarters (why are there never any Hindquarters?). Army trestle tables covered in clean, white cloths were laid out for the thirty guests, with gunner mess waiters in attendance. It was a plain but wholesome meal: roast beef, Yorkshire pudding, roast potatoes and Brussels sprouts; followed by a Mrs Beeton-style trifle nearly a foot high, then the wedding cake with a small icing sugar model of a bride and a gunner bridegroom mounted on the top surrounded by lots of silver cashew nuts.

*

Back in London the newlyweds rented a house at 22 Gabriel Street – a Victorian terraced house in Honor Oak Park, London, SE26. Florence Sparrow kept the little home lovely and clean: the doorstep was always white – the brass knocker and letterbox on the front door were polished every morning with Brasso – the fireplace was black-leaded with Zebo every day and the brass coal scuttle shone like the sun. The lace window curtains were washed once a week with Sunlight soap and rinsed in Reckitts blue.

† In the storming of the Kashmir Gate.

Every morning Mrs Sparrow got up at half past five to stoke up the iron stove in the kitchen and put the big black iron kettle on the hob to boil. In wintertime, when it was a dark morning, she'd light the gas mantle while she cooked Leo Sparrow's breakfast of porridge and toast, and he shaved with his cut-throat razor in the kitchen sink; in those days, there were no bathrooms and the toilet was outside in the garden, so in cold weather nobody stayed in there very long!

Mrs Sparrow was a very good Catholic, so before they ate breakfast she would always say grace. 'Bless us, O Lord, and these Thy gifts, which we are about to receive.'

After breakfast Sparrow would get out of his nightshirt and put on his khaki Royal Artillery uniform. He had two bombardier chevrons in gold braid on each sleeve, a round wheelwright's badge, and shiny brass buttons down the front of his jacket, each button stamped with a cannon. Then he put on his big blue Melton overcoat with a red flannel lining so he was nice and warm and would kiss Florence goodbye. He would walk down the street, to the main road, and catch a horse-drawn tram to Woolwich. He would go upstairs – it was cheaper because it was an open top, if it rained you got wet. Bombardier Sparrow worked as a wheelwright in the farriers' shop at the Woolwich Garrison. His job was to mend gun-carriage wheels – in those days, the guns were towed by six horses, and the streets of London were cobbled – so the wheels used to get lots of wear and tear. Bombardier Sparrow's friend was Bombardier Alan Mills – he was the blacksmith who shoed the horses. Bombardier Sparrow was teaching young recruits how to maintain wheeled vehicles.

In those days the British Army was very big, with regiments and garrisons all around the world – India, Burma, Africa, China, Belize, Malta, Gibraltar, Aden – and soon these young recruits would be posted there. One day Bombardier Sparrow was called in by his Commanding Officer, Major Skipton Climo. 'At ease, Sparrow,' he said as the Bombardier saluted. 'Look, how would you like to go to India?'

'By boat, sir,' he said.

The Major groaned and repeated the question.

Bombardier Sparrow's heart missed a beat – India, he thought,

how marvellous! In his life he'd never been further than Southend. India! He'd never been to an India. Sparrow was lost for
words.

'Well, Sparrow,' said the Major, 'lost yer tongue, man?'

'No, sir, just the words. Yes, I'd love to go to India.'

The Major smiled. 'Good,' he said, 'you'll leave on . . .' he flicked
through his diary 'Ah, here we are, you sail from Tilbury on 14
December, so you've a month to get ready.'

Sparrow saluted, and knocked his hat off.

When Bombardier Sparrow went home that night, it was very,
very foggy; the tram was very, very slow and Bombardier Sparrow,
on the top deck, was freezing.

'My, you're late tonight, Leo,' said Mrs Sparrow. 'I was getting
worried.'

'While you were getting worried, I was getting cold,' he said as
he took his greatcoat off. 'Terrible fog – had a man with a brand
walking in front of the tram half the way.'

Leo opened the stove's fire-box, showing a red glow – he held his
hands in front and rubbed them together. He faced Florence, who
was doing something in the sink. 'How'd you like to go to India,
Kiddy?'

She turned with a bemused smile on her face. 'India,' she said.
'India?'

'India,' he repeated, then told her.

'Well, blow me down,' she said.

Bombardier Sparrow didn't try to blow her down as he knew she
was too heavy. Over their supper of boiled halibut, potatoes and
spinach they talked and planned their new adventure. 'It'll be hot
out there,' said Leo, who right then was cold in here.

So they prepared for their great trip. They stored all their furniture with Florence's brother, Bertram, who owned a warehouse.

'How long are we going to be out there?' said Florence.

Leo shrugged his shoulders. 'I don't know. I'd say about two years,
that's about the normal time – unless you ask to stay longer.'

'We'll have to see if we like it out there.'

The weeks that followed saw the first snow in November. Florence spent the days packing for the trip. At weekends they went and said goodbye to friends and relatives.

'You'll like it in India,' said Alfred Kettleband. 'Nice sunshine but it can get hot.'

Mrs Kettleband poured the tea from the big brown stoneware teapot.

'And you can get servants cheap.'

Mrs Sparrow smiled. 'Servants?' she said. 'What – like to look after things?'

'Oh yes,' said Alfred Kettleband, sipping tea from a moustache cup. 'We had two when I was stationed in Kirkee. Did everything – cooking, washing, stealing.'

'House cleaning as well,' added Mrs Kettleband, handing round the home-made fruit cake.

'Can you trust 'em?' said Bombardier Sparrow.

'Well,' said Mr Kettleband, 'you have to watch 'em.' He emptied his cup into the white slops bowl, then held his cup out.

'A drop more, Mother,' he said.

'Is it expensive out there?' said Florence.

'No. Oh no,' said Mrs Kettleband, 'a lot cheaper.'

'And,' added Alfred Kettleband, 'you'll be getting an overseas allowance.'

At that Bombardier Sparrow laughed. 'Sounds better before we even get there.'

There was a pause in the conversation as Alfred shovelled more coal on the fire; what a pity, setting fire to that lovely coal, he thought. Florence Sparrow admired the coloured tile slips on the burnished iron fireplace, green with white magnolias.

'Mind you, it's not all milk and honey out there,' Alfred was saying. 'You got to look out for mosquitoes, always put yer mossy net up before sunset and,' here he sipped his tea, then squeezed the drops from his moustache back into the cup, 'never drink the milk or water without boiling it.'

Mrs Kettleband chipped in, 'Oh yes, and you must keep food under cover – the flies are terrible.'

The tea finished with the Kettlebands concluding all the remaining advice on India. It was getting dark, Mrs Kettleband lit a taper and ignited the bracket gas lamps each side of the over-mantel mirror as Alfred lowered the wooden slatted blind, then drew the blue velvet curtains. He didn't want people looking in at his moustache.

'Well,' said Bombardier Sparrow, standing up, 'time we were going, Flo.' They entered the brown lino-covered hall with its smell of Mansion polish.

'You need every bit of that,' said Mr Kettleband as he helped his daughter on with her heavy Paisley shawl, while Bombardier Sparrow tightened his web belt and adjusted his pillbox hat at a jaunty angle.

Alfred opened the door on to the cold gaslit street. 'Oh, it's 'taters out there,' he said. Leo looked but couldn't see any potatoes. Alfred Kettleband must be imagining. Bidding their good-nights, the Sparrows left with Florence fastening her bonnet ribbon. As the 74 tram trundled them along, the Sparrows debated what future lay for them in that distant, mysterious land.

The Voyage

Early on 14 December the Sparrows loaded their three suitcases and hand baggage on to a Hackney carriage drawn by a black horse.

'Where to, sir?' said the driver.

'Well,' said Leo, 'eventually India. Right now, Waterloo Station will do.'

'You sure?' said the driver. The Sparrows climbed into the cosy, upholstered, buttoned interior.

Through the roof hatch the driver said, 'What time you got to be there?'

'We have to catch the nine-fifteen boat train to Tilbury.'

The driver shook his reins, cracked his whip and the horse started to trot – down Brockley Rise he trotted past the Brockley Jack – down New Cross past the Marquis of Granby. The morning mixture of horse-drawn and early motor traffic was getting heavier – by the time they drove over Waterloo Bridge the rush hour was at its peak. At Waterloo a policeman was controlling the traffic and his temper. Through the window Bombardier Sparrow saw a porter and called him over; the porter said his name wasn't 'Over', it was Sebastian.

'Which platform, sir?' said Sebastian.

'Tilbury boat train,' said Bombardier Sparrow springing open his fob watch; the Roman numerals on its enamelled face said eight-forty-six. The driver handed down the luggage.

'How much, driver?' said Sparrow.

'Six and threepence, sir.'

Bombardier Sparrow dipped into his pocket and handed the driver two half crowns, a shilling and a threepenny bit. The driver took it, raised his top hat, displacing the hackle which fell into the street.

'You dropped something,' said Bombardier Sparrow grinning and handing it back to him.

'I'm coming to pieces,' laughed the driver. What he meant to say was what about a bloody tip.

'This way,' said Sebastian trundling his iron trolley. 'Mind yer backs,' he shouted, killing people as he went.

The station was crowded with commuters hurrying to work and men from Her Majesty's Services catching the boat train – among them Bombardier Sparrow recognized Bombardier George Millington and his wife, Sophie.

'Hi, George,' called Sparrow.

'Oh, Leo! Don't tell me you're on the same draft!'

'All right,' joked Bombardier Sparrow, 'I won't tell you!'

He turned to Florence. 'Look who's here, Flo,' he said, so she looked who was here. Florence threw her hands up in surprise and caught them as they came down. 'Fancy, you two and your daughter, Saria.' The little girl, all embarrassed, hid behind her mother.

They jostled through the crowd carrying hand luggage with the big P&O labels 'WANTED ON VOYAGE'. They passed through the barrier, the inspector scanned each green ticket, then clipped a 'V' in them with his clippers. At the platform, the Great Southern Railway train stood shining in its green, yellow and black livery.

They searched for the third-class compartment marked 'RESERVED FOR RA PERSONNEL'.

'Here we are,' shouted Bombardier Millington, opening the carriage door. As they entered the carriage with its black leather seats, they felt the warmth of the steam heating coming from under the seats. They piled their luggage on to the racks above.

'Well,' said Bombardier Sparrow, plonking himself down on the seat, 'so far so good.' He loosened his belt and slipped his pillbox hat off.

'Paper – morning paper!' a Cockney news vendor was walking rapidly along the platform.

'Here, son,' shouted Bombardier Millington out the window. 'The *Morning Post*. What would you like, Leo?' he said back through the window.

'Oh, I'll have – I'll have – er – what would you like, Flo?' Flo would like the *Family Herald*.

'The *Family Herald* and *Tit-bits*, son,' said Millington.

With expertise the lad withdrew the two papers from under his arm and with a flick handed them up. 'Oh,' said the lad taking the two-shilling piece, ''aven't you got anything smaller, it's tuppence?'

Millington fingered through the loose change in his hand. 'Here,' he said, 'I've only got a threepenny bit, keep the change.'

The lad did a pretend spit on it. 'Oh, good luck, guvnor,' he said.

As he did a porter ran along the platform slamming the open doors – the guard at the end was looking at his big chrome watch, a green flag in his hand, ready to go.

'We're nearly off,' informed Bombardier Millington.

There followed a shrill whistle from the guard – the carriage lurched forward as the driver eased the throttle forward, the great train, hissing gouts and gushes of steam from its burnished sides, pluming throats of black smoke from its tall brass funnel, eased forward.

'We're on our way,' said Florence with an excited upward inflection; all faces in the carriage were radiant with expectation.

Slowly they pulled from the busy station; the great journey had started.

~

RACHMANINOV'S 3RD PIANO CONCERTO

We are drinking cupped Sonatas like wine,
The red glow, the cut throat of Sunset.
Like a tungsten locked Icarus
I charge my mind with heaven fermented grape
that grow to Caesar's Royal Purple in my brain,
Trim my logic as I may
The tyrant Onos unbraids my thoughts
      like maidens' tresses at eve
I am wafting across mindless heavens
'Where am I,' I ask the Lotus maiden,
She says 'Singapore Air Lines –
      Economy Class'.

– from *Open Heart University*

~

from It Ends with Magic

Voyage of the SS Plassey

On board the SS *Plassey*, Florence kept a diary which her mother and father gave to her as a going-away present; inside they had written 'To our fond daughter, Florence'.

14 December 1885

Boarded SS *Plassey* at Tilbury, lots and lots of noisy soldiers and their wives boarding as well, Leo was glad to see some friends from his battery sailing with us. We have a nice, clean cabin. We are sharing it with Bombardier Bill Eggit and his wife Emily. The women will sleep in the lower bunks and the men in the upper. Our Cabin B111 is one deck below the main deck – it is an outside cabin so we have a porthole. To start with it was very confusing with everyone looking for the right cabin. At six o'clock a man went round shouting 'All visitors ashore', at six-thirty they took in the gang plank, then they let go the hawsers and two black tugs started to push the *Plassey* into midstream. Then the gong went and a steward went round saying, 'First sitting for tea.' That meant us so we eventually found the dining room, it was very crowded. We had bread, butter, apricot jam and tea. Surprise, at our table was George Millington and his wife.

As the night closed in, the *Plassey* moved slowly downstream; past Canvey Island, Southend-on-Sea and Shoeburyness, passengers stood on deck watching the black shapes and lights ashore as they slid past, the ship was vibrating now as the engines went slow ahead, everyone seemed excited at the coming trip. Up on the bridge the Captain, Donald Chaterjack, called, 'Steady as you go'; the leading seaman shouted down the speaking tube to the engine room, 'Steady ahead.'

'Steady ahead it is,' came the reply. At first the ship travelled very smoothly down river, but then it started to roll a little as they reached the open sea.

'We're in the Channel, I think,' said Leo to Flo as he peered down at the black foam-topped waves. It was getting chilly so most people went down to the lounge, which just had long wooden tables with benches, but it was lit by the new electric lights. Some passengers were standing close to them examining the new-fangled bulbs and puzzling out how they worked; some of the men played cards or dominoes, while the women talked or knitted. At eight-thirty the gong went. 'First sitting for dinner,' shouted the steward as he walked briskly around the ship's corridors.

SS *Plassey*   14 *December 1885*

Menu

Potato Soup
and Mutton Stew
Boiled Potatoes
Carrots – Peas
and
Roly Poly Pudding
Tea – Coffee

The sleeping arrangements were pretty hysterical. So that the ladies could prepare themselves for bed, the men had to wait outside in the corridor, looking very silly to passing passengers, to whom Leo said, 'We're – we're waiting, aren't we, Bill?' The man was a fool.

Indeed, when George Millington came by, he said, 'What in God's name are you doing?'

Sure enough, Leo said, 'We're waiting, aren't we, Bill?' The man was a fool.

When the ladies were in their night-clothes the men had to undress. For this they turned the lights off; in the dark there were thuds and groans as the two men collided while taking off their trousers, accompanied by stifled laughs from the ladies. 'Go on, laugh,' said frustrated Leo, and so they went on and laughed. In the middle of the night, when Bombardier Sparrow fell from the top berth, they had another good laugh.

TEETH

English Teeth, English Teeth!
Shining in the sun
A part of British heritage
Aye, each and every one.

English Teeth, Happy Teeth!
Always having fun
Clamping down on bits of fish
And sausages half done.

English Teeth! HEROES' Teeth!
Hear them click! and clack!
Let's sing a song of praise to them –
Three Cheers for the Brown Grey and Black.

– from *Silly Verse for Kids*

from It Ends with Magic

Just then the dark lady arrived with a tray on which was a big, brown Worcester-ware teapot and two of the blue and white teacups. In a silver-plated rack were six slices of hot toast, a pat of butter and another pink pot containing strawberry jam. 'Just the job,' said Leo rubbing his hands together.

'I'll be mother,' said Florence, pouring the tea through a large mesh strainer.

'That must be quite a strain,' said that fool of a man.

'Oh, I forget the milk,' said the dark lady, hurrying off. She returned with a little white fluted milk jug. 'There you are,' she said. 'Anything else,' she said, 'you call me.' What they should call her, she never said. Leo and Florence sipped their tea and talked about their day on the rock.

'How did those monkeys get there?' said Florence.

'Well,' said Leo, 'there's a story that they were brought here when the Moors invaded; then, there's another story, that they came from Africa in a tunnel that runs under the sea and comes out in the big caves in the rock.'

'Big caves?' said Florence.

'Yes, big,' said Leo and for some reason spread his arms. 'There's big caves on the rock, it says here,' and he turned the pages of his P&O guidebook. 'Look,' he said showing a page with illustrations.

'Oh, they do look interesting,' she said.

'Yes, the illustrations look interesting,' he repeated. Why?

Leo there and then decided that the caves would be more interesting than the illustrations. It was the place to visit, Leo said. 'The only way to see them is go there.'

He's getting worse, thought Florence.

They finished up their tea and toast; Leo paid the bill. 'Not bad,' he said, 'one and sixpence.'

Outside they caught another landau. 'Ah, you like the caves,' said the driver. His horse was done up in a straw hat, coloured ribbons, and lots of decorations on his harness. Unlike the last landau, all the brass and harness were brightly polished and the driver wore a crisp, white, well-ironed jacket.

'You have a very smart turnout here,' said Bombardier Sparrow admiringly.

'Yes, I first class,' said the driver with a Spanish accent. 'I like keep my horse and carriage very clean.' At that point, unfortunately, the horse did a steaming wee.

'Oh, dear,' said Leo. 'I'm sorry.'

'Why,' said Flo, '*you're* not doing it.' Leo was embarrassed. That horse! 'The poor thing can't help it,' said Flo.

'Oh, he doesn't need any help, he can do it on his own,' said Leo.

The incident over, the horse plodded on to the great caves. The driver gave them some more information.

'This place first called by Arabs, Djbel Altar, that mean, tall mountain. But now *not* Djbel Altar, G*i*bra*ltar*, English call G*i*-bral-*tar*.' He laughed as though it was a great joke, which, of course, it wasn't – ask any Spaniard.

Arriving at the cave mouth the landau pulled over. 'Shall I wait for you for some anything, you bloody fool?' said the driver raising his top hat and letting out the steam.

Bloody fool? Where did he learn that? He had learned that from soldiers who had told him it meant 'sir'.

'Yes, I think we better keep you,' said Leo.

'Thank you – you bloody fool,' said the driver.

A military guide was at the entrance to the cave, a fellow gunner, it was admission free but, 'If you want a guide,' said the gunner, 'it's sixpence for half an hour.' Actually, the guide was free, but we all have to make a living; all right, they'd have a guide.

'Raymondo,' the gunner called over to three guides sitting on a bench.

One stood up and came across. He smiled and said, 'Yes, I am Raymondo, you bloody fool.' He'd met the soldiers too. He was a small man aged about forty-five with a black moustache hung under his nose like a coat hanger; he wore a Panama with a band that had the letters 'Girl Guide'. Into a long, rocky passage he led them along some duck boards over a deep gorge. 'However did ducks get over these?' said Leo. The inside of the cave was lit by gas with tinfoil reflectors behind each of the quadruple mantles; it cast a fitting, eerie glow. The guide carried a brand which he lit with a box of Captain Webb matches. As they went deeper in, the cave opened out into a huge size with great stalactites hanging from the roof, like stone organ pipes; water dripped slowly from them to the floor.

Raymondo pointed to them. 'It take million years for them to form,' he said. How the hell did he know? He was only forty-five. At one point in the cave he stopped and said 'Listen' and shouted out 'Helloooo . . . !' There was a pause and then his voice echoed back ten times, 'Helloooo . . . helloooo . . . helloooo,' each one getting fainter and fainter. 'You try,' he said. Leo tried and he became fainter and fainter. Florence cupped her hands to her mouth. 'Hellooo!' she said, back came the amazing echo.

'Let me try again,' said Leo; he shouted 'hello', then 'stand easy', then he called his name, his inside leg measurement, a receipt for jelly. Finally, Florence sang a few notes – all came floating back; it was a new experience for them. Deep in the cave they reached a railed-off gallery, from which the great cave descended hundreds of feet into total darkness.

'Here we don't know how deep, people go in there many years ago – never come back.' It was like Brixton. 'Very dangerous, now government say no one allowed.' He held up his lighted brand as the Sparrows peered into the great unknown depths. 'They say,' said Raymondo, 'that through here come the apes from Africa.'

'They must have been trying to avoid customs.'

In half an hour the tour was over; it was cold in there and they were glad to get out into the warm evening sunshine where their landau awaited, albeit with the driver asleep in the back. Leo gave him a light poke in the belly. He stayed asleep, so Leo gave him a heavy poke in the belly, then the knee, then the chest, the buttock, the spine, the pelvis etc. . . . . The man finally screamed.

'Sorry, I asleep. Sun very hot, make you tired,' he said. 'Ayeup-pahh!' he shouted to his horse, cracked his whip vigorously. Suddenly, with a terrible noise, the horse broke wind, reducing Florence and Leo into helpless laughter.

*

5 Climo Road
Old Sappers Lines
Poona
India

May 1892

My dear Mum and Dad,

Well, by now you know that you're both going to become grandparents, I hope you don't mind! I'm now on a sergeant's rhino, so that will help with the extra mouth to feed, though I must say, life out here is so much better than serving in England.* The Indian Army are very lenient about working conditions. I get quite a bit of time off to do gaffs, otherwise we start work at the dufta early mornings while it's cool, then we have the afternoon off when it's hot, then do a few hours in the evening.†

As a sergeant I am allowed a horse and a syce. Every morning my syce, Pushram, brings me my horse Kitty, she is an Australian whaler, a horse they breed in Queensland especially for the Indian Army, so before work I have a lovely gallop to Ganishkind, then ride to the Southern Command Offices where another syce stables my horse. These days we have a most pleasant social life, we have tennis courts, a racecourse, polo, hockey and football matches, hockey seems to be the favourite game among the Indians. The current champions are the Poona Rifles, formed from Anglo-Indians with British Officers. My only sport is boxing where exercise consists of getting your face punched in, then waiting for it to come out again. When I arrived here my fame had gone ahead of me, it must have travelled on a faster boat, yes, they knew I had boxed for the Artillery back in Wonderful Woolwich. Last month they asked me to enter the Southern Command championships where for three months men clout each other and whoever is left alive wins. By ducking frequently I survived

---

* Rhino = Rhinofelt = Gelt.
† Dufta = office.

the preliminaries, then came the semi-finals. This was open to those left alive. Now I weigh ten stone six pounds, I stand five foot eight, my God when my opponent got in the ring he was six foot and weighed thirteen stone. For three rounds I ran backward screaming help, then he caught me with a right cross. When I regained consciousness the lights were out and everybody had gone home. Well that's about all for now.

> *Love to all*
> *Leo*

PS. I'm thinking of becoming a Mason!

'Ah, Mrs Sparrow,' said Doctor Tookram in that sing-song Indian accent, wagging his head like it was on a spring. 'With the baby coming, I am thinking you are too thin with thinness. Oh dear, no, you must building yourself up, now. I am knowing that from what soldiers say that the drinking of the Guinness is good for you, so if you are finding some, you must be taking it into your body, like that!' He charged Florence five rupees. So, for many evenings to come, Florence sat with Leo in front of their house and drank 'the Guinness into your body, like that'. She went on for a month drinking the stuff, she never got any fatter just drunker and drunker as the Guinness 'went into the body like that'.

'Look,' said Leo, 'you'll drown the bloody baby, I can't let you go on, you're becoming an alcoholic.'

'It's all right, dear,' said Florence, staggering naked around the front garden. 'I confessed it to the priest.'

'What does he say?' said Leo.

'He said where can he get it.'

The RAMC doctor, Captain Parkinson, had a different cure for Florence's thinness. 'Arrowroot,' he said. 'Have some at bedtime.' So at night, while Leo sipped his shandy, Florence was eating cold arrowroot. One evening they were visited by friends. It was dark when they arrived. Florence said, 'What would you like?'

They said, 'Oh, whatever you're having', so they had cold arrowroot – they never came again.

⌢

ME

Born screaming small into this world –
Living I am
Occupational therapy twixt birth and death –
What was I before?
What will I be next?
What am I now?
Cruel answer carried in the jesting mind
        of a careless God.
  I will not bend and grovel
  When I die. If He says my sins are myriad
  I will ask why He made me so imperfect
  And he will say 'My chisels were blunt'.
  I will say '*Then why did you make so*
        many of me'.

Bethlehem Hospital
Highgate 1966

– from *Small Dreams of a Scorpion*

BAD REPORT – GOOD MANNERS

My daddy said, 'My son, my son,
This school report is bad.'
I said, 'I did my best I did,
My dad my dad my dad.'
'Explain, my son, my son,' he said,
'Why *bottom* of the class?'
'I stood aside, my dad my dad,
To let the others pass.'

– from *Unspun Socks from a Chicken's Laundry*

THE ABC

T'was midnight in the schoolroom
And every desk was shut,
When suddenly from the alphabet
Was heard a loud 'Tut-tut!'

Said A to B, 'I don't like C;
His manners are a lack.
For all I ever see of C
Is a semi-circular back!'

'I disagree,' said D to B,
'I've never found C so.
From where I stand, he seems to be
An uncompleted O.'

C was vexed, 'I'm much perplexed,
You criticize my shape.
I'm made like that, to help spell Cat
And Cow and Cool and Cape.'

'He's right,' said E; said F, 'Whoopee!'
Said G, ''Ip, 'ip, 'ooray!'
'You're dropping me,' roared H to G.
'Don't do it please I pray!'

'Out of my way,' LL said to K.
'I'll make poor I look ILL.'
To stop this stunt, J stood in front,
And presto! ILL was JILL.

'U know,' said V, 'that W
Is twice the age of me,
For as a Roman V is five
I'm half as young as he.'

X and Y yawned sleepily,
'Look at the time!' they said.
'Let's all get off to beddy byes.'
They did, then, 'Z-z-z.'

or

alternative last verse

X and Y yawned sleepily,
'Look at the time!' they said.
They all jumped in to beddy byes
And the last one in was Z!

– from *Silly Verse for Kids*

from Indefinite Articles and Scunthorpe

Eccentrics

According to Cassell's three-page dictionary for computerized idiots, the word eccentric means: 'Deviating from the centre; an oddity; a mechanical contrivance for converting circular into reciprocating rectilinear motion, especially that operating the side valve of a steam engine.' Having been accused by the Boulting Brothers of being an eccentric, I am puzzled as to why they didn't give me my correct title, i.e. a mechanical contrivance for converting circular into reciprocating etc. etc. etc. . . .

So . . . when Willy Davis said, 'Milligan, kneel down, I the God of *Punch* dub thee Writer, go, write something about Eccentrics,' I began to wonder just why I was one and had never noticed it. I mean, when I read Oliver St John Gogarty's description of a gentleman waiting to cross Sackville Street dressed in a top hat, a football jersey, evening dress jacket, cricket pads, a girdled cavalry sword and holding a red guard's van flag, I thought *that* was an eccentric – but no, apparently nobody even noticed him, so who were the eccentrics – him, or the passing pedestrians? It's difficult to say; however, racing back through my boyhood I realized that my whole family were, as I said, mechanical contrivances for converting circular into etc. etc. . . .

Let's start with my father. For a start I thought every football fan who listened to his team (Arsenal) on the wireless, like my father wore a red and white football jersey, and carried a football rattle and took swigs from a beer bottle. When T V started and he could see the game, he added a referee's whistle. Even on that he had a variant; he would turn off the T V sound, blindfold himself and listen to the radio commentary, every now and then stealing a glance at the screen to see if the commentary tied up with the game.

The night before the match he would unroll a small plan of a football pitch, and, using sugar lumps dipped in red ink for Arsenal, he would lock himself in the parlour. We could hear him shouting out instructions. 'It's the long ball down the middle that will do it . . . forget flank penetration, there's too many in the goalmouth, it's the headed ball *over* the defence . . . 3 goals and you're on to a bonus of 10 shillings a man . . . you can live it up . . .' and so on. For economy's sake my mother had to use the inked sugar cubes, and all through the soccer season I drank red tea.

My mother's side, the Kettlebands, were also mechanical contrivances etc., especially my late Uncle Hughie, who would try and see how far he could walk without opening his eyes. He once managed three-quarters of a mile. For this he chose a large, barren, treeless plain in Hyderabadsind, but it took him so long he was stricken with sunstroke. He moved to London where there were no large treeless plains; trying to break his record he was knocked down by a tram in Catford, SE6. When he was discharged from Lewisham Hospital, he took up another test of self-control, holding his breath underwater. He calculated the less pressure on the body the less exertion and therefore a longer duration of breath retention, so he would lie on his bed face down, his head hanging over the foot of the bed. He also believed that cold water absorbed body energy (true), consequently the water had to be at body temperature, 98.4 degrees. So that he could time it to perfection, he bought a waterproof stop-watch that he placed at the bottom of the bucket; this was so that no time was lost in having to take head from water to look at stop-watch. He managed up to two minutes but this brought on nosebleeds and terminated his attempts.

He then settled for seeing if it was possible to sleep in the upright position, and many's the night I awoke to see him standing on his bed at three in the morning. After two weeks he still hadn't managed it. He persisted and then one night, in the early hours, I heard a terrible THUD and a groan; he had fallen asleep, his legs had collapsed and he had been catapulted to the concrete floor which split his head open. 'Must have lost control,' he said as we bandaged his head.

This, dear reader, is not all. His mother, the late Margaret Burnside-Kettleband (my grandmother), who looked the epitome of normality, left behind her a trail of yellow powder. She swore she had never had arthritis in her legs because every morning she poured two ounces of sulphur into her socks. When she and grandpa did the Lancers at the gallop at the Governor's Ball (Poona) they were soon swirling in a knee-high yellow dust. My grandpa, Trumpet-Major Alfred Henry Kettleband MM, was all in the same mould.

A respectable, rich Hindu lad, one Percy Lalkaka (Urdu translation: 'Red Dung') fell madly in love with my Auntie Eileen, but he was frightened off. My grandfather would frequently appear in his wife's floral nightgown. Holding a boiled egg in a spoon, he would glide past them, grinning and saying. 'There's going to be frost tonight in Quetta,' and disappear into the bathroom where he could be heard pouring buckets of water into the WD bath. A pause, then he would reappear, clad in shorts, now holding a spoonful of curry powder: 'But . . . it's going to be damned hot tonight.' It terminated the romance.

All that I have told you I accepted as normal. I was five at the time. I became personally involved in eccentricity (that's off-peak electricity), when my father, owing to his strange behaviour in India, was posted to Rangoon as a Sergeant in the Port Defence. One day he came to me. 'Son,' he said, 'the jungles are full of Dacoits, you must learn to defend yourself, come with me.' He placed me behind a rock and gave me an old Lee-Enfield filled with blanks, while he, wearing a dragon mask, plunged into the undergrowth. 'When you see me, fire, and I will judge if you have scored a hit.' As he ran hither and thither I blazed away. Occasionally he would shout, 'A hit, a hit,' and then stick a red adhesive spot on his body or face.

Came three o'clock, he was a mass of red spots and exhausted, but worse was to come. A nursing mother kite-hawk (wing span five feet) dove on him and clawed off his wig and flew away. It was a puzzled coolie who saw a man covered in red spots, with a bald and bleeding head, shouting up at the sky and throwing rocks in the air. The next day my father decided not to be the target, so he got several puzzled coolies to surround him holding *lathis* (police sticks) and, wielding two blank cartridge pistols, he blazed away, forcing the victims to stick on red spots when 'hit'.

Many of you may think that all I tell you is lies, but a picture was taken of the last incident. I leave you now to return to my life as a mechanical contrivance for converting circular etc. etc. Oh yes, the caption on the back of the photo, which is my father's own, reads, 'Picture taken in Burma in 1930 shows Captain Leo Milligan practising "Custer's Last Stand", which he learnt in New Mexico as a boy, using his own Lascars as the enemy and shooting soap bullets with a reduced charge.' Any questions?

⌒

INDIA! INDIA!

As a boy
I watched India through fresh Empirical eyes.
Inside my young khaki head
I grew not knowing any other world.
My father was a great warrior
My mother was beautiful
        and never washed dishes,
        other people did that,
I was only 4, I remember
        they cleaned my shoes,
        made my bed.
'Ither ow'
'Kom Kurrow'
Yet, in time I found them gentler
        than the khaki people
They smiled in their poverty
After dark, when the khaki people
        were drunk in the mess
I could hear Minnima and
        her family praying in their godown.
In the bazaar the khaki men
        are brawling
No wonder they asked us to leave.

– from *Open Heart University*

I ONCE – AS A CHILD

I once – as a child – saw Mahatma Ghandi
Walk past the Old Sappers Lines, Climo Road –
He was on his way to Yeroda Gaol. 'He's not
As black as he's painted' said my kind Grandmother –
But I found out he was not painted –
It was his real colour.

– from Small Dreams of a Scorpion

GROWING UP I

Even tho' they are my tomorrows
Do they know my yesterdays
    are wrapped up in them?
Those golden yesterdays.
Was there ever a sound
    like child laughter,
Was there ever such talk
    as theirs,
That lily pure truth on their lips?
Grown you are, yet I only see
    the child in you.
It is past reality, it is a haunting,
I cannot live without the
    memory of it.
At the going of those yesterdays
    my todays ended.

– from The Mirror Running

⌐∽

from Depression and How to Survive It

My father and mother loved theatricals. They were given time in the army in those days. But they rowed – the sound of rows always upset me. I can remember my mother and father having a row in Rangoon which upset me. I can still hear it ringing in my ears, this terrible screaming and shouting. I have always been hypersensitive to noise. We had just come from Poona to Rangoon, where my father had already been posted in advance of us, and I think he had been having an affair with an Anglo-Indian girl, a slant-eyed temple maiden of Kipling, and he was saying 'I only took her out dancing' and this screaming match went on which frightened me very much.

[Mother] was always either hugging me close and loving me to death or hating me and screaming at me. I couldn't understand it. I didn't understand the extremes of temperament. I couldn't cope with it at all.

When I stopped going to Church – I was eighteen at the time – she started an unending attack on me every Sunday as to why I wouldn't go to Church such that eventually I left home and went to stay with Harold Fagg [a friend]. She could be very demanding.

I was about six and a picnic was going on. She was very beautiful and I remember one of the chaps who was with her pulled her head right back and it upset me so much that I ran inside the house and cried, I don't know why. Did I love her? Was she my girlfriend deep down? I was jealous.

She seemed to fuss over me all the time. In fact I wasn't able to take responsibility. She did it all, everything. She used to make my bed in the morning, clean my shoes, make my breakfast and I used to take it as normal.

[Father] was a soldier and he was away a lot from home. My mother was very highly strung and not cruel but used to beat me sometimes quite violently, and I think there was this resentment that I didn't have anybody to go to. I thought when you got beaten by your mother you went to your father and vice versa. I don't know – it's a mystery. I'd like to be put to sleep one day and asked about it.

I don't know what it was all about. I believe I wished my father was with me more. I think I wanted some extra attention. I remember it was very awful lying there all wet. And then I remember being picked up and dried and powder being put on and clean pyjamas, and then being tucked up again in fresh sheets, and it was a very wonderful thing indeed to be put back to sleep again, clean and dry and warm.

He would come back and we would all have a jolly time shooting deer. Actually I didn't like that. I remember one was pregnant and it was like an arrow in my head. I think that is why I am a vegetarian.

I suppose I was four or five. I remember being given a *chota bazri* – the Indian for small breakfast – on a tennis court where our beds had been taken out at night because of the great heat. And I remember the toys my father gave me, he had them carved out of wood for me by his Indian carpenter – but I had one toy I really loved, he was called Mickey, a huge donkey – a caricature of a donkey – who used to sit up at the front whenever we all went for a ride in a gharry or a Victoria or a tonga. I don't know what happened to him. My parents always threw everything out, gave everything away. I'm surprised they never threw me away. That's why I've always kept my children's things. My parents had no feelings for belongings.

I remember leaving Rangoon, I was fourteen, and I stood on the deck of the ship and I burst into tears but my mother never knew nor my father, nobody ever knew. I didn't let on. I kept that sort of thing to myself. Odd thing but the only other time I remember crying like that was when I was on the boat that was going to take us on the invasion of North Africa. It was late night in Liverpool and all the soldiers had gone down below deck to their hammocks and I stayed on deck looking at the water and I burst into uncontrollable fits of crying. Perhaps I recalled the previous trip. I am not very good at leaving things.

⌒‿

from Scunthorpe Revisited, Added Articles and Instant Relatives

Christmas in India 1923

My own particular memory of Christmas was more fragrant: it had curry smells. My first recollection was when I was four and living in the Cantonment of Poona, a well-known wog-beating area. In the baking heat of 120 degrees in the shade I observed my parents sticking little blobs of white cotton wool on the windows. Never having seen any, I never knew it was meant to be snow. On reflection, how much more appropriate to have dotted the windows with curry paste and slicked banana portions.

My little questioning mind asked my parents how Father Christmas came and was told 'Down the chimney'. When I pointed out we hadn't any they changed tack. Ah yes, no, this Father Christmas would come via the back door. That's why they left the back door open, and that, dear reader, is why we were burgled. Alas, the thief, being a Hindu, had no idea that in the early hours my parents would be actively placing the presents at the bed end. They both collided in the parlour, my father grabbed the thief, naked except for a loin-cloth, while my mother phoned the police. Hearing the noise, I and my brother arose from our beds to see turbaned policemen manacling and hitting the unfortunate Hindu with their fists until he apparently told them he was a Harijan (Untouchable). When they reverted to sticks, the Hindu fell to his knees clutching my father's legs.

My little brother said to me, 'Is that Father Kwismus?' I didn't know.

Seeing us, my mother shushed us back to our beds with the story that a naughty man had tried to steal all Father Christmas's toys, and on that we went to sleep again.

I tell this story because the following year, by which time the family were in Rangoon (The Rangoon Show), come Christmas my little brother said, 'Are the hitting men coming tonight?'

My mother, who had forgotten the incident, said, 'What hitting men, dear?'

'You know, Mummy, the hitting men and the man with no clothes on who cried!'

Should she take him to a child psychiatrist? No, no hitting men came that year. Instead, at five minutes to midnight on Christmas Eve, the earthquake came. My parents leapt from their beds and rushed us into the garden as the crows, disturbed from the trees, sent up a great cawing. Yes, that was another Merry Christmas.

---

from Indefinite Articles and Scunthorpe

Some Like It Hot

There are many ways of keeping warm. It all depends on how much money you have. Let's start at the bottom, that is the bottom of the social scale. There are those gentlemen of the road who at midnight can be seen sleeping peacefully on the embankment in cold weather. The secret is the English Newspaper, which is wrapped around the inside of the outergarments, the *Financial Times* being a favourite; as one tramp said, 'Like bein' wrapped in dreams.'

I myself was working-class and keeping warm was different in each room. The outside WC in winter was a formidable affair, so when I saw my father putting on long underwear, a heavy sweater, overcoat, muffler and gloves I knew what his next function was. My brother had his own method: he would do vigorous exercises until he was boiling hot, then rush to the WC, abort at speed and get back before he grew cold. The only room with heat was the kitchen where a great iron stove glowed red, fed with all the rubbish in the house; on its hot plate kettles steamed and whistled, pots boiled, conkers hardened, chestnuts popped and socks and under-wear steamed in the scarlet heat, and grandma's shins scorched in the inferno. No, there was no heating problem for the poor in the kitchen, but the rest of the home was clutched in Stygian ice.

The habit of staying up late only came into being when people stopped sleeping in the kitchen or, to be exact, in pre-industrial times the kitchen, bedroom and living-room were all one room. But came the age of the separate bedroom and late nights started. My own family would start to disrobe in the kitchen, start putting on flannelette nightshirts, pyjamas, bed socks, etc., and finally, each one clutching a hot water bottle, we would get on our marks and at a signal run screaming to our freezing beds, from where we would all groan and scream, 'O Christ I'm freezin', cor stone a crow, Brrrrrrrr, etc., etc.,' until the bed became warm. Winter mornings were agony; the thought of getting out of bed was as pleasant as hara-kiri. So I would pull my suit into bed and, when it was warm, undress and dress under the bedclothes; mind you my suit looked like a concertina, but I was warm.

Now the article is about keeping warm, so let's bring it into the present. I give up. I don't know *how* to keep warm. Keeping warm with central heating is very difficult, because most of the time is spent roasting. As a result one spends the evening adjusting the thermostat, opening and closing windows, taking off jackets or pullovers, so there is as much difficulty keeping warm with central heating as if you were in a freezing room. If it were up to me, I would abolish all central heating; it destroys furniture, floors, walls, and your respiratory system. No, a big cosy armchair, a pair of thick woollen socks, carpet slippers and a roaring coal fire (or logs) are the answer. In the street, people only get cold if they walk like cripples (as most of the English do). I walk very fast; as a result I arrive at work warm as toast and exhausted for the day.

2
Boys with Guns

I'm a hero . . .
. . . with coward's legs.

– 'Spike on Spike', *Memories of Milligan*

In 1933 the family returned to England. Spike's first job, at the age of fourteen, was as a clerk to a book-keeper at Stone's Engineering Company. Meanwhile, he joined a local band, the New Era Rhythm Boys, where he learned to play the bass. He was sacked from Stone's Engineering but soon got a job as a van boy delivering confectionery and sweets.

'After eating so many Bassett's liquorice allsorts I had the shits for a whole week, so I left.'

Evenings he played in local bands, and then joined Tommy Brettell's New Ritz Revels, playing every week at St Cyprian's Hall, Brockley. By this time, he'd found another day job as a work hand at the Chislehurst Laundry.

Like his father he started to enter talent contests and won a 'Bing Crosby Singing Contest'. Now seriously practising his trumpet, he was promoted to solo trumpet player.

Back to the day job as shop assistant in S. Straker's stationery shop on Queen Victoria Street. He was fired for unpunctuality. His next day job was as a stockroom assistant at Keith Prowse in Bond Street.

'It was soul destroying, and all that kept my sanity was playing evenings with the New Ritz Revels. I'd started to croon with the band.'

Another day job was as a skilled labourer at the Woolwich Arsenal, while playing evenings on his illegally obtained Besson trumpet with the Harlem Club Band. He said he had started to earn good money.

By now it was 1939. Alas, came the Adolf Hitler Show.

For me, Spike was the original free spirit, which I could never quite square with his love of the army and all its discipline. Yet he dearly loved its camaraderie and his army life. June 1940 was the beginning of that love affair when he attended the Yorkshire Grey pub in Eltham for his medical. Grade 1 saw him on his way to Bexhill, home of the army cadets.

Of course, he took his trumpet with him and soon he formed 'D Battery Band'. These musicians became lifelong friends: Doug Kidgell on drums, Harry Edgington on piano, Alf Fildes on guitar and Milligan on trumpet. This quartet played all through the war.

A memorable year was 1943 in Italy, when he first met Harry Secombe. Later that year, in a concert party with Army Welfare's 'Central Pool of Artists', they met again when Spike was performing, playing his trumpet and guitar. Instant rapport.

January 1944, Spike was wounded, labelled 'Battle Fatigue' and sent to see a psychiatrist. 'This was a time of my life that I was very demoralized. I was not really me any more.'

from Adolf Hitler: My Part in His Downfall

One day an envelope marked OHMS fell on the mat. Time for my appendicitis, I thought.

'For Christ's sake don't open it,' said Uncle, prodding it with a stick. 'Last time I did, I ended up in Mesopotamia, chased by Turks waving pots of Vaseline and shouting "Lawrence we love you" in Ottoman.'

Father looked at his watch. 'Time for another advance,' he said and took one pace forward. Weeks went by, several more OHMS letters arrived, finally arriving at the rate of two a day stamped URGENT.

'The King must think a lot of you son, writing all these letters,' said Mother as she humped sacks of coal into the cellar. One Sunday, while Mother was repointing the house, as a treat Father opened one of the envelopes. In it was a cunningly worded invitation to partake in World War 2, starting at seven and sixpence a week, all found. 'Just fancy,' said Mother as she carried Father upstairs for his bath, 'of all the people in England, they've chosen you, it's a great honour, son.'

Laughingly I felled her with a right cross.

I managed to delay the fatal day. I'll explain. Prior to the war, I was a keep-fit addict. Every morning you could see people counting the bones in my skinny body at Ladywell Recreation Track, as I lifted barbells. Sometimes we were watched by admiring girls from Catford Labour Exchange; among them was one with a tremendous bosom. She looked like the Himalayas on their side. The sight of this released some kind of sex hormones into my being that made me try to lift some impossible weight to impress her. Loading the barbell to one hundred and sixty pounds (about $70) I heaved at the weights, Kerrrrrrissttt!! an agonized pain shot round my back into my groin, down my leg, and across the road to a bus stop. Crippled and trying to grin, I crawled, cross-eyed with agony, towards the shower rooms. Screams of laughter came from the girls.

'Ohhh yes,' said our neighbour Mrs Windust, 'you've got a rupture comin'. My 'usband 'ad one from birth. Orl fru our courtin' days 'e managed to keep it a secret, 'course, on our 'oneymoon 'e 'ad to show me, and then I saw 'e was 'eld together wiv a Gathorne and Olins advanced leather truss. 'E 'ad to 'ave it remodelled before we could 'ave sectional intercourse.'

Terrified, I hied me to my Hearts of Oak Sick Benefit Hindu Doctor, who had a practice in Brockley Rise. 'Oh yes Milligan! You are getting a rupture! I can feel it!' he said inserting curry-stained fingers like red hot pokers in my groin. That diagnosis from a son of the BMA was thirty-five years ago. I'm not ruptured yet. Perhaps I'm a late starter. Rupture! the thought filled me with lumps of fear, why? For three years I had been trumpet player with the Ritz Revels, a bunch of spotty musicians held together with hair oil. They paid ten shillings a gig;* of this I gave Mother nine, who in turn gave seven to the church for the Poor of the Parish. I couldn't understand it, *we* were the Poor of the Parish.

Blowing a trumpet puts a strain on the groin up to chest height, so, every time we did a gig I improvised a truss. I stuffed rags into an old sock until it was packed tight. I then placed it in the predicted rupture spot and attached it to my groin with lengths of tape and string; this gave me a bulge in my trousers that looked like the erection of a stallion. Something had to be done, I mean, if some woman saw it, I could never live up to it, so I tried to reduce the bulge by putting leather straps round me and pulling them tight; nothing happened except my voice went up an octave. It still looked obscene, but Mother came to the rescue; she sewed on an additional length of dyed black curtain which covered the bulge

---

* A one night stand.

but brought the jacket half way down my thighs. Embarrassed, I explained it away by saying, 'This is the latest style from America, Cab Calloway wears one.' 'He must be a cunt,' said the drummer.

I had bought the evening dress from my Uncle Alf of Catford for thirty-eight shillings; the suit was tight, but so was money, so I bought it. For weeks I played in my leather harness trussed up like a turkey.

After a month I got saddle sores and went to the doctor, who passed me on to a vet; in turn, he reported me to the police as a Leather Pervert. The pain in my back persisted, sometimes I couldn't move for it. What I had was a slipped disc, a condition then unknown to the world of medicine. But to get a 'bad back' at the same time as your call-up rings as hollow as a naked wife in bed with the lodger saying the laundry's late. (In my case it was true, the laundry was late.) I was put in Lewisham General Hospital under observation. I think a nurse did it through a hole in the ceiling. Specialists seeking security in numbers came in bunches of four to examine me. They prodded me, then stepped back to see what happened. 'He's still alive,' said one. They then hit me all over with rubber mallets and kept saying to each other, 'what do you think?' Days later a card arrived saying 'Renal Colic'.

The old man in the next bed leaned over and said in a hoarse voice, 'Git aht of here son. I come in 'ere wiv vericose veins and they took me 'pendix aht.'

'Thanks,' I said, 'my name's Milligan.'

'Mine's Ethel Martin,' he said.

'Ethel? It says Dick on your chart.'

'I was when I come in, somewhere between there and 'ere.' He pointed in an obvious direction.

'The unkindest cut of all?'

'They got me mixed up with someone who wanted to be sterilized. How do you tell your wife you ain't what she thinks you are?'

'Don't tell her, show her!'

'I'll think about it.'

'From now on that's all you will be able to do about it.'

Those sons of fun at the hospital, having failed to diagnose my

ailment, discharged me with a letter recommending electrical treatment, and headed 'To whom it may concern' – I suppose that meant
me. It was now three months since my call-up. To celebrate I hid
under the bed dressed as Florence Nightingale. Next morning I
received a card asking me to attend a medical at the Yorkshire Grey,
Eltham. 'Son,' said Father, 'I think after all you better go, we're
running out of disguises, in any case when they see you, they're
bound to send you home.' The card said I was to report at 9.30 a.m.
'Please be prompt.' I arrived prompt at 9.30 and was seen promptly
at 12.15. We were told to strip. This revealed a mass of pale youths
with thin, white, hairy legs. A press photographer was stopped by
the recruiting sergeant. 'For Christ's sake don't! If the public saw a
photo of this lot they'd pack it in straight away.' I arrived in the
presence of a grey-faced, bald doctor.

'How do you feel?' he said.

'All right,' I said.

'Do you feel fit?'

'No, I walked here.'

Grinning evilly, he wrote Grade 1 (One) in blood red ink on my
card. 'No black cap?' I said. 'It's at the laundry,' he replied.

The die was cast. It was a proud day for the Milligan family as I
was taken from the house. 'I'm too young to go,' I screamed as
Military Policemen dragged me from my pram, clutching a dummy.
At Victoria Station the RTO gave me a travel warrant, a white
feather and a picture of Hitler marked 'This is your enemy.' I
searched every compartment, but he wasn't on the train. At 4.30,
2 June 1940, on a summer's day all mare's tails and blue sky, we
arrived at Bexhill-on-Sea, where I got off. It wasn't easy. The train
didn't stop there.

⌒

[The organizers of the Lewisham Jazz Festival wrote to Spike asking him for a letter of support for their jazz festival.]

9 Orme Court
London W2

18 July 1983

Dear Jazzers,

It's a long time since that day in 1936/7, when at the Lewisham Town Hall I was given a silver medal by Benny Carter for the best jazz soloist in the Melody Maker Dance Band contest.

So, it's almost a complete circle to be asked to write a letter supporting this occasion.

Of course, jazz is a great and happy music, even the blues are good news. Everything about jazz I love, except when they put it through ten microphones and 50,000 watt amplifiers and deafen you, so I do hope you are not doing this on this particular occasion. Nevertheless, even if you are, I wish the occasion great happiness.

From an old jazzer, still blowing a lonely 'B' flat cornet in the corners of dark pubs, to barmaids with big boobs, hoping they have a key to A flat.

Love, light and peace
Spike Milligan

⌒

CONKERER

I'm going to march on Poland
And then I'll march on France,
Next I'll march on Germany,
I'll lead them such a dance.

I'll smash my way through Russia,
I'll storm all over Spain,
Then I'll go *back* to Poland
And do it all *again*!

I'll conquer all of Asia
From Sweden to the Med.
And then I'll really have to stop,
Mum says it's time for bed.

Hadley Wood
September 1980

– from *Unspun Socks from a Chicken's Laundry*

⌒

from 'Rommel?' 'Gunner Who?'

Algeria

The ground was like rocks. The nights were rent with gunners groaning, swearing, twisting, turning and revolving in their tents.
Temperatures fluctuated. You went to sleep on a warm evening, by dawn it dropped to freezing. We had to break our tents with hammers to get out. Dawn widdles caused frost-bitten appendages,

the screams! 'Help, I'm dying of indecent exposure!' We solved the problem. I stuffed my Gas cape with paper and made a mattress. Gunner Forest wrapped old *Daily Mirrors* round his body, 'I always wanted to be in the News,' he said, and fainted. Others dug holes to accommodate hips and shoulders.

At night we wore every bit of clothing we had, then we rolled ourselves into four blankets. 'We look nine months gone,' said Edgington. 'Any advance on nine,' I cried.

We slept warmly, but had overlooked the need to commune with nature; it took frantic searching through layers of clothing to locate one's willy, some never did and had to sleep with a damp leg. Gunner Maunders solved the problem! He slid a four foot length of bicycle inner tube over his willy, secured it round his waist with string, he just had to stand and let go. Jealous, Gunner White sabotaged it. As Maunders slept, fiend White tied knots in the bottom of the tube.

*

23 Jan.
19 Bty
56 Heavy Regiment, RA
BNAF

My dear Des,

In Africa we are all playing silly buggers. We are on a course teaching us how to 'Leap' anything that stands in our way. I think this could be introduced at home to encourage fitness among the Wartime civilian population. For example 'Leaping Stones' could be installed in the home. The stone, about three feet high by two feet wide, could be cemented in all the doorways in the home, including one at the foot of the stairs.

A Leapo-meter is attached to the ankle of every member of the family, which records the number of leaps per person, per day. Those who show disinterest can have a small explosive charge fixed to the groin, which detonates should the person try climbing round the stone, this will cause many a smoke-blackened crotch, but with our new spray-on 'Crotcho!' – a few squirts leaves the groins gleaming white, and free of fowl pest. Think of the enervating joys of the Leaping stones! Sunday morn – and the whole household rings with shouts of Hoi Hup! Ho la! Grannies, uncles, mothers, cripples all leaping merrily from one room to another for wartime England – ah, there's true patriotism! We have high hopes that more progressive young politicians with an eye to eliminating senile MPs intend to have a 'Great Westminster Leaping Stone' that will be placed dead centre of the great entrance doors on opening day. Mr Churchill could start the leaping, those failing will of course be debarred. You can try and assist the failed member over the leaping stone by applying hot pokers to the seat, thus the smell of scorched flesh, burning hairs and screams can bring a touch of colour to an otherwise dull wartime England. I don't know when I will post this letter, I might deliver it tomorrow by hand, ankle, foot and clenched elbow.

As ever,
Your loving brother
  Terry

*

27 January 1943: The services of the Battery Band were called for. 'There's ten acts on the bill and we'd like yeow to do a twurn!' said the District Entertainments Officer. He had a very high effeminate voice. 'I used to be counter-tenor at the Gwarden,' he said. 'It must have been Welwyn Garden,' whispered Edge. That evening, a highly polished staff car calls for us. 'Don't touch it,' I cautioned, 'it's a trap, it's only for our instruments, we're supposed to run alongside.'

We were driven at great speed to a massive French Colonial Opera House where at one time, massive French colonials sang. A sweating Sergeant was waiting.

'Ah,' he said with obvious relief. 'I'm Sergeant Hope.'

'What a good memory you've got,' I said.

'I'm the compère. You are the Royal Artillery Orchestra?'

'Yes,' I said.

'Where's the rest of you?'

'This is all there is of me, I'm considered complete by the MO.'

'We had been expecting a full orchestra.'

'We are full – we just had dinner.'

'That will do,' he said leading us to the wings.

On stage an Army PT Instructor was doing a series of hand stands, leaps, and somersaults; the conclusion of each trick was standing to attention and saluting. 'You don't salute without yer 'at on, cunt,' said a voice from the khaki rabble. Sgt Hope took down details of our 'act'.

'Name?'

'Milligan.'

'Rank?'

'Gunner.'

'Regiment?'

'I'm sorry,' I said, 'under the Geneva Convention of 1921 all I need give is my name, rank and number.'

'Look son, I've had a bloody awful day, I'm at the end of my tether,' he said. 'Save the jokes for the stage, I was told you were a twenty-piece regimental orchestra and you were going to play Elgar's Pomp and Circumstances.' He walked away holding his head.

The PT Sergeant finished his leaping act, and was given a reception that he had never had before or since. He came into the wings grinning with triumph. 'I think I'll turn pro after the war,' he triumphed. The next time I saw him was 1951, he was a furniture remover in Peckham. 'Changed your mind?' I said. He threw a cupboard at me.

The worried compère was now the other side of the curtain saying 'Thank you, the next act is – er – the 19th "Battalion", Royal Artillery Dance Band, under its – er – conductor Gunner Spine Millington!' Behind the curtain we were rupturing ourselves trying to get a massive French colonial piano on the stage. I shouted 'We're not bloody well ready.' 'Well,' said the sweating Sergeant, 'as you can hear they're not quite bloody well ready yet ha-ha but – er – they ha-ha – er – won't be long now, and then –' he put his head through the curtain. 'Hurry up for Christ's sake!' 'Keep ad libbing,' I said, 'you're a natural.' He continued 'Well, they're – er – nearly – er – not quite – ready, ha-ha and soon we'll be . . .'

Not waiting for him to finish, we launched into our up tempo signature tune, 'The Boys From Battery D', which Harry Edgington had written.

> We're the boys from Battery D
> Four Boys from Battery D
> We make a rhythmic noise
> We give you dancing joys
> And sing the latest melody.
>
> Now we make the darndest sounds
> As we send you Truckin' on down
> And if it's sweet or hot
> We give it all we've got
> And boy! we got enough to go around.
>
> We'll set your feet tapping with a quick step
> We've a waltz that'll make you sigh
> And then the tempo we've got
> For a slow fox-trot
> Would make a wallflower wanna try.
>
> Come on along you he and she
> It's the dancers' jamboree
> Come on and take a chance
> Come on and have a dance
> To the band of Battery D.

Not exactly Cole Porter, but we weren't getting his kind of money. To our amazement we got an ovation. Three more jazz numbers and they wouldn't let us go; to cool them off I got Doug Kidgell our drummer to sing Toselli's Serenade. When he came to the line:

> 'Deep in my heart there is Rapture'

forgetfully we sang our customary version:

> 'Deep in my guts I've got Rupture
> But for that dear
> I'd have upped yer.'

We realized our mistake too late, and a great roar of laughter stopped the song in its tracks. We finished up with me impersonating Louis Armstrong doing the St Louis Blues, and took unending curtain calls. Old soldiers reading this may remember that occasion.

Driving back in the staff car, we sat silent in the aura of our unexpected success. To our left the Bay of Algiers was bathed in moonlight. 'I never dreamed,' said Harry, 'that one day, I would be driven along the Bay of Algiers by moonlight.'

'Didn't you?' I said. 'The first time I saw you I said, "One day that man is going to be driven along the Bay of Algiers by moonlight."'

'You're asking for a thud up the hooter,' he said.

'No I wasn't! What I said was, "The first time I saw you I . . ."'

'All right Milligan, stick this in yer dinner manglers.' He gave me a cigarette. Old sweats will shudder and fall faint when I mention the brand, 'V's'! They had appeared in our rations when we landed in Algiers. 'This is,' I said, 'living proof that the British soldier will smoke shit, and that goes from Sanitary Orderly Geordie Liddel to General Alexander.'

Alf Fildes, our guitarist, disagreed. 'Liddel, yes, he lives near it, he'd smoke shit, yes, but I bet a bloke like Alexander wouldn't wear it.'

There followed a classical argument on smoking shit, that resolved in the agreement that General Alexander *would* smoke shit provided it was offered him by the King. The story went round that 'V's' were India's contribution to the war. Churchill asked Ghandi if there was a natural commodity that was going to waste, and Ghandi said, 'Yes, we got plenty of cows' shit.' 'Right,' said Churchill, 'we're sending you a million rupees to turn it into tobacco.'

Two years went by; Churchill, anxious for news, phones Ghandi:

CHURCHILL: 'Ghandi? How's the Ersatz tobacco coming along?'
GHANDI: 'All right but we need more money.'
CHURCHILL: 'Good God, you've had a million!'
GHANDI: 'Yes, you see, so far it *looks* like tobacco – it *smokes* like tobacco – but –'
CHURCHILL: 'But what?'
GHANDHI: 'It still smells like shit.'

DIVERTISSEMENT SEPTEMBER 1973
As I sit in a suite on the 13th Floor of the Eurobuilding in Madrid, writing this volume, I reflect on that time thirty years ago, and the emotional analysis of those khaki days, have left such a deeply etched impression, that the whole spectrum actually re-inhabits my being with such remarkable freshness that the weight of the nostalgia is almost too much to bear, feelings that I had incurred in those days, towards people, incidents, nature, which I thought of as almost trivial, were really of Titanic proportions, and ones, that I now realize were to stay fresh, and become more poignant as the years passed, and the desire to experience them all once again, be they good, bad or indifferent, became a haunting spectre that suddenly, during the course of a day, takes you unawares, a particular word, a scent, a colour, or song could trigger it off. It could be at, say, Ronnie Scott's Club with a companion. Without warning someone plays a tune, and immediately, the surroundings and the companion become total strangers, and you long for those yester-ghosts to snatch you and rush you back to that magic day it happened. I used to scoff at my father's looking forward to his annual World War 1 reunions, but now I know, you *have* to have them! In fact I was instrumental in getting

our own D Battery reunions started, and lo and behold, the attendance increases every year.

Despite the friendships I have made since the war, it is always those early ones that have weight, understanding, confidence and mutual experience that I cling to. Though my best friend Harry Edgington has emigrated to New Zealand, we are closer than ever, I know that a particular tune will automatically make him think of the time we played it together, and the same applies to me. Our correspondence is prodigious, his letters fill three boxfiles, likewise recorded tapes, in which he sends his latest compositions, asking my opinions. He sends me tapes that send me into gales of laughter and yet all these occasions are not really happy, and yet I welcome them, they give a most soul-warming effect, it savours of satisfaction, and yet is emotionally inconclusive, it has become, like cocaine, addictive. Is it because with the future unknown, the present traumatic, that we find the past so secure?

*

I yawned one of those yawns that makes the back of your head touch your shoulder blades and push your chest out. Tomorrow the new Gun Position. Oh no! *not* tomorrow . . . *at midnight* we were beaten awake with rifle butts, our erections smashed down with shovels. We were to move *now*.

'This isn't war,' screamed Edgington, 'it's Sadism. S-a-d-e-s-e-a-m' etc. The convoy crawled along in pitch darkness, the moon having waned. 'Where are we going, sir?' I asked.

'It's a place called Map Ref. 517412,' said Lt Goldsmith.

'They don't write numbers like that any more, sir.'

We passed the bombed shattered village of Toukabeur, full of Booby Traps. Seven Sappers were killed during clearing. Outside the village was our new position. At night it looked like the surface of the moon, or Mae West's bum the moment the corsets came off.

In front of us was a rocky multi-surfaced outcrop eighty feet high and 100 yards long, behind us a ledge dropping sheer fifty feet to a granite plateau fifty yards long, then another thirty-foot drop into a valley, in fact two giant steps. The canvas command post erected, I pitched my tent on the edge of the first drop, because shells falling behind me would drop fifty feet down and I would avoid being subdivided by the Third Reich. However, if shells landed in front of me, I'd suffer the quincequonces. The guns were pulled, heaved and sworn into position. Wireless network opened with 78 Div. HQ and 46 Div. OP line laid and contact made. Jerry dropped an occasional Chandelier flare. Kerrashboom-kerak! Our first rounds went off at 22.00 hours. I was on Command Post duty all night.

In between fire orders a running argument developed between Lt Beauman Smythe, Gnr Thornton and self.

THORNTON: 'There's been heavy casualties on Bou Diss.'

ME: 'I'm glad it's not me.'

B-SMYTHE: 'That's a selfish view.'

ME: 'Selfish, sir? All I said was I'm glad it wasn't me that died.'

B-SMYTHE: 'That's not something to be glad about!'

THORNTON: 'I think –'

ME: 'Sir! You want me to say, "I'm sorry it wasn't me that got killed"?'

B-SMYTHE: 'It's better than being *not* sorry. Someone's got to get killed in wars.'

ME: 'Well, someone was, it's just that it wasn't me.'

THORNTON: 'I think –'

B-SMYTHE: 'I still say your attitude to death was selfish.'

ME: 'Look, sir, mother went thru' a lot of pain to have me, I was a 12 lb baby, 11 lb was my head, me father spent a fortune for a Sergeant on my education, some days it was up to threepence a day, I'm not throwing all that away. My father still goes round with a begging bowl.'

THORNTON: 'I think –'

B-SMYTHE: 'I still say your attitude to death was selfish.'

MILLIGAN: 'Shellfish?'

THORNTON: 'I think –'

ME: 'Sell? What do you think?'

THORNTON: '. . . Oh Christ – I've forgotten.'

ME: 'Well be a good boy, go outside and get killed to cheer up Lt Smythe.'

Off duty at 06.00 hours, went straight to bed and I think I died.

———

LONGSTOP HILL, 22 APRIL 1943

That April day
Seems far away
The day they decided to kill
Lieutenant Tony Goldsmith RA
On the slopes of Longstop Hill.

At Toukabeur
The dawn lights stir,
Whose blood today will spill?
Today it's Tony Goldsmith's
Seeping out on Longstop Hill.

One can't complain
Nor ease the pain
Or find someone to fill
The place of Tony Goldsmith
Lying dead on Longstop Hill.

In Germany
There still might be
A Joachim, Fritz or Will
Who did for Tony Goldsmith
That day – on Longstop Hill.

– from *The Mirror Running*

⌒

THERE WAS A YOUNG SOLDIER CALLED EDSER

There was a young soldier called Edser
When wanted was always in bed sir:
One morning at one
They fired the gun
And Edser, in bed sir, was dead sir.

– from *Silly Verse for Kids*

⌒

from Mussolini: His Part in My Downfall

Salerno

Thursday, 23 September 1943

My diary: Still at war! Early closing in Catford. Read letter from Mother saying Chiesmans of Lewisham are so short of stock, the manager and staff sit in the shop miming the words 'Sold Out'.

Dear Reader, the beds in the Dorchester Hotel are the most comfortable in England. Alas! neither Driver Kidgell nor Lance-Bombardier Milligan are in a bed at the Dorchester – no! they are trying to sleep on a ten-ton Scammell lorry, parked on the top deck of 4,000-ton HMS *Boxer*, inside whose innards are packed 19 Battery, 56th Heavy Regiment, all steaming in the hold; from below comes the merry sound of men retching and it's all from Gunner Edgington. We are bound for Sunny Salerno. For thirteen days since the 5th Army landing, a ferocious battle had ensued on the beach-head. Even as we rode the waves we knew not what to

expect when our turn came. The dawn comes up like Thinder.
*Thin*der? Yes, that's Thin Thunder. 'Shhhhhh,' we all shout. The
chill morning air touches the khaki somnambulists sleeping hero-
ically for their King and Country. We are awakened by Gunner
Woods in the driving cab, who has fallen asleep on the motor horn.
A puzzled ship's Captain is wondering why he can hear the sound
of a lorry at sea. Kidgell gives a great jaw-cracking yawn and that's
him finished for the day. He stretches himself but doesn't get any
longer. Deep in his eyes I see engraved the word, 'TEA'. 'Wakey
wakey,' he said, but didn't. The ship is silent. The helmsman's face
shows white through the wheel-house.

'It is Dawn,' yawns Kidgell.

'My watch says twenty past,' I yawned.

'Yes! It's *exactly* twenty past Dawn,' he yawned.

We yawned. Like a comedy duo, we both stand and pull our
trousers on; mistake! he has mine and vice versa. The light is growing in the Eastern sky, it reveals a great grey convoy of ships,
plunging and rising at the dictation of the sea. LCTs. LCTs, some
thirty of them, all flanked by navy Z-Class destroyers. The one on
our port bow is stencilled B4. Imagine the confusion of a wireless
conversation with it.

'Hello B4, are you receiving me?'

PAUSE.

'Hello B4 answering.'

PAUSE.

'Hello B4, why didn't you answer B4?'

'Because we didn't hear you before.'

In the early light the sea is blue-black like ink. Kidgell is carefully folding his blankets into a mess, 'I haven't slept that well for
years.'

'How do you know?' I said. 'You were asleep.'

He chuckled. 'Well, it *feels* like I slept well.'

'Where did you feel it, in the legs? the elbows? teeth?' I was
determined to pursue the matter to its illogical conclusion; I mean
if *sane* people are going around saying 'I slept well last night', what
would lunatics say? 'I stayed awake all night so I could see if I slept

well'? I mean – we are interrupted by the shattering roar of aircraft!! 'Spitfires!' someone said, and we all got up again.

'Thank God they weren't German,' says Kidgell.

'Why thank him,' I said. 'He doesn't run the German air force, thank Hitler.'

'All right, clever Dick.' He giggled. 'This is going to sound silly – thank Hitler they weren't Germans.'

The helmsman's face showed white through the wheel-house.

I produce a packet of Woodbines. I offer one to Kidgell. I have to . . . he's got the matches. My watch says 12.20; that means it's about seven o'clock. We stow our gear into a lorry full of sleeping Gunners with variable pitch snoring; three of them are snoring the chord of C Minor. We decide to walk 'forrard'. The *Boxer* makes a frothy swathe as her flat prow divides the waters. The sky is turning into post-dawn colours – scarlet, pink, lemon. It looked like the ending of a treacly MGM film where John Wayne joins his Ghost Riders in the sky. (Personally I can't wait for him to.) It's chilly; we wear over-coats with the collars up. Kidgell looks pensively out towards Italy.

'I was wondering about the landing.'

'Don't worry about the landing, I'll hoover it in the morning.'

He ignored me, but then everybody did. 'I've been thinking.'

'Thinking? This could mean promotion,' I said.

'I was thinking, supposing they land us in six foot of water.'

'Then everyone five foot eleven and three quarters will drown.'

'That's the end of me, then.'

'I thought you were a champion swimmer!'

'You can't swim in army boots.'

'You're right, there is not enough room.'

'What *are* you talking about?'

'I'm talking about ten words to the minute.'

A merry matelot approaches with a Huge Brown Kettle. 'You lads like some cocoa?'

We galloped at the speed of light to our big packs and returned to meet the merry matelot as he descended from the Bridge. He pours out the thick brown remaining sludge. The gulls in our wake scream as they dive-bomb the morning garbage. We sip the cocoa, holding the mug with both hands to warm them. A change from holding the mug to warm the Naafi tea. Another cigarette, what a lunatic habit! 'Here we are,' I said. 'We go to these bastards who make this crap and we say 'We will give you money for twenty of those fags', we smoke them, we make the product *disappear*! Ha! Supposing you bought a piano on the same basis? Suddenly, in the middle of a concert it disappears, you have to belt out and buy another one to finish the concerto. It's lunacy.'

In the deck-house, a red-faced officer scans the horizon ahead. 'I wonder exactly where we are,' says Kidgell.

'I think we're on the ancient sea of Tyrrhenum Sive Inferum.' That finishes him.

'When we reach Sicily we will hug the coast to afford us air cover and the way things are, I'd say we could *just* afford it.'

We are travelling one of the most ancient trade routes in history, Carthaginians, Greeks, Romans, Mamelukes, Turks and Mrs Doris Hare. 'Fancy us being part of history,' I said. 'I don't fancy it,' said Kidgell.

The Tannoys crackle. 'Attention, please.'

A Gunner faints. 'What's up?' we ask.

'I thought I heard someone say please.'

'Attention . . . This is the Captain speaking . . . (What a good memory he had) . . . In three minutes the Ack-Ack guns will be firing test bursts . . . this is only a practice, repeat, practice.'

Soon the sky was festooned with erupting shells, black puffs of smoke with a red nucleus from the barrels of the multiple Pom Poms. The Tannoy again.

'Hello this is your –' a burst of amplified coughing follows.

'It's the resident consumptive,' I said.

The coughing ceases. 'Attention, that practice firing will be repeated every morning at –' Coughing – coughing – 'at' – coughing . . .

The helmsman's face showed white through the wheel-house.

'I feel a sudden attack of roll-call coming on,' I said.

I was right. Sgt King lines us up on deck. We answer our names and anyone's that isn't there; even if they called 'Rasputin' a voice answers 'Sah.'

'Milligan?'

'Sah!'

'Devine?'

'Sah!'

'Edgington? . . . Edgington?'

From the deck below comes a weak voice 'Sah!' followed by retching.

Britannia rules the waves, but in this case, she waives the rules. A roar of engines, the Spitfires return, we all get up again. They repeat roaring back and forth through the day, we get used to it, we get so used to it that when a Focke Wolfe shoots us up, we're all standing up, aren't we? Breakfast is happening in the galley.

'I have been a slave to breakfast all my life but breakfast *and* a galley slave never!' says Kidgell.

We lined up head on to a trio of Navy cooks, who doled out Spam Fritters, Bread, Marge, Jam and Tea and avoided looking at it when they did. We ate on top deck enjoying the sea breeze, the pleasant weather . . . were we *really* going to war or were we on our way to Southend for the day?

24 September 1943

I was awake at first light, and I heard gunfire. I sat bolt upright, we were down to about three knots, very slow, granny-knots. We were pulling into the Bay of Salerno! All the beaches look remarkably peaceful. Good! we'd have a quiet landing. The still waters of the Bay were a carnival of ships, some 200, all shapes and sizes rode at anchor. The amazing American Amphibian DWKs were ferrying supplies ashore. Looming large among all this was HMS *Valiant* and HMS *Warspite*. Suddenly one let fly a devastating salvo which thundered around the bay and rocked the warship some fifteen degrees off her axis.

'That's not going to do Jerry any good,' said a sailor and added, 'It's not doing the *Warspite* any good either.'

In the morning mistiness we make out hyper-activity on the beaches – lorries, tanks, half-tracks, beach-masters waving flags, pointing, lifting, lowering, signalling, shouting – all involved in the logistics of the war. The shells from *Warspite* were bursting inland on the hills behind Pontecagnano, which dominated the landing beaches. Why wasn't Jerry replying? We drop anchor; immediately trouble, the chain has wrapped around the propeller shaft, fun and high jinks. We cheer as a diver goes down. A boat from the beach approached with a purple-faced Officer who shouted rude things through a bull-horn at our Captain, whose face incidentally showed white through the wheel-house. To make it more difficult for our Captain, the destroyers lay a smoke-screen around us, and the Tannoy crackles: 'Hello – click – buzz-crackle – it's – click-buzz-crackle – later.' End of message.

'It's all getting a bit silly,' said Harry. 'All we had was the view and now that's been bloody obscured!'

Now is the time for action! I take my trumpet from its case. There must be men still alive who remember the sound of 'The Last Post' from the smoke-shrouded *Boxer*. The Tannoy crackles.

'Whoever is playing that bugle, please stop,' said a piqued Navy voice.

The anchor chain is finally freed. The smoke-screen lifts to show we are now facing away from the beach.

'They're takin' us back again,' says Gunner Devine.

'Of course not, you silly Gunner, no, the Captain has turned his ship around in the smoke to show us how clever he is.'

There are laconic cheers as the diver surfaces.

'Caught any fish?' someone says.

He holds up two fingers.

'Is that all?'

The engines start up again, the ship swings slowly round and points toward Italy, I mean, he couldn't miss it. Sub-Section Sergeants are going around telling us to 'Get ready to disembark.' Drivers are unchaining the restraining cables that secure the vehicles to the deck. The day is now a delightful mixture of sun and a cool wind. The *Warspite* lets off another terrifying salvo. It thunders around the bay. We watch it erupt among the hills.

'That'll make the bastards sit up,' says Sgt 'Jock' Wilson.

'I'd have thought', I said, 'it would have the opposite effect!'

'Oh hello, Spike,' he says. 'How you bin enjoying the sea trip?'

'Well, Sarge, Yes and No.'

'Wot do ye mean Yes or No?'

'Well, Yes I am, and No I'm not, but mostly No I'm not, otherwise, Yes I am.'

He frowned. 'You'll never get promotion.'

Wilson was a Glaswegian, he was 'Fitba' (Football) mad, and his family at home were hard put to it to send him all the news cuttings on the Scottish Matches*.

September 24 1943

REGIMENTAL DIARY: *HMS* Boxer *landed first party on Red Beach, Salerno Bay at 0940 hrs.*

The ship touched the beach very gently, so gently I suspect it's not insured. 'Sorry about the bump, gentlemen,' said a chuckling Navy voice on the Tannoy. A cheer arose from the lads as the landing ramp was lowered. Another salvo from *Warspite*. At the same time an American supply ship starts to broadcast Bing Crosby singing 'Pennies from Heaven' over its speakers. To our right, over the Sorrento peninsula, a German plane is flying very high; pinpoints of high bursting Ack-Ack shells trace his path.

Time 9.30. Sea calm.

The Tannoy crackles. Another coughing demo? No.

'Hello, is it on? – Hello, Captain Sullivan speaking.'

'Give us a song, Captain,' shouts Gunner White.

'Attention, will all men without vehicles, repeat, without vehicles, please disembark first?'

'I think I'm without vehicles,' I said to Harry.

'How about you?'

'No, I haven't got vehicles, but they might be incubating,' says Edgington, who is, now that the sea is calm, back to his cheery self; the roses haven't come back to his cheeks, but he tells me they're

* Scottish Matches = ones that won't strike.

on their way. 'They have reached my knees and are due in me navel area this afternoon.'

The Tannoy: 'Will men without vehicles disembark now?'

'We've been spoken for, Harry,' I said as we trundle down the gangways to the 'Floor' of the *Boxer*. We were about to set foot on Italy. The jaws of the *Boxer* are opened on to a sunlit beach.

'I could never have afforded all this travel on my own,' I say. 'It had to be the hard way, World War 2. I've always wanted to see Russia, I suppose that would mean World War 3.'

I don't believe it, we were walking down the broad ramp on to the Salerno beaches, no bullets! no shells! and I didn't even get my feet wet, as I leave my first footprint in the sand. I shout loudly 'TAXI!' and point in the direction it's coming from. 'The woods are full of them,' I add.

We move in a milling throng on to the beach. I start the sheep bleating and soon we are all at it, much to the amusement of the seamen watching from top deck. The scenery by L/Bdr Milligan: the beaches are a mixture of volcanic ash and sand, the colour of milky coffee, it stretches left and right as far as the eye can see. Strewn along the beaches is the debris of a battle that had raged here; an occasional German long-range shell explodes in the bay. There are no hits. The beaches vary from twenty to thirty yards deep. Back from this is a mixture of pines, scrub, walnut trees and sand hillocks mounted with Tuffa grass. Bulldozers have made clearways flanked by white ribbons denoting them mine-free. There is activity the length and breadth of the shores. Great ammo dumps are, as we watch, getting higher and bigger. Just inland, Spitfires are refuelling and about to take off from a makeshift airstrip. American Aero-Cobras are revving their engines, turning into the wind and taking off in the direction of Naples.

We congregated by the sand hillocks, dumped our small kit and started to explore the area. Hard by was an American Lightning plane that had crash-landed half in the sea; a glimpse inside showed a blood-saturated cockpit. 'He must be very anaemic by now,' said Sherwood. There are slit trenches everywhere, water bottles, helmets, empty ammo boxes, and spent-cartridge cases by the hundreds.

'Must have been a hot spot,' said Bdr Fuller.

At the bottom of a trench I spot a Scots Guard cap badge, several pieces of human skull with hair attached, and a curling snapshot of two girls with an address somewhere in Streatham. I put it in my paybook intending to forward it to the address. We come across thirty or so hurried graves with makeshift wooden markers. 'Private Edwards, E', a number, and that was all. Fourteen days ago he was alive, thinking, feeling, hoping . . . If war was a game of cards, I'd say someone was cheating.

~

SOLDIER, SOLDIER

There was a little soldier
Who went off to the war
To serve the King,
Which is the thing
That soldiers are made for.

But then that little soldier
Was blown to bits, was he.
All for his King
He did this thing:
How silly can you be?

– from *Startling Verse for All the Family*

~

24 September 1943

My diary: Cool night, a touch of autumn chill in the air. Had very disturbed sleep. Kept waking up in a cold sweat, took swig at water

*bottle, had a fag. What a bloody life. I finally dropped off into a black
sleep, like death. Am I the black sleep of the family?*

25 September 1943

I awoke at first light, sat up, yawned. I felt as tired as though I had
not slept. A morning mist is rapidly disappearing. It swirls around
the head of Monte Mango. I start the ritual of folding my blankets.
A voice calls, 'Hallo, Terry.' Terry? I hadn't been called that since I
turned khaki. It was Reg Lake, a Captain in the Queen's Regiment.
He had been sleeping about thirty yards away. Reg was the pre-war
manager of the New Era Rhythm Boys, one of the best semi-pro
bands in London. He was the one who gave me my first break as a
'crooner'. Last time I had seen him was on a 137 bus going from
Brockley to Victoria.

'My God, Terry, what are you doing in this God-forsaken place?'

'I'm helping England win the war.' What a silly bloody question.
'Reg,' I said, 'or do I call you sir?'

'How long you been here?' he said.

'Came yesterday – I thought it was a day trip.'

'I was here on the landings, you missed all the fun.'

'I'll try and make up for it.'

It was difficult to make conversation. I couldn't say, 'Where's the
band playing this week?' I asked what had happened to the boys in
the band.

'All split up.'

'That must be painful.'

'Most of them are in the services – remember Tom the tenor
player with only one lung? They took him.'

'They took me and I've only got two.'

He was called away by a Sergeant. I never saw him again, I've no
idea if he survived the war. If he reads this book, I hope he gets in touch.

A voice is calling across the land, 'Bombardier Milligan.'

'Bombardier Milligan is dead,' I call in a disguised voice.

The voice replied, 'Then he's going to miss breakfast.'

Good God! it's nearly nine! I just get to the cookhouse in time to have the remains of powdered eggs, bacon and tea that appears to have been all cooked together.

'You slept late,' says Edgington.

'I'm training for sleeping sickness.'

We are now gathered around the Water Wagon doing our ablutions. Edgington is at the lather stage, peering into a mirror the size of a half crown propped on a mudguard. He was moving his face clockwise as he shaved. I had stripped to the waist, which brought cries of 'Where are you?' I had my head under the tap enjoying the refreshing cascade of chlorinated cold water, at which time, twelve FW 109s are enjoying roaring out of the sun, guns hammering, there's a God-awful scramble, we all meet under a lorry. I caught a glimpse of the planes as they launched their bombs on the 25-pounder regiment behind us.

'Look out,' warns Edgington, when the planes were half way back to base. He hurled himself face down. 'All over.' We stand up. Edgington presented a face, half lather, dust and squashed grapes.

What was *I* laughing at? One moment I was well. Next moment I was on my knees vomiting. It was unbelievable. I became giddy, kept seeing stars and the Virgin Mary upside down.

'Report sick,' says Bombardier Fuller.

'You're so kind,' I said.

They took me to the Doc, who said I had a temperature of 103.

'What *have* you been doing?' he said.

'I was washing, sir.'

Having a temperature of 103 allowed you to stop fighting. No but seriously, folks, I was ill! Oh I *was ill*!! The war would have to go on without me! In a bren carrier they took me shivering with ague to the Forward Dressing Station. It was a small tented area off a rough track; a Lance-Corporal, tall, thin with spectacles, took my details, tied a label on me, I think it was THIS WAY UP.

'That stretcher there,' he said.

So, they were going to stretch me! I felt a bit of a fraud. Around me were seriously wounded men. Some were moaning softly. A chubby Catholic priest, about forty-five, red faced, blond hair going grey, walked among us.

'What's wrong with you, son?'

'I got fever.'

'Fever?'

'Yes. Disappointed, father?'

He grinned, but it didn't wipe the sadness off his face. He told me they were awaiting the arrival of some badly wounded men from the Queen's.

'They were trying to take that.' He nodded towards Monte Stella.

Three jeeps arrive with stretcher cases. Among them is a German, his face almost off. Poor bastard. There was a trickle of wounded all afternoon, some walking, some on stretchers, some dead; the priest went among them carrying out the last rites. Was this the way Christ wanted them to go? The most depressing picture of the war was for me the blanket-covered bodies on stretchers, their boots protruding from the end. For my part I kept falling into a delirious sleep, where I told General Montgomery to sing 'God Save America' with his trousers down. When I awoke it was evening. I'd been lying there about four hours.

'Are they going to take me?' I asked an orderly.

'Yes, you're next, Corporal,' he comforted. 'We had a lot of badly wounded, we had to send them off first.'

With the sun setting, and the tent sides turning pink in the light, I was loaded aboard an ambulance in the top bunk. The top bunk! It all came back to me, the top bunk, that's the one my parents always put me in during those long train journeys across India on the old GIP* Railway . . . all seemed so long ago . . . The ambulance bumped and jolted through the narrow mountain roads. I recalled those bright sunlit Indian days, as a boy, where every day *was* like a Kipling story . . .

'Like a drink of water, Corporal?'

'Yes.'

The attendant poured water into a tin mug. I gulped down two, it tasted like nectar.

It was four stretchers to an ambulance; in between with his back

* Great Indian Peninsula.

to the driving cab sat an orderly. The inside was painted white. The vehicle smelt new. A blood plasma bottle was attached to the soldier on the lower bunk, his chest swathed in bandages. The orderly constantly checked the flow of the plasma. The German kept groaning. It all seemed to be coming to me through a heat-charged mist. I was hovering twix delirium and reality. I doze off.

The ambulance stops, nearby artillery are banging away, the doors open, it's dark, voices mixed with gunfire, I am being unloaded. I'm on the ground, from there a large municipal building with a flat roof is silhouetted against the night sky. Covered with ivy, it looks like the setting for *Gormenghast*. I am carried up stairs along corridors, more stairs, and finally into a dim-lit ward of about thirty beds, all with mozzy nets down. I am placed on the floor.

'Can you undress yourself?' says an overworked orderly.

Yes, I can.

'The pyjamas are under the pillow,' he points to a bed.

My God, it looked good, already turned down, white sheets and pillows, TWO PILLOWS, being ill was paying dividends. I pulled on the standard blue pyjamas.

'Where's the karzi?' I said weakly.

He pointed out the door. 'Dead opposite.'

I wasn't quite dead but I went opposite; that journey over, I pulled my body under the sheets. I was desperately tired and feverish, but stayed awake to enjoy the luxury of sheets. Another orderly; they all wear gym shoes so you don't hear them coming, he took my pulse, temperature, entered them on a board that hung on the foot of my bed.

'Like some tea?' He spoke Yorkshire.

'Aye,' I said in Yorkshire.

'Anything to eat?'

'Yes, anything.'

He came back with a plate of tomato soup and bread. On the tray were four white tablets.

'Take these when you dun, they'll help bring temperature down.'

'I don't want it down, I want it up for the duration.'

I gulped it down. Took the tablets, brought them all up. Who said romance was dead? So much for my first forty-eight hours in Italy.

26 September 1943, 0600 hrs

Awakened by a nurse. A *female* nurse, all pink and scrubbed in spotless uniform smelling of Pears soap.

'Darling, I love you, marry me,' I said.

'Good morning,' she said, threw back the mozzy net and before I could answer had stuffed a thermometer in my gob.

'It's down,' she said.

'What's down?' I said.

'You're only a 100.'

She bent over the next bed, and showed two shapely legs, one would have been enough. I felt my temperature go up again. I really was ill. I fell asleep, an orderly woke me up with breakfast. The ward was coming to life, I wasn't; orderlies were taking down the last of the blackouts, those patients who could were putting the mozzy nets up, trailing out to the ablutions, others were swallowing medicines, here comes mine, four white tablets, what are they? The orderly doesn't know.

'I don't have to,' he says, 'then if you die it's not my fault.'

Cheerful bugger. For the first two days my temperature goes up and down, and so I'm not alone, I go with it. At night it was worst with delirium and terrible dreams. However, gradually I start to recover. The nurse (I wish I could remember her name) tells me of an incident. In the officers' section there's a Colonel from the RAOC; he's due for a hernia operation, the matron has been given the job of shaving him, she knocks on the door.

'Come in,' says the Colonel.

The matron throws back the bedclothes, lathers all around his willy, shaves him and starts to leave. The Colonel says, 'Pardon me, matron, but why did you bother to knock?'

In the next bed is a Marine Commando, Jamie Notam. He's in with our old friend 'Shell Shock', received during the landings around Marina. He was forty-one, a bit old for a Commando.

'I used to be a Gentleman's Gentleman,' he's speaking with a broad Scots accent.

Jamie is sitting on the edge of his bed, he is in his battle dress, his boots highly polished, a hangover from his gentleman's gentleman days. His bed was immaculate, his eating irons and mess-tins shine like silver. He basically wanted to *do* things; if he folded a newspaper it was always perfectly square, but there the creation stopped. He could never *make* anything. It was always *do* but what he did was perfect. He must have been the ideal servant.

THE BATTLE

Aim! said the Captain
Fire! said the King
Shoot! said the General
Boom! Bang! Ping!

Boom! went the Cannon
Bang! went the Gun
Ping! went the Rifle
Battle had begun!

Ouch! said a Prussian
Help! said the Hun
Surrender! said the Englishman
Battle had been won!

Melbourne
April 1980

– from *Unspun Socks from a Chicken's Laundry*

~⟡~

The Battle of Spion Kop
from *More Goon Show Scripts*, Woburn Press 1973

The Goon Show, no. 250 (9th Series, no. 9)
Transmission:
Monday, 29 December 1958: 8.30–9.00 p.m. Home Service
Wednesday, 31 December 1958: 9.30–10.00 p.m. Light
*   Programme*
Studio: Camden Theatre, London

Can England be saved by the British Army's rendition of 'Good-Bye Dolly I must leave you'? Will what saved Lord Nelson at Waterloo, likewise save Willium 'Mate' Cobblers from a fate worse than bananas? . . . And is French Neddie's accent convincing? These and answers to other vital questions will not be revealed in the following pages. However, the full Technicolor spectacle of British military dinners under fire, Bloodnok's secret woman recipe, and Moriarty's socks are here to be observed in microscopic detail, along with the full story of how the peaceful hamlet of Poknoips became the turbulent battleground of Spion Kop!

THE MAIN CHARACTERS

Ned Seagoon	Harry Secombe
Major Denis Bloodnok	Peter Sellers
Captain Jympton	Spike Milligan
Eccles	Spike Milligan
Recruiting Sergeant	Harry Secombe
Moriarty	Spike Milligan
Grytpype-Thynne	Peter Sellers
Member of Parliament	Spike Milligan
Henry Crun	Peter Sellers
Minnie Bannister	Spike Milligan

Bluebottle	Peter Sellers
French Neddie	Harry Secombe
Moriarty Bonaparte	Spike Milligan

The Ray Ellington Quartet
Max Geldray
Orchestra conducted by Wally Stott
Announcer: Wallace Greenslade
Script by Spike Milligan
Produced by John Browell

BILL: This is the BBC Light Programme. Now here is a variation on that. This is *the* BBC Light Programme.

OMNES & ORCHESTRA: MURMURS OF APPROVAL.

PETER: The old night school's paying off there, Wal.

HARRY: Yer, chat on more on it there Wal lad.

BILL: I continue my recital of announcements. The BBC is open to the public on Thursdays and Wednesday afternoons, or, on Wednesday afternoons and Thursdays.

SPIKE: Thank you Jim, now here folks is Chief Ellinga to say Thursday in Swahali.

RAY: Ma ar la toola, yarga toola marngo, me ar gar tula la margu uta meel tick arrs fargoola tol dommmmmmmm . . .

SPIKE: You see how long the days are in Africa folks. Forward Mr Seaside with your New Year's resolutions.

SEAGOON: Thank you. Hello folks, hello folks, it is me folks. Next year folks I hope to give up 1958 permanently.

PETER: *(As elder statesman)* Ungrateful beast, after all 1958 has done for you, you discard it like an old boot, I won't hear it.

SEAGOON: Let me warn you hairy sir, of the many dangers and dongers of keeping on old years after it's worn out. Mrs Greenslade's husband will now tell you why.

BILL: It was the year 1907 and here is the orchestra to play it.

1923. Leo and Florence, showing their equestrian skills.

April 1928. The gun belt was a birthday present from his father.

1930. His first suit. So normal – what happened?

1940. He loved the army life. His smile says it all.

1945. The Bill Hall Trio and the start of it all for Spike. He wrote sketches for the show.

1946. The Bill Hall Trio with Milligan on guitar. Where's his beloved trumpet?

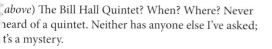

(*above*) The Bill Hall Quintet? When? Where? Never heard of a quintet. Neither has anyone else I've asked; it's a mystery.

(*right*) 1948. The year he hoped to go solo but joined another trio: the Ann Lenner Trio.

(*below*) 1948. Ann auditioned him for a 'singing spot' and they toured Europe.

1950

IF LOVE COULD FIND A WAY

SONG

WORDS AND MUSIC

BY

~~JACK JORDAN,~~ } 1%
~~JAMES GRAFTON~~
& TERENCE MILLIGAN 99%

EDWARD COX MUSIC Co.LTD.
142, CHARING CROSS R9, LONDON,W.C.2

Made in England.

1950. His first attempt at songwriting and music. Typical Spike; he loved his alterations.

1951. His big break, as a vocalist with Joe Loss.

Shepherds Bush Empire

Chairman	...	...	...	...	...	PRINCE LITTLER
Supervisor	...	...	...	...	...	JOHN CHRISTIE
Manager	...	...	...	...	...	J. H. CHRISTIE, Jnr.

BOOK BY 'PHONE ... ... SHEpherds Bush 4531 (3 lines)

6.30 TWICE NIGHTLY **8.40**
MONDAY, FEBRUARY 19th, 1951

1 OVERTURE

2 THE VERNON SISTERS
Dancing Around

3 BOB WAYNE & BARBARA
" Slightly Insane "

4 THE CARSONY BROTHERS
Sensational Hand Balancers

5 The Life and Soul of the Party
GEORGE DOONAN
" Smatterwitchew ?"

6 INTERMISSION
CHARLES HENRY with the EMPIRE ORCHESTRA

7 THE SKATING DEXTERS
A Boy & A Girl in a Whirl

8 LESLIE ADAMS
" Eve's Delight "

9 " IN THE MOOD "
Britain's King of Rhythm In Person

JOE LOSS

presents his new 1951 BAND SHOW

PERSONNEL

Conductor	...	...	...	JOE LOSS
Vocalists	...	...	...	Howard Jones
				Elizabeth Batey
				Tony Ventro
				Irene Miller
				Spike Milligan
Saxophones	...	...	Manny Prince—Alto
			Danny Miller—Alto
			Joe Temperley—Tenor
			Bill Unsworth—Tenor
			Tony Beck—Baritone & Sax
Trumpets	...	...	Sid Pollitt
			Reg Arnold
			Joe Ward
Trombones	...	...	Don Clark
			George Wilder
			Clair Welsh
Piano	...	...	Syd Lucas
Bass	...	...	Syd Burke
Percussion	...	...	Phil Seamon

Manager : William Treacy   Secretary : Miss R. Wright
Arranger : Leslie Vinall

| COLISEUM | DRURY LANE |
| CHARING CROSS | THEATRE ROYAL |

Commencing THURS. MAR. 8th
JACK HYLTON presents
'KISS ME KATE'
MUSIC by COLE PORTER
Every Evening 7.30. WED. & SAT. 2.30

CAROUSEL
A RODGERS and HAMMERSTEIN
Musical Success
EVENINGS AT 7.15
MATS. WED. & SAT. 2.30

STOLL THEATRE, Kingsway
Commencing MON. FEB. 26th.
EVENINGS at 7.30
MATS. : WED. & SAT. 2.30

The ' Gay ' and ' Exciting '
SPANISH BALLET of
TERESA and LUISILLO
And Their
Company of
Spanish Dancers
and Musicians

1951. Signing the contract for 'The Crazy People', the first series of what became *The Goon Show*.

(*right*) 1952. Now recording as *The Goon Show* – and in suits and ties!

(*below*) 1952. Practising his Minnie Bannister voice.

A rare card – the only one I know of with all of their signatures. It must be late 1952 because Michael Bentine had already left the show. (By kind permission of the *Goon Show* Preservation Society.)

1953. On the set of *The Harry Secombe Show*, famous for Spike and Eric's 'Mirror Routine'.

1960. Spike gave me this photo and said, 'We were happy then.' Said with such sadness.

1962. Spike and his father in the gun room at Woy Woy. He loved the times they shared together in that room.

1965. John Bluthal's Christmas card to Spike.

"No More Swing"
by
Jock Strap
and his
Elastic Band

Merry Christmas
Happy Chanukah
Jack Blumenthall

(*above left*) 1967. *Ben Gunn* at the Mermaid Theatre. Women found him attractive!

(*above right*) *Son of Oblomov* broke all box office records at the Comedy Theatre.

(*centre left*) April 1966. Maggie Jones's Restaurant, last-night party of *Son of Oblomov*.

(*below left*) 1968. *Curry and Chips* – a TV programme written by Johnny Speight. Spike loved the role of 'Paki Paddy'.

ORCHESTRA: NEW MAD LINK ALL OVER THE SHOP. SINGING IN THE MIDDLE. SOUND F.X. IN MUSIC. FINISHES ON A CHORD.

SEAGOON: Ohhh what a year that was . . . the South African war had broken out and was now in its second year.

OMNES & ORCHESTRA: SING HAPPY BIRTHDAY –
(Fade)

SEAGOON: Knock knock knock on a door in Africa.

BLOODNOK: Knock knock on a door in Africa . . . Gad, that's the address of my door – come in!

SEAGOON: Effects door opens . . .

BLOODNOK: Ahhh 'effects Ahhh'.

SEAGOON: May I introduce myself?

BLOODNOK: Of course.

SEAGOON: *(Announcing)* Ladies and Gentlemen! The man in the blue corner is Neddie Seagoon.

SEAGOON: *(Normal)* Thank you. I'm 5th Lieutenant Seagoon reporting from Sandhurst SW9.

BLOODNOK: Oh, sit down on that chair in Africa SE16.

F.X.: DUCK CALL.

SEAGOON: Thank you. I was told to hand this envelope to you with a hand . . .

BLOODNOK: Oh . . . Pronounced . . .

GRAMS: BLOODNOK Oooooooooooooh!!!

F.X.: ENVELOPE OPENING.

BLOODNOK: Oh, these are your secret orders.

SEAGOON: What do they say?

BLOODNOK: Standddddd Attttttt . . . Ease . . .

GRAMS: REGIMENT STANDING AT EASE.

SEAGOON: *(Relief)* Oh, that feels much better sir.

BLOODNOK: Yes, and it suits you what's more. Now to military matters, of milt. Captain Jympton?

GRAMS: MAD DAHS OF COCONUT SHELLS HORSES HOOVES VERY BRIEF, VERY FAST, APPROACHING TO FOREGROUND.

JYMPTON: Ah *(stutters)* . . . sorry I'm late sir, I . . . was quelling a native with ah . . . quells.

BLOODNOK: You'll get the military piano and bar for this, ah . . . now explain the victorious positions of our defeated troops.

JYMPTON: Ah . . . intelligence ah . . . has established that the ah . . . people attacking us ar . . . are . . . are . . . the enemy.

BLOODNOK: So that's their fiendish game is it?

SEAGOON: Gentlemen, do the enemy realize that you have this information?

BLOODNOK: Oh no, we got 'em fooled, they think that *we're* the enemy.

SEAGOON: What a perfect disguise.

JYMPTON: Ha ha ha, yes you see Lieutenant Seagoon we have a plan – a plan of plin and ploof. The South Africans are magnificent fighters, and it's our intention to persuade them to come over to our side.

SEAGOON: Then that would finish the war sir!

JYMPTON: Oh no! Ha ha ha. Oh dearie no!

SEAGOON: Then how would you keep it going?

JYMPTON: England, my dear sir, is never short of enemies!

BLOODNOK: Of course not the waiting room's full of 'em. Now Seagoon, sit down, tell me what's the time back in England?

SEAGOON: Twenty to four sir.

BLOODNOK: Ah . . . it's nice to hear the old time again . . . Singhiz?

SINGHIZ: Yes sir?

F.X.: SLAPSTICK.

BLOODNOK: Now get out will you! You see, Seagoon, how bad things are! That banana for instance . . . It's only been eaten once, and look at it!

SEAGOON: But sir, back in England they told me all was well.

BLOODNOK: Back in England, all *is* well. It's *here* where the trouble lies.

GRAMS: EXPLOSION.

BLOODNOK: *(Over above)* Oh – what the – eh – what?

GRAMS: APPROACH OF OLD CAR BACK FIRING. GRINDING OF GEAR. PARPING ON BULB HORN. CAR EXPLODES . . . GUSHER OF STEAM. FALLS TO BITS . . . YELLS.

ECCLES: Well . . . I think I'll pull-up here.

BLOODNOK: I say you . . . you with the apparent teeth.

ECCLES: Ohh a soldier . . . Hello soldier . . . Bang . . . Bang . . . Bang Bang . . . Bang – you're dead soldier!

SEAGOON: Let me talk to him. I speak Idiot fluently . . . *(Does Eccles impression)* Hello Ecclesssss.

ECCLES: Oh? . . . You must be from the old country . . . Oh hohoh!

BLOODNOK: Neddie allow me to humour him with this mallet.

SEAGOON: No no no, leave it to me. *(As Eccles)* Tell us Mad Dan, wha' are you doing in Africa . . . Wha'n 'u doin' Afric-aaa . . .

ECCLES: 'What are you doing in Africa' I translated. I'm here as an adviser to the British Army.

SEAGOON: *(As Eccles)* Splendid, what are you going to advise them?

ECCLES: Not to take me.

BLOODNOK: Oh, I respect your cowardice, it warms my heart

and gives old Denis a real smart idea. Come over here and warm yourself by this Recruiting Sergeant.

SERGEANT: *(Cockney)* 'Ello 'ello 'ello my lad, you look a likely lad.

ECCLES: HELLO, hello, hello my laddddd. Yourn loonk linke a ohn *(Rubbish)* . . .

SERGEANT: Very gude, very gude . . . 'ere lad, 'ow would you like to 'ave a grandstand view of the opening night of the Battle of Spion Kop dere.

BLOODNOK: Just a moment Sergeant . . . Spion Kop! He can have my place I tell you!

SERGEANT: Oh ho ho?

BLOODNOK: Yes, just by chance Sergeant I have a vacant uniform in the front rank, he'll see everything from there.

SERGEANT: Now then, you 'eard that very fair offer from the nice Major dere.

ECCLES: Yes, he's a nice Major – ah a nice man. How much do you want fer it?

BLOODNOK: Well, usually it's free, but just this once it will be seven shillings, so . . . ah shall we say a pound?

ECCLES: A pound?

BLOODNOK: You said it.

ECCLES: Oh . . . I've only got a five-pound note.

BLOODNOK: Well, I'll take that and you can pay me the other four later.

F.X.: TILL.

BLOODNOK: Oh, the old Military till.

SERGEANT: You're a very lucky ladddd . . . I'll have a regiment call for you at six tomorrow morning. Meantime here is the well known 'Conks' Geldray. A sittin' target.

MAX: Boy, in the war my conk holds its own.

MAX & ORCHESTRA: MUSIC.

(Applause)

ORCHESTRA: DRAMATIC 'RETURN TO THE STORY' LINK (PRE-BATTLE).

GRAMS: HORSE ARTILLERY TROTTING UP THE LINE. DISTANT TRAMP OF SOLDIERS PLODDING ALONG ROUGH ROAD.

BILL: At Dawn the British attack was mounted, not very well stuffed but beautifully mounted. And then suddenly through the stilled British front line, a lone voice is heard.

MORIARTY: *(Approaching)* Lucky charms . . . get your lucky charms before the battle . . . get your lucky charmsssssss. *(Sings)* Get your self a charm today, and save yourself from harm today.

WILLIUM: 'Ere . . . 'ere mate . . . charm man? 'Ere.

MORIARTY: What is it merry drummer man.

WILLIUM: Them charms, are they any cop mate?

MORIARTY: Ah, they're . . . they're real cop mate – Nelson bought one for Waterloo.

WILLIUM: He weren't at Waterloo.

MORIARTY: Of course not, he was in my shop buying a lucky charm. You see how lucky they are.

WILLIUM: How much is a good one then?

MORIARTY: Well certainly, what part don't you want to be wounded in?

WILLIUM: I don't want any of me parts wounded.

MORIARTY: I know, you want the all parts comprehensive charm.

WILLIUM: Hurry up then – how much??

MORIARTY: Three shillings, a bargain . . .

WILLIUM: THERE – I pins it on me chest so me chest won't get killed.

F.X.: PISTOL SHOT.

WILLIUM: Owwwwwwwwwwwwww Mateeeeeeeee.

F.X.: THUD OF BODY.

MORIARTY: Good shot Grytpype.

GRYTPYPE-THYNNE: Unpin the lucky charm and back on the tray with it. Off you go.

MORIARTY: Charms, second-hand lucky charms. *(Fading)* Only used once . . .

GRYTPYPE-THYNNE: There he goes, a true son of France and Hyde Park. Who knows what mystic thoughts are whispering in the mossy glades of his krutty shins.

HARRY: *(Hooray off)* I say, do you mind taking your hat off, old chap? The battle's about to begin, and we can't see you know.

GRAMS: BATTLE STARTS – FIRST THE VOLLEYS OF MUSKETRY, THEN DISTANT CANNONS. THE RETURN FIRE OF THE ENEMY IS EVEN MORE DISTANT. FADE DOWN & UNDER. FADE IN BIG BEN CHIMING. FADE.

ELDER STATESMAN: Gentlemen of the house, the Battle of Spion Kop opened last night.

OMNES & ORCHESTRA: Hear Hear! Long Live the Empire!

ELDER STATESMAN: Ahh, but I fear it got very bad notices in the Press.

M.P.: You're not thinking of taking it off are you, Mr Prime Minister?

ELDER STATESMAN: Well, unless Robert Morley puts some money in I can see no other way . . .

M.P.: But what about Binkie and his backers, they'll lose their money.

ELDER STATESMAN: Patience sir, patience. We have here Lieutenant Seagoon, who will proceed to give us the reason for the disaster.

SEAGOON: Thank you, Hon Members. The reason for it flopping was obvious . . . there isn't one decent song in the whole battle.

PETER: *(As another statesman)* But soldier fellow, the Battle of Spion Kop isn't musical!

SEAGOON: And that's where we went wrong. If the Americans had been running it they'd have had Rex Harrison, and the other wrecks.

ELDER STATESMAN: Do you know any good composers of battle scores?

SEAGOON: Just by chance and careful planning, I have an auntie in Grimsby who sits among the cabbages and plays an elastic water tank under supervision.

ELDER STATESMAN: *(Ecstatic)* I didn't know there were any of her kind left you know. Now off you go and tell your auntie the good news.

GRAMS: RUNNING FOOTSTEPS & HARRY SINGS 'LAND OF HOPE AND GLORY' SPEEDING UP INTO THE DISTANCE.

ORCHESTRA: DRAMATIC CHORDS.

F.X.: HAMMERING OF A METAL SPOON ON ANVIL.

CRUN: *(Over hammering mutters)* Ohh, dear . . . there . . . now that's got the spoons in fine-spoons fettle Min.

F.X.: QUICK TWO SPOONS TOGETHER À LA BUSKERS.

CRUN *(Sings)* 'Na ahah, ahah, ahah, ah'. Now Min, get inside the piano and select me a tuning A.

GRAMS: ONE SHEEP BLEATING.

CRUN: Again Min.

GRAMS: ONE SHEEP BLEATING AGAIN.

CRUN: Oh, they don't make pianos like that any more.

MINNIE: Isn't it time we had it shorn Henery?

CRUN: No, not yet Min, the winters aren't upon us yet, you know. Hand me my knuckle oils.

MINNIE: Now Crun rub it well into the knuckles . . . it's mixed with Indian brandyyy.

BOTH: *(Cries of brandyyy brandyyy)*.

CRUN: Oh Min.

F.X.: AGONIZING KNUCKLE CRACKING.

CRUN: *(Muttering over)* It's no good Min, I've got flat-feet in the third knuckle you know Min . . . Ah! . . . Ah well – Now to try for the Paganini variations for spoons arranged – Crun!!!!

GRAMS: DISC OF VARIATIONS. CRUN PLAYS SPOONS AND WHISTLES.

CRUN: Stop! Stop stop! This spoon is out of tune, Min. Have you been eating with it again?

MINNIE: No.

CRUN: *(Power)* Then what's that you're stirring the soup with?

MINNIE: A violin.

CRUN: She's always got an answer the old cow. Now to compose the last tune for the Battle of Spion Kop.

F.X.: BUSKER SPOONS IN TEMPO. MINNIE & CRUN SING 'DOLLY GREY' FADE.

GRAMS: FADE UP BATTLE NOISES. EXPLOSIONS. ETC.

BLOODNOK: Aaaaaaaahhhh . . . aaahhh . . . ahhhhhhh. Ellinga . . . turn the volume of that battle down.

F.X.: DOOR BURSTS OPEN.

SEAGOON: Major! The enemy are . . .

BLOODNOK: Aaahhhhh . . . Ah!

GRAMS: WHOOSH.

SEAGOON: Good heavens, he's gone. Ah here are his boots, they're still warm, he can't be far.

BLOODNOK: *(Slightly off)* Aaahhh, there ain't nobody here but us chickens I tell you.

SEAGOON: The voice came from a cowardly red-face on the top of a chicken wardrobe.

BLOODNOK: Oh, it's you Seagoon, you you coward.

SEAGOON: Why have you deserted your post?

BLOODNOK: It's got woodworm sir.

SEAGOON: Old jokes won't save you.

BLOODNOK: They've saved Monkhouse and Goodwin, and that's good enough for me.

SEAGOON: Major, there's still hope. Crun's vital battle songs have arrived.

BLOODNOK: It won't be easy sir. The enemy have just attacked in E-Flat. And we had to retire to G-Minor.

SEAGOON: Never mind sir, these old songs are all written in six-sharps.

BLOODNOK: The most powerful brown key of them all. Get Ellinga and his Zulu bones to dash off a chorus towards the enemy.

SEAGOON: Fire – !

RAY ELLINGTON QUARTET: MUSIC

(Applause)

ORCHESTRA: DRAMATIC CHORDS.

GRAMS: BUGLE CALL AT VARYING PITCHES, MURMURS OF TROOPS TAKING UP POSITIONS.

SEAGOON: At dawn under cover of daylight we took up our positions with our teeth blacked out.

SPIKE: *(Woeful)* Every man has his ammunition pouches bulging with offensive military songs and spoons at the ready.

SEAGOON: Right. We'll just have to sit and wait.

(Long pause)

BLUEBOTTLE: You tink we're goin' to win, Captain?

SEAGOON: Never was victory more certain little lad.

BLUEBOTTLE: Oh . . . then why have you got that taxi waiting for you at the end of the trench.

SEAGOON: Ha ha . . . here's half-a-crown little lad. I think we can forget all about it now.

BLUEBOTTLE: No . . . I can't forget about it.

F.X.: COLOSSAL CLOUT.

BLUEBOTTLE: Ahh . . . I forgotten about it.

SEAGOON: Now explain to me why you're lying down two inches below the level of the ground and speaking through a tombstone.

BLUEBOTTLE: Well, I was doing an impression of a zebra crossing when . . . squelch! . . . a taxi ran over me breaking both my boots above the wrist.

SEAGOON: What agony igony ogony oogany mahogany . . . Did it hurt you?

BLUEBOTTLE: No because I'm making it all up. Ha hee . . .

SEAGOON: Taxi!

GRAMS: TAXI APPROACHES AT TERRIFIC SPEED. JELLY THUD SOUND.

BLUEBOTTLE: Oooh. You've taxied me. Look, the Christmas string's coming off my legs.

SEAGOON: Swallow this first-aid book and custard. I'll have your legs relacquered free and exported to Poland.

BLUEBOTTLE: You're a fair man, sir . . . Merry Krudmas.

ECCLES: Ooh, Bottle. What you doing under that taxi?

BLUEBOTTLE: It ran over me, Eccles.

ECCLES: You must be rich . . . I can only afford to be run over by buses.

BLUEBOTTLE: Well my man when you're in the big money you know, you can do things like this.

ECCLES: You see, one day I'll have enough money to be run over by a Rolls-Royce with a chauffeur.

BLUEBOTTLE: Well, pull me out then.

ECCLES: Right. Hold this.

BLUEBOTTLE: What is it?

ECCLES: I don't know, but I got it cheap.

SEAGOON: Let me see what you got cheap?

GRAMS: TIGER GROWL.

SEAGOON: Good heavens it's a genuine hand operated 1914 tiger!

BLOODNOK: Seagoon, put that tiger back in its stripes . . . we don't want any scandals during ladies' night.

JYMPTON: Pardon me, sir. All the men are ready with their music.

BLOODNOK: Good, let's have those spoons then lad.

ORCHESTRA: EACH MAN ISSUED WITH TWO SPOONS. THEY MAKE NOISE LIKE BUSKERS.

BLOODNOK: Oooh . . . what a terrifying sound. It's a good job nobody heard it.

SEAGOON: Now men, to your military Crun music and take up your vocal positions with your voices facing outwards.

BLOODNOK: And don't sing men until you see the whites of their song sheets. Bugler, sound the elephant.

GRAMS: INFURIATED HIGH-PITCHED TRUMPETING BY SINGLE ELEPHANT.

BLOODNOK: Ohhh . . .

JYMPTON: Here they come now, sir.

BLOODNOK: Quick, me spoons and me music. I'll show 'em . . .

F.X.: TWO SPOONS BUSKING IN TEMPO TO BLOODNOK SINGING 'GOODBYE DOLLY, I MUST LEAVE YOU'.

BLOODNOK: 'Goodbye Dolly, I must leave you.' *(Shouts)* Come on you fools, there's more where that came from. *(Continues singing)* 'Off we go and fight the foe.' *(Shouts)* Sing up lads!

OMNES & ORCHESTRA: ALL JOIN IN SINGING AND RATTLING SPOONS.

GRAMS: SHELLS START BURSTING IN THEIR MIDST. STARTING SLOWLY & INCREASING IN INTENSITY. BLOODNOK CONTINUES TO SING BUT GRADUALLY HIS MORALE IS DESTROYED. HE BREAKS OFF.

BLOODNOK: Run for it lads . . . Oooh, these songs aren't bullet proof.

GRAMS: WHOLE ARMY RUNS AWAY YELLING IN TERROR. SPEED UP AND FADE.

(Pause)

GRAMS: ARCTIC GALE HOWLING. OCCASIONAL WOLVES. THEN APPROACH OF RUNNING ARMY STILL YELLING & PANTING. ALL GRADUALLY SLOW DOWN BY SLOWING RECORD.

BLOODNOK: That's far enough lads, where are we?

SEAGOON: The South Pole sir.

BLOODNOK: No further, we don't want to back into them. Oh . . . plant the Union Jack will you? The national flag of the Union of Jacks. I claim the South Pole in the name of Gladys Ploog of 13 The Sebastibal Villas, Sutton.

SEAGOON: Who is she, sir?

BLOODNOK: I don't know, but obviously we're doing her a big favour.

SEAGOON: There's still a chance of victory. Look what I've got in the brown paper parcel.

F.X.: RUSTLING OF PAPER.

BLOODNOK: Good heavens white paper, what a glorious
victory for England.

SEAGOON: Look under the stamp.

BLOODNOK: What? A fourteen-inch naval gun.

ECCLES: And guess what's in the barrel?

BLOODNOK: I've no idea.

SEAGOON: Major, inside the barrel are photographs of a
British military dinner.

BLOODNOK: Really . . . Keep it going lads, keep it going.

SEAGOON: I intend to fire that photograph at the enemy
canteen during their lunch break. When they see the size of
British military dinners they'll desert.

BLOODNOK: I know . . . half our men deserted when they saw
the size of 'em. However it's worth a try. Take aim . . . fire!

**GRAMS: COLOSSAL EXPLOSION. FOLLOWED BY PILES
OF BONES FALLING ON TO THE GROUND.**

BLUEBOTTLE: Ah . . . that's the last time I kip in a barrel.
Collapses, and is left out of show from now onwards. Goodnight everybody.

GRAMS: CHEERS, APPLAUSE.

BLUEBOTTLE: Oh . . . by popular request I come back again.

F.X.: SLAPSTICK.

BLUEBOTTLE: Ahhh . . .

SEAGOON: All we can do is to wait and see what effect that
photograph of a military dinner has on the enemy. Meantime a sound effect.

GRAMS: WIND UP AND WOLVES HOWLING.

BILL: Meantime in Parliament the British Government had
written off the Battle of Spion Kop as a dead loss.

HARRY: *(Statesman)* Gentlemen, um, um . . . to save face and the honour of England, we're going to bring back that old favourite um, ah . . . the Battle of Waterloo.

OMNES & ORCHESTRA: ANCIENT MURMURS OF APPROVAL.

ELDER STATESMAN: Gentlemen, we shall send out immediate notification to the original cast.

ORCHESTRA: MARSEILLAISE-TYPE LINK.

MORIARTY BONAPARTE: *(Snoring).*

F.X.: DOOR OPENING.

FRENCH NEDDIE: Mon Emperor, wake up!

MORIARTY BONAPARTE: How dare you wake the Emperor Napoleon up in the middle of his retirement.

FRENCH NEDDIE: Wonderful news . . . by special request we have to do an encore of the Battle of Waterloo.

MORIARTY BONAPARTE: What . . . but we lost it.

FRENCH NEDDIE: This time we've got a British backer.

MORIARTY BONAPARTE: Get my trousers oiled and unwrap a fresh Josephine . . . ahh, there's going to be fun tonight.

F.X.: THWACK.

GRYTPYPE-THYNNE: Down Emperor down . . . back to your grave. You know you're not allowed out after your death.

MORIARTY BONAPARTE: Blast these silly rules.

GRYTPYPE-THYNNE: My card Neddie.

SEAGOON: This is a piece of string.

GRYTPYPE-THYNNE: Have you no imagination lad. I am Lord Ink.

SEAGOON: Not Pennan?

GRYTPYPE-THYNNE: Yes Pennan Ink.

ORCHESTRA: CHORD IN C.

SEAGOON: Don't worry folks, it's getting near the end now. All pay-offs will be gratefully received.

GRYTPYPE-THYNNE: One coming up, Ned. Unfortunately my client Moriarty is appearing in 'The Death of Napoleon' at the local nackers yard . . . it looks like being a very long run.

SEAGOON: It looks like being a long run? What does?

GRYTPYPE-THYNNE: Ten miles.

F.X.: PISTOL SHOT.

GRAMS: TWO PAIRS OF RUNNING FEET.

SEAGOON: *(Panting)* As we ran we discussed the contract for the Battle of Waterloo. Later at Preston Barracks Brighton, we auditioned for the part of the Duke of Wellington.

GRAMS: FADE IN PETER SINGING LAST PART OF 'ANY OLD IRON' MATE.

SEAGOON: Thank you. Wait inside the piano one moment will you. What do you think?

GRYTPYPE-THYNNE: He's not the Lord Wellington type you know.

SEAGOON: Yes *(Calls out)*, I say – we'll write and let you know.

WILLIUM: Let me know what?

SEAGOON: That you're no good for the part.

WILLIUM: Rite – I won't take another job till I hear that, then.

SEAGOON: Next please.

ECCLES: *(Sings)* I'll follow my secret heart till I find you . . .

SEAGOON: One moment. *(Aside)* Where's my pistol?

GRYTPYPE-THYNNE: No Neddie no one moment . . .

MORIARTY BONAPARTE: Grytpype . . . with Eccles playing the part of Wellington this time the French are bound to win the Battle of Waterloo.

GRYTPYPE-THYNNE: Right . . . Eccles? Button the hat and sword. Now Charge . . .

GRAMS: GREAT GALLOPING OF HORSES INTO

**DISTANCE WITH SHOTS, SCREAMS AND MORE
SHOTS.**

SEAGOON: *(In tears)* No . . . we've . . . we've lost the Battle of
Waterloo.

MORIARTY: New history books . . . get your new history
books here . . . read all the truth about Waterloo.

F.X.: PHONE RINGS.

SEAGOON: Hello?

BLOODNOK: Seagoon, look here, a right twitt you made of
yourself firing that photo of a dinner at the enemy. Do you
know what they've fired back?

SEAGOON: What?

BLOODNOK: The photograph of an empty plate.

SEAGOON: Well, there you are folks, the old anti-climax again.

ORCHESTRA: 'OLD COMRADES MARCH' PLAYOUT.

from Mussolini: His Part in My Downfall

Towering above the countryside, with vines growing on its lower
slopes, was the ominous shape of Vesuvius; like me it smoked heavily.
At night, from my bed, I could see the purple-red glow from its throat;
it looked magnificent. At one time it had looked so to those doomed
people, the Pompeians, but I wasn't a Pompeian, I was Irish, how could
Vesuvius wipe out Dublin? No, I was perfectly safe, but Vesuvius
wasn't. I discovered that Pompeii was but three miles as the crow flies.
This incredible relic of a Roman city free of camera-clicking tourists
was a situation I had to thank Hitler for. Thank you, Hitler!

HITLER: 'You hear zat, Goebbels? Milligan is visiting Pompeii.
Keep all tourists out, and zer ruins *in*!'

After roll-call, accompanied by a Private Webb, we hitched and walked till we arrived at the gates. There was no one about, save a sleepy unshaven attendant, who said he had no tickets and charged twenty lire to go in, which he put straight into his pocket. It was a day I shall treasure, a day I met the past, not only the past but the people from it, be it they were now only plaster casts. I had read Pliny the Younger's account of that terrible day of destruction, *Gells Pompiana* and several text-books, so I was reasonably well informed. We had gone in the entrance that opened on to the amphitheatre and the Grande Palestra on our right. The excitement it generated in me was unbelievable, and it stayed with me all day. I don't think there are many sights as touching as the family who died together in the basement of their home, off the Via Vesuvio, the mother and father each side of three little girls, their arms protecting them this two thousand years. There were the lovers who went on banging away even though being suffocated. He *must* have been a Gunner. What a way to go!

All through that warm dusty day I wandered almost in a dream through the city, now almost deserted save for an occasional soldier.

It was late evening when we finally arrived at the Porta Ercolano that led into the Via dei Sepolcri. We sat in the mouth of one of the tombs and smoked a fag. Webb was knocked out.

'Bloody hell,' he said. 'I never heard of the place, I never knew it existed, they don't say a bloody word about places like this at school. Alfred the Great, Henry the Eighth, Nelson, Queen Victoria and that's the bloody lot.'

I discovered that the Americans had actually bombed it! They believed German Infantry were hiding in it! Not much damage had been done, museum staff were already at work trying to repair it. Bombing Pompeii!!! Why not the Pyramids, Germans might be hiding there? Or bomb the Astoria Cinema, Wasdale Road, Forest Hill, that's an ideal hiding-place for Germans? Or bomb Mrs Grollick's boarding house, Hagley Road, Birmingham?

Webb afforded me amusing incidents during the day; we approached the front of a house in the Via de Mercurio; another shabby unshaven attendant was standing outside. He looked like a bag of laundry with a head on. He indicated a boxed partition on the wall. '*Vediamo questo?*' he said, and the innuendo was that of something 'naughty'.

'*Si*,' I said fluently.

We gave him ten lire each, and with a well-worn key he opened the door. It revealed a male figure dressed as a Roman soldier; holding up his kilt from under it was an enormous phallus that rested on a pair of scales, the other scale held a bar of gold. Very interesting, but the point of it all escaped me.

'Wot's 'ee weighing 'is balls for?' said Webb, the true archaeologist.

'I think it's something to do with wartime rationing.'

The Italian explains the message, the man is saying, 'I would rather have my prick than a bar of gold.' Wait till he's sixty, I thought.

Another diversion is the Lupanarium.

''Ere, isn't that a man's prick sticking out over the door?'

'Well, it certainly isn't a woman's.'

It was a monster made of concrete and about a foot long.

'What's it doin' up there?' says Webb.

I demonstrate by hanging my hat on it.

'A hat-stand? Get away.'

'Well, it's a stand of some kind,' I explained, 'and this is a house of ill repute.'

Webb grinned from ear to ear. 'Ahh, that's why they got that bloody great chopper sticking out, then.'

'You should have been a Latin scholar,' I said.

The Lupanarium: around the walls were paintings, or rather a catalogue of the various positions that the clients could have; there was everything but standing on the head. I observed that the cubicles the ladies had to perform in were woefully small, one would have to have been five foot four or a cripple. It must have been an interesting sight that day of the eruption, all fourteen cubicles banging away and suddenly Vesuvius explodes, out the door shoot men with erections and no trousers followed by naked screaming tarts. You don't get that stuff in the film versions.

The sun was setting when we retraced our footsteps. I was loath to leave but I was to return here again in exciting circumstances. We hitched back on several lorries including one American with a coloured driver, yellow.

'Ain't you limeys got any fuckin' transport?' he said.

'Yes, we have lots of transport, trams, buses, but they're all in Catford.'

He didn't know what I was talking about and he said so. 'What are you talkin' about, man?'

He hated me. I hated him. It was a perfect arrangement. We were just in time for dinner. I took mine to the billet (the walk did it good) and ate it in the semi-reclining position; when in Rome . . . Another occupant of our billet stumbled in. Corporal Percival, he's smelling of beer.

'Where have you been?'

'I been to Naples,' he said.

Naples wow! The big time! The Catford of Italy.

'I went to the Pictures, I saw . . . Betty Grable and Cesar Romero in *Coney Island*. Bai she's got lovely legs.'

'What about his?'

'Fook off.'

'Of course, I'll pack at once.'

Percival was a North Country lad, all 'Eeeee bai Gum'. He doted on Gracie Fields.

'Gracie Fields,' I guffawed, 'she's as funny as a steam roller going over a baby.'

'You must be bludy thick, she's a scream.'

'Yes, I scream every time I hear her sing.'

'Ooo do you think is foony then?'

'W. C. Fields, Marx Brothers.'

'Oooo?'

He'd never heard of them.

'I bet they're not as foony as Gracie, you put 'em next to her and she'd lose 'em.'

The mind boggled, Gracie Fields meets the Marx Brothers! Help! I tried to demonstrate to him how Groucho walked.

'Wot 'ee walk like that fur? It looks bludy daft.'

'It's supposed to, you nana, look! North Country humour is *all* bloody awful, all Eeeee bai Gum, flat hats and boiled puddens. I mean, you must be all simple to think George Formby's funny, I get the same feeling from him as if I'd been told my mother was dead.'

The onslaught silenced him, then he spoke. 'Milligan? That's Irish isn't it.'

'Yes, well I'm half Irish.'

'That's bludy truble . . . that's what keeps you simple minded.'

'Bernard Shaw and Oscar Wilde were Irish.'

'What bludy good did they do?'

'They were recognized as great writers.'

'Not by me, fook 'em.'

'Listen, mister, the worst thing in life I can think of is being tied to a post and forced to listen to George Formby . . .'

'All right, 'oo do you think is a gud singer?'

'Bing Crosby.'

''Im? 'ee sounds like 'ee's crapped 'imself and it's sliding down wun leg.'

'Yes . . . he *would* sound like that to you; I suppose you think Gigli is a load of crap as well.'

'Gigli? Who's she?'

'*He*'s a great opera singer.'

'Gracie Fields could sing opera standing on her head.'

'If she did, it would be the first time I'd laugh at her.'

Arguments like this were frequent; there seemed to be a love-hate relationship between the North and South, the South loved themselves and the North hated them for it. Percival had been down with sandfly fever like myself.

'Were you on the landings?'

'Nay, we cum in ten days after to lay Sumerfield Track for fighter planes ter land on, but ship with the stoof on were soonk by Jerry radio-controlled bomb.'

Percival had once brought me to the verge of tears; one night, he came in pissed as usual.

'Ever seen a white-eared elephant?' he said.

No, I hadn't. Whereupon he pulls the linings of his two trouser pockets out, opens his flies and hangs his willy out. I cried with laughter, who in God's name invented these tricks? and all the others like the swan flies East, sausage on a plate, sack of flour, the roaring of the lions, there was a touch of obscene genius about them all.

∼

THE SOLDIERS AT LAURO

Young are the dead
Like babies they lie
The wombs they blest once
Not healed dry
And yet – too soon
Into each space
A cold earth falls
On colder face.
Quite still they lie
These fresh reeds
Clutched in earth
Like winter seeds
But these will not bloom
When called by spring
To burst with leaf
And blossoming
They will sleep on
In silent dust
As crosses rot
And memories rust.

Italy 1943

– from *Small Dreams of a Scorpion*

⌐⌐⌐

THE YOUNG SOLDIERS

Why are they lying in some distant land
Why did they go, did they understand?
Young men they were
Young men they stay
But why did we send them away, away?

written during Korean War
30 March 1955

– from *The Bedside Milligan*

⌐⌐⌐

from Mussolini: His Part in My Downfall

Gunner Edgington's Public Appearance

'Crabs! They've got crabs!' the cry runs through the serried ranks.

The 'Theys' were the crew of Monkey 2, it was the first mass outbreak of crabs in the Battery; how proud we were of them, at last the label dirty bastards could be added to the Battery honours. The only other mass outbreak of crabs was Gunner Neat in Bexhill. He told the MO he got them off a girl in Blackpool. 'I brought them south for the sun, sir,' he said.

Among the crab-ridden is Gunner Edgington. Let him recount the grisly details.

We hadn't had our clothes off for some considerable time, much less our underwear, such as it might have been, and as I've said, a bath was something we only vaguely remembered from long ago. My hair was a matted lump. The whole world we knew at that time was to get phone lines out and keep them going – all else was sleep and food and a good deal of the latter was often scrounged from strange outfits we encountered while out on the line.

Not surprisingly we began to smell strongly and then to scratch: the irritation became incessant and something obviously had to be done: I don't think Bentley came to us . . . it was just arranged by phone calls, that we go over to RHQ.

I think there *must*'ve been more than the M2 team, for the 'crab-ridden' were taken in a three-tonner to where some showers had been erected in the corner of a field. The showers were a Heath Robinson contraption mounted under a tin roof on angle-iron supports, but they were thoroughly efficient.

Capt. Bentley, keeping a distance, called down instructions from the safety of his room on an upper floor of an adjacent building.

'Strip off!' he called to us, and this was just the Monkey 2 gang at this point. 'Have a thorough wash-down all over as hot as you can possibly stand it.'

In the middle of this field, in full view of civilians and soldiers alike, we disported ourselves joyously under four very efficient jets of steam and near-boiling water to the accompaniment of screams, yells and cackles.

'Blimey, you can see the bloody things! See 'em moving under the skin? Those little bastards.'

Sure enough, I could see my collection in the skin of my belly just above the 'short-and-curlies'.

Some five minutes, and Bentley calls: 'OK, that's enough – get up here like lightning!'

Away we went in a tight bunch for the steps which led up the side of the building; these being only wide enough to permit one at a time, it meant some of us had to ease back to create a single-file rush up the stairs, all naked and freezing. Into a small bare room we thundered, its only furniture a bare table, on which stood in a row seven empty cigarette tins, and a large dob of cotton wool alongside – no sign of Bentley though.

Looking round puzzled, we see his grinning face peering round a distant door at the far end of the room – he had no wish to get near us. The legend 'crabs can jump six feet' still lingered on.

'Right! Each man grab a tin and a blob of cotton wool. Dip the cotton wool into the tin and dab it generously all over the affected parts . . . quickly now, quickly!' He slammed the door, in case any escaped.

Looking in my tin I saw a clear mauve liquid. The lads were all still chortling and crying in mock agony – 'Unclean! Unclean!', the war-cry we had been bellicosely hollering from the lorry that brought us – and ringing imaginary handbells.

The fluid was liberally applied – backs, balls and bellies as well – not one of us having guessed what it was, it took about ten to fifteen seconds to act. Then everyone's balls caught fire. It was raw alcohol.

The first 'Cor-mate!' was rapidly echoed all round, followed by a growled 'Awww! Gawd blimey!!' Faces were transfixed with pain and cross-eyed agony, they yelled, they screamed, they fell and rolled, they jumped, they ran back and forth, they twisted, cannoned into walls – each other – they fell over the table. At the height of the chaotic fandango I was sat on the floor, knees drawn up, left arm wedging my trunk half upright, right hand fanning my 'wedding-tackle', when through the melée of flailing arms, legs and prancing bodies I saw the inner door open again slightly and Bentley's face appear in the narrow gap. 'Merry Christmas,' he said and was gone!

For Edgington to remember that occasion in such detail thirty-five years after the event is quite a feat of memory. Mind you, one doesn't get crabs every day, not even at the fishmongers.

*

We set off single file on the road towards Castleforte, which sits in the near distance on a hillside full of Germans. We turn left off the road into a field; we pass a Sherman Tank, a neat hole punched in the turret; a tank man is removing kit from inside.

Laying on a groundsheet is the mangled figure of one of the crew.

'What a mess,' says the Tankman in the same tones as though there was mud on the carpet.

I grinned at him and passed on. Above us the battle was going on full belt; coming towards us is Thornton, dear old thirty-five-year-old Thornton; he looks tired, he has no hat, and is smoking a pipe.

'Hello, what's on?'

He explains he's been sent back. 'I'm too old for that lark. I kept fallin' asleep.'

I asked him the best way up. He reaffirms, 'You go up a stone-lined gully; when it ends start climbing the hill, it's all stepped for olive trees. Of course,' he added, 'if you're in the gully and they start mortaring, you've had it.'

'Thanks,' I said, 'that's cheered us up no end.'

He bid us farewell and we went forward, we reached the gully. In a ravine to the left were Infantry all dug into the side; they were either 'resting' or in reserve. So far so good. We reach the end of the stone gully and start climbing the stepped mountain – each step is six foot high, so it's a stiff climb. CRUMP! CRUMP! CRUMP! – mortars. We hit the ground. CRUMP CRUMP CRUMP – they stop. Why? Can they see us? We get up and go on, CRUMP CRUMP CRUMP – he can see us! We hit the deck. A rain of them fall around us. I cling to the ground. The mortars rain down on us. I'll have a fag, that's what. I am holding a packet of Woodbines, then there is a noise like thunder. It's right on my head, there's a high-pitched whistle in my ears, at first I black out and then I see red, I am strangely dazed. I was on my front, now I'm on my back, the red was opening my eyes straight into the sun. I know if we stay here we'll all die . . . I start to scramble down the hill. There's shouting, I can't recall anything clearly. Next I was at the bottom of the mountain, next I'm speaking to Major Jenkins, I am crying, I don't know why, he's saying, 'Get that wound dressed.'

I said, 'What wound?'

I had been hit on the side of my right leg.

'Why did you come back?' He is shouting at me and threatening me, I can't remember what I am saying. He's saying, 'You could find your way back but you couldn't find your way to the OP'; next I'm sitting in an ambulance and shaking, an orderly puts a blanket round my shoulders, I'm crying again, why why why? Next I'm in a forward dressing station, an orderly gives me a bowl of hot very sweet tea; 'Swallow these,' he says, two small white pills. I can't hold the bowl for shaking, he takes it from me and helps me drink it. All around are wounded, he has rolled up my trouser leg. He's putting a sticking plaster on the wound, he's telling me it's only a small one. I don't really care if it's big or small, why am I crying? Why can't I stop? I'm getting lots of sympathy, what I want is an explanation. I'm feeling drowsy, and I must have started to sway because next I'm on a stretcher. I feel lovely, what were in those tablets . . . that's the stuff for me, who wants food? I don't know how long I'm there, I wake up. I'm still on the stretcher, I'm not drowsy, but I start to shiver. I sit up. They put a label on me. They get me to my feet and help me to an ambulance. I can see really badly wounded men, their bandages soaked through with blood, plasma is being dripped into them.

When we get to one of the Red Cross trucks, an Italian woman, all in black, young, beautiful, is holding a dead baby and weeping; someone says the child has been killed by a shell splinter. The relatives are standing by looking out of place in their ragged peasants' clothing amid all the uniforms. An older woman gives her a plate of home-made biscuits, of no possible use, just a desperate gesture of love. She sits in front with the driver. I'm in the back. We all sit on seats facing each other, not one face can I remember. Suddenly we are passing through our artillery lines as the guns fire. I jump at each explosion, then, a gesture I will never forget, a young soldier next to me with his right arm in a bloody sling put his arm around my shoulder and tried to comfort me. 'There, there, you'll be all right mate.'

from Indefinite Articles and Scunthorpe

Christmas 1944

I was a Lance Bombardier at an observation post on the forward slopes of Monte Sperro in Italy. With me was Lieutenant 'Johnny Walker' and his assistant Bombardier Eddie Edwards. It was Christmas Eve, the rain fell in sheets, it was icy cold and we sat in our slit trench sitting on wooden boxes with water slopping around our boots. We took it in turns to try and empty out the water in a small tin. As darkness fell a man from the battery scrambled down the slope; it was mail from home!

'Bombardier Milligan?'

'Yes,' I said.

'Nothing for you,' he said with a cheery laugh (the bastard). One letter for Walker (lucky bastard).

By a covered torch he read it aloud: 'Oh my God,' he said, 'I've been burgled.' We couldn't help it, we laughed.

To add to the festive cheer a German 155mm gun started to lay down harassing fire; we tried to doze. As it drew near to midnight an infantryman from a nearby slit trench must have watched the clock reach midnight and started to sing: Silenttttt nighttt (CRASH BOOM A SHELL) Holyyyyy nighttt all is peace (WEEEEE BOOM!) Round yon manger (WEEEEEE BOOM).

The last one landed just above the trench and threw up a column of mud that descended on us. By the light of the torch we saw that Lieutenant Walker had got it right in the face and, looking like Paul Robeson, said, 'Hello dere! A Werry Merry Christmas.'

Ah! They don't have Christmases like that any more.

from Where Have All the Bullets Gone?

Stop the festivities! The Germans have broken our lines in the Ardennes, all our washing is in the mud! Yet another it's-going-to-be-over-by-Christmas-promise gone. Still, it could be worse. Like poor old Charlie Chaplin who was in a paternity suit – unfortunately it fits him.

Steve Lewis looks up from his newspaper, stunned! How can this happen? Will Hitler win after all? Should he telegraph his wife and say, 'Sell the stock, only take cash.' Stay cool. Help is coming. Is it John Wayne? No, it's Sheriff Bernard Law Montgomery. He is going to 'tidy up' the battle, which ends with him claiming he's won it, and he will shortly rise again from the dead. Eisenhower is furious. He threatens to cut Monty's supply of armoured jockstraps and Blue Unction. Monty apologizes: 'Sorry etc., etc. You're superior by far, Monty.'

Christmas came and went with all the trimmings, tinned turkey, stuffing, Christmas Pud, all served to us by drunken Sergeants. Now we were all sitting round waiting for 1945. It had been a good year for me. I was alive.

January 1945

Cold and rain.
Letter from home.
Very quiet month.

Then, on 23 February 1945, this drastic message was flashed to the world from the pages of *Valjean*, the O2E house magazine.

TRUMPETER

Is there no stylish trumpeter in the ranks of the Echelon? At present the O2E Dance Orchestra is handicapped to a certain extent by the lack of one of these only too rare musicians. Ex-trumpeter 'Spike' Milligan, who has now gone on to the production line, had to hang up his trumpet on medical grounds, so if there is a trumpeter in our midst please contact SQMS Ward of R/O.

Milligan has hung up his trumpet! A grateful nation gave thanks!

It started with pains in my chest. I knew I had piles, but they had never reached this far up before. The Medical Officer made me strip.

'How long has it been like that?' he said.

'That's as long as it's ever been,' I replied.

He ran his stethoscope over my magnificent nine-stone body. 'Yes,' he concluded, 'you've definitely got pains in your chest. I can hear them quite clearly.'

'What do you think it is, sir?'

'It could be anything.'

Anything? A broken leg? Zeppelin Fever? Cow Pox? La Grippe? Lurgi?

'You play that wretched darkie music on your bugle, don't you?'

'Yes, sir.'

'You must give it up.'

'Why?'

'I hate it.' He goes on to say, 'It's straining your heart.'

Bloody idiot. It's 1985, I'm a hundred and nine, and I'm still playing the trumpet. He's dead. At the time I stupidly believed him and packed up playing.

The first Saturday Music Hall of the New Year was a split bill. The first half variety, the second half a play, *Men in Shadow*. It was seeing the latter that prompted me to do a lunatic version of our own. We timed it to go on the very night after the play finished, using all the original costumes and scenery.

MEN IN GITIS

Tomorrow the chief attraction at the Concert Hall will be the super, skin-creeping, spine-tingling production 'Men in Gitis'. In it are the craziest crowd of local talent that one could imagine. Spim Bolligan, the indefatiguable introducer of this new type of show, describes it as 'colossal'.

I wrote the script with Steve Lewis and Len Prosser. It was total lunacy, starting the play before the audience came in; several of the actors outside the hall doing the first act to the queue; the curtain going up and down throughout the play; the orchestra coming into the pit calling out 'Bread . . . give us bread,' then proceeding to tune up every ten minutes. Bodies were hauled up to the ceiling by their ankles asking for a reduction in rent; people came through trap doors, and all the while a crowd of soldiers done up as Hitler tried to get a grand piano across the stage, and then back again. It ended with the projection of the Gaumont British news all over us, with the music up loud, while the band played 'God Save the King' at speed. As the audience left we leapt down among them with begging bowls, asking for money, and shouted insults after them into the night. How were we received? See below.

ENTERTAINMENTS — contd. from page 1
MUSIC HALL

Last Saturday's Musical Hall was one of the best ever presented. The highspot was undoubtedly 'Men in Gitis' – a
satirical sequel to 'Men in Shadow'. This type of show is
either liked or hated, and quite a few did not care for it
at all, but the majority of people present gave the distin-
guished performers a really good ovation. 'Spike' Milligan
was at his craziest and the show was a cross between
'Itma' and 'Hellzapoppin'.

The entry of Major Bloor, Major New and the RSM
added to the enjoyment of this burlesque which culminated in the 'Mass Postings' poster being exhibited.

I love that 'good ovation' as against a bad one, however it wasn't
bad for lunatics. Spurred by success, like vultures we prepared to
wreck the next play. This was . . .

FUTURE ATTRACTIONS

Tonight and tomorrow there is the well advertised
'White Cargo' showing in the Concert Hall. This play,
which some may remember seeing in pre-war days, has a
first class story running throughout and should definitely
not be missed.

The innocent actor-manager putting it on was Lt Hector Ross.
No sooner was *White Cargo* over than *Black Baggage* was on its way.
With maniacal relish we went on to destroy the play piecemeal. The

best part of it was that we had persuaded Hector Ross to keep appearing and saying lines from the original show, then bursting into tears and exiting. It was uproarious fun. I didn't know it, but I was taking my first steps towards writing the *Goon Show*. For this I have to thank Hitler, without whose war it would never have happened.

SOMEWHERE IN THE GULAG ARCHIPELAGO 1984 NINETY-YEAR-OLD HITLER IS SHOVELLING SHIT AND SALT.

HITLER: 'Hear zat? You must let me be free. I am zer inventor of zer Coon Show. Ven zer Queen hears zis she will giff me zer OBE and ein free Corgi.'

~

SAID THE GENERAL

Said the General of the Army,
'I think that war is barmy'
So he threw away his gun:
Now he's having much more fun.

– from *Silly Verse for Kids*

~

from Where Have All the Bullets Gone?

We have driven through Naples, turned left at the bottom of Via Roma up the Corso San Antonio, which goes on for ever in an Eastern direction. Finally we arrive at a broken-down Army Barracks complex. The walls are peeling, they look as if they have mange. I report to a Captain Philip Ridgeway, a sallow saturnine fellow with a Ronald Colman moustache who looks as if he has mange as well. He sits behind the desk with his hat on. He is the son of the famous Ridgeways' Late Joys Revue that led to the Players Theatre. He looks at my papers. 'So, you play the trumpet. Do you play it well?'

'Well, er loudly.'

'Do you read music?'

'Yes, and the *Daily Herald.*'

He smiled. He would find me a place in 'one of our orchestras'. I was taken by a Corporal Gron, who looked like an unflushed lavatory, and shown to a billet on the first floor, a room with forty single beds around the walls. In them were forty single men. This being Sunday, they were of a religious order that kept them in kip until midday. I drop my kit on a vacant bed, and it collapses to the floor. 'That's why it's vacant,' laughed Corporal Gron, who laughed when babies fell under buses. Next bed is Private Graham Barlow. He helps me repair the bed with some string and money. Nice man – he played the accordion. Noël Coward said, 'No gentleman would ever play the accordion.'

I had no job as such, and as such I had no job. Breakfast was at 8.30, no parade, hang around, lunch, hang further around, tea, extended hanging around, dinner and bed. The CPA Complex had the same ground plan as the Palace of Minos at Knossos, consisting of rehearsal rooms, music stores, costume stores, scenery dock and painting area, Wardrobe Mistress, Executive offices. People went in and were never seen again. The company was assembled from soldier artists who had been down-graded. They would be formed into concert parties and sent on tour to entertain those Tommies who weren't down-graded. The blind leading the blind. The facilities were primitive, the lavatories were a line of holes in the ground. When I saw eighteen soldiers squatting/balancing over black holes with straining sweating faces for the first time, they looked like the start of the hundred yards for paraplegic dwarfs.

My first step to 'fame' came when I borrowed a guitar from the stores. I was playing in the rehearsal room when a tall cadaverous gunner said, 'You play the guitar then?' This was Bill Hall. If you've ever seen a picture of Niccolò Paganini, this was his double. What's more, he played the violin and played it superbly; be it a Max Bruch Concerto or 'I've Got Rhythm', he was a virtuoso. But bloody scruffy. We teamed up just for the fun of it, and in turn we were joined by Johnny Mulgrew, a short Scots lad from the Recce Corps; as he'd left them they were even shorter of Scots. Curriculum Vitae: Pre-war he played for Ambrose and the Inland Revenue. In the 56 Recce in N. Africa. Trapped behind enemy lines at Madjez-el-Bab. Lay doggo for forty-eight hours in freezing weather. Got pneumonia. Down-graded to B2 . . .

Together we sounded like Le Hot Club de France. When we played, other musicians would come and listen to us – a compliment – and it wasn't long before we were lined up for a show.

In the filling-in time, I used to play the trumpet in a scratch combination. It led to my meeting with someone from Mars, Gunner Secombe, H., singer and lunatic, a little myopic blubber of fat from Wales who had been pronounced a loony after a direct hit by an 88mm gun in North Africa. He was asleep at the time and didn't know about it till he woke up. General Montgomery saw him and nearly surrendered. He spoke like a speeded up record, no one understood him, he didn't even understand himself; in fact, forty years later he was knighted for not being understood.

The Officers' Club, Naples. We were playing for dancing and cabaret, the latter being the lunatic Secombe. His 'music' consisted of some tatty bits of paper, two parts, one for the drums and one for the piano – the rest of us had to guess. We busked him on with 'I'm just wild about Harry'. He told us he had chosen it because his name was Harry, and we said how clever he was. He rushed on, chattering, screaming, farting, sweat pouring off him like a monsoon, and officers moved their chairs back. Then the thing started to shave itself, screaming, chattering and farting; he spoke at high speed; the audience thought he was an imported Polish comic, and many wished he was back in Warsaw being bombed. Shaving soap and hairs flew in all directions, then he launched into a screaming duet with himself, Nelson Eddy and Jeanette Macdonald, but you couldn't tell him apart. A few cries of 'hey hup' and a few more soapy farts, and he's gone, leaving the dance floor smothered in shaving soap. His wasn't an act, it was an interruption.

The dance continues, and officers are going arse over tip in dozens. 'No, not him,' they'd say when Secombe's name came up for a cabaret.

Bill Hall. A law unto himself. He ignored all Army discipline, he ignored all civilian discipline. His regiment had despaired of him and posted him to CPA with an apology note.

Take kit parade. We are all at our beds, kit immaculately laid out for inspection. The Orderly Officer reaches Gunner Hall. There, on an ill-made bed, where there should be nineteen items of army apparel, are a pair of socks, three jack-knives, a vest, a mess tin and a fork. The officer looks at the layout. He puts his glasses on.

OFFICER: 'Where is the rest of your kit?'
GUNNER HALL: 'It's on holiday, sir.'

Apart from Gunner Secombe, CPA contained other stars to be, including Norman Vaughan, Ken Platt and Les Henry (who later formed The Three Monarchs).

Civilian Status

The Central Pool of Artists is changed to The Combined Services Entertainment. Why? I suppose it's the result of a 'meeting'. In its wake we, the Bill Hall Trio, are being offered officer status and wages if, when we are demobbed, we sign with the CSE for six months. Hedonists, we all say yes. Officer status? Cor Blimey! All the bloody months in the line and you become Lance-Bombardier. Play the guitar in perfect safety, you become an officer. If I learned the banjo and the tuba I could become a Field-Marshal!

I wrote home and told my delighted parents. Mother proudly informed the neighbours that her son was a 'Banjo-playing Officer'.

*

Lieutenant Priest seeks me out. Tomorrow Bill Hall and I are to report to Villach Demob Camp to be issued with civilian clothes, how exciting! Next morning a 15 cwt truck takes us to the depot. Giant sheds loaded with military gear. We hand in our papers and discharge sheets, then we are given the choice of three suits – a grey double-breasted pinstripe suit, a dark blue ditto or a sports jacket and flannels.

I had chosen clothes three times too large for me and Hall had chosen some three sizes too small. The distributing sergeant was pretty baffled. We duly signed our names and walked out. England's heroes were now free men. No more 'yes, sir, no, sir', no more parades. Back at the guest house, we have our first meal as civilians. As I remember it was spaghetti.

We had one more demob appointment. That was with the Army MO. This turns out to be a watery-eyed, red-nosed lout who was to medicine what Giotto was to fruit bottling.

'It's got you down here as B1,' he says.

'That's right, I was downgraded at a medical board.'

'It says "battle fatigue".'

'Yes. "Battle fatigue, anxiety state, chronic".'

'Yes, but you're over it now, aren't you?'

'No, I still feel tired.'

'So, I'll put you down as A1.'

'Not unless I'm upgraded by a medical board.'

'Oh, all right. B1.'

He then asks me if my eyesight is all right.

'As far as I know.'

'You can see me, can't you?'

'Yes.'

'Then it's all right.'

It ended with him signing a couple of sheets of paper and showing me the door. Why didn't he show me the window? It was a nice view.

That was it. I was a civilian and B1.

3
Earning a Living

All I ask is the chance to prove that money can't buy you happiness.

– 'Spike on Spike', *Memories of Milligan*

After the 'Adolf Hitler Show' Spike didn't return to England. He was demobbed in May 1945 but stayed in Italy and toured with the Bill Hall Trio. Their show was called *Barbary Coast*. During this tour he started to perform sketches that he had written – the beginning of the *Goon Show*s?

He returned to England in 1946, still touring with the Bill Hall Trio, but wanted to go solo. After arguments and a less than amicable split with Bill Hall, he went. But before he could get a solo gig, he joined the Ann Lenner Trio playing the guitar, which took him on another European tour that ended in Vienna. By now he was determined to go solo.

Jimmy Grafton, who owned a pub called the Grafton Arms, was writing for a comedian, Derek Roy, who performed there. Grafton heard Spike had appeared with the Bill Hall Trio and had written some 'funny material', so he asked Spike to join him writing for Derek Roy. This was in 1948. The BBC got wind of this and asked Jimmy and Spike to write for a radio show, *Hip Hip Hoo Roy*.

Harry Secombe and Spike remained friends after the war, and Spike went to see him perform at the Hackney Empire. In the bar after the show, Harry introduced Spike to another up-and-coming comedian, Peter Sellers. Harry was friendly with Jimmy Grafton and so the pub became their meeting place.

Peter had worked at the BBC and knew a producer, Pat Dixon. They met, and Pat asked Spike to write a script – the first *Goon Show* – but when the show aired on 28 May 1951 it was called 'The Crazy People'. It changed to *The Goon Show* at Spike's insistence for the second series.

The pressure of writing a *Goon Show* every week caused him to have a nervous breakdown, which eventually ended his marriage to June Marlow. At the end of 1959 he wrote: 'It had been the most traumatic year of my life. I had become famous and successful but deeply unhappy. God please help me.'

from The Murphy

Showing at the local cinema was a silent film of *Tarzan*, played by Frank Edwards, an actor with a magnificent torso, but painfully thin legs. This they overcame by having him wear a long leopard skin back and front from the waist down. In the film, Tarzan manfully strangled a gorilla with his bare hands and also killed a lion that was stuffed.

A newsreel followed, showing strikes in America.

'Ah, America!' sighed Murphy. 'Dat's der place fer strikes.'

His uncle had gone to America and become a policeman. He married a huge German woman who beat the shit out of him every night.

'America's der land of opportunity!' exclaimed Murphy, as he and Molly walked home.

'Den why don't you go dere?' asked Molly.

'I don't want an opportunity,' he answered. 'I might not like it . . . I won't be a moment,' he added, disappearing into a public toilet.

He swiftly reappeared. 'Oh, what a filthy mess! None of the dirty buggers had pulled der chain.'

He reported the condition to the Council Sanitary Officer, Adam Ripley, who immediately went round and pulled all the chains – a man of action. Murphy admired that. He determined to become a man of action and took a new job at the Sligo Funeral Parlour. He had to show customers the entire range of coffins, from the reinforced cardboard 'Powell', to the mahogany 'Churchill'. He sold a lot of 'Powells' but never a 'Churchill'.

'People can't afford to die in style these days,' he said, sadly. He was on commission.

Mrs Priscilla Doyle came seeking a coffin for her husband.

'Is he dead?' asked Murphy.

'No, he's not,' she said, 'but I don't want to leave it till the last moment.'

In fact, Mr Doyle was only twenty-three. She chose the 'Powell'. It was put on the back of an open-topped lorry and driven back to her house in the rain. When they arrived, the cardboard had softened and collapsed.

'It'll be all right when it dries out,' Murphy advised by phone. 'Put it in front of der fire.' She did. It burned to the ground.

'Oh, bugger,' Murphy advised by phone. 'Well, we'll replace it when it stops raining.'

'What if it dies before he does?' said Mrs Doyle.

'Oh, bugger,' muttered Murphy, who didn't know the answer to that one. Eventually he sold her his first 'Churchill'. She kept it in a warm, dry room awaiting her husband's death.

The job held, people went on dying, most were buried in the 'Powell', which generally held together quite well. Murphy was often heard quietly praying in the funeral parlour's chapel of rest, 'Just don't let it bloody rain!'

Financially he was doing well; his wage was three pounds a week plus a percentage of coffins sold. On a good week he could make fifteen to twenty pounds. He never told Molly that – she'd have had all of it. Ironically, when the rainy winter months ended, coffin sales declined. The bronchitis season was over and people just refused to die! Murphy's income plummeted.

Money, bloody money. One thing would solve the problem – a robbery. Murphy thought deeply on it and gradually an idea came into his head. Sligo Castle – Lord O'Neill – he'd have money. Now, inside the castle there were suits of armour. If he could get into one and wait for nightfall . . .

Pretending to be the man who read the gas meter, Murphy was allowed entry, despite the fact that the real man who read the gas meter never visited Sligo Castle. They were all-electric. Murphy spotted the suit of armour straight away. There was nobody about. Furtively, he hid all of his clothes in a large chest. Slowly he got into the suit; it was quite comfortable, if cold. He shivered. He sounded like one of those strings of tin cans they tied behind wedding cars. Settling down for a long wait, he tried not to think of the cold. He tried not to think. He was good at that.

Eventually he heard the hall clock strike twelve. The house was silent. Now for action – the safe! Stealthily he crept up the stairs. CLANG! Blast, an arm fell off – no one seemed to have heard. As he walked there was a slight squeaking from the joints. Finally he reached the study. He opened the visor. It slammed shut. He took the helmet off. That was better, now he could see. There on the wall was a picture, behind it, the safe! Now if he could only get the combination right . . . well, he had all night. He proceeded to try various combinations with no luck whatsoever. In the end he tried his old army number, 954042. My God, it worked! The safe opened – there was money inside! He counted it feverishly. It totalled three pounds ten shillings. Surely there must be more? There was, but it was in the Bank of Ireland. Well, so be it. Clutching the money, he put his helmet back on and tiptoed downstairs.

He tried to take the armour off but, curse it, it wouldn't shift. He was still trying to remove it when the early morning butler found him.

'Who are you in there, sir?'

'Mick Murphy,' the armour replied.

'What are you doing in there, Murphy?'

'I'm trying to get out,' said Murphy.

'I'll have to inform the police, sir,' said the butler.

'No, now don't be troublin' yourself by doin' dat. Just help me off wid it and I'll go.'

'No, it's no good, sir, it won't come off. You'll need a plumber,' said the butler, and phoned for one.

Roy Coe, the plumber, assessed the job. It was a tricky one, but it was better than being up to his elbows in shit unblocking some poor diarrhoeic sod's toilet. 'It needs an acetylene torch, but that would burn him to death.'

'Not der torch!' screamed the armour. 'Not der torch!'

Inside, despite the chill of the metal suit, Murphy was pouring with sweat. The plumber decided to cut him out with a hacksaw. First he cut the legs free, revealing Murphy's fat hairy legs.

By now Lord O'Neill was watching. 'Why in God's name, man, did you do this?'

'I was going to a fancy dress ball, sir,' lied Murphy from behind his visor.

By midday, most of the armour was off, but the police had arrived.

'Do you wish to press charges, sir?' asked Garda Michael Milligan, number 213.

The garda were numbered in case they got lost. This was one of the most exciting things ever to have happened in Garda Milligan's short and inauspicious career in law enforcement. Sligo was a dead town. No one was clever enough to be a criminal.

'There's no one to arrest,' he had once complained to his sergeant.

'Oh, dear,' said Garda Sergeant Drew. 'You can always arrest someone for pissing in a doorway.'

Was that true? Milligan had pondered. 'Right, then!' He kept a watchful eye out that night as he was patrolling the street and he caught a couple fornicating in the doorway of a shop.

'And what would youse be doin'?' he asked.

'We're having a shag,' was the answer.

'Is dat so?' nodded Milligan. 'Well, it's a good job youse were not having a piss or I'd have got yer!'

The man in the suit of armour, though, was a different matter altogether. Here was a clear crime in progress. 'So, sir, do you wish to press charges?' repeated Garda Milligan.

'Well, he nicked my elbow wid dat hacksaw, but I'll let him off dis time . . .' said Murphy.

'Not you,' hissed the policeman. 'Your Lordship?'

'Oh, no, officer. I think this is just a joke gone wrong,' he chuckled.

'We can have him for trespass . . .' insisted the policeman.

An hour and a half later, the armour was finally off, revealing Murphy in his vest and underpants, which sent O'Neill into paroxysms of laughter. Sheepishly, Murphy retrieved his clothes from the chest.

'Would sir like a cup of tea?' asked the footman.

Oh, yes, dat was what was needed. Murphy sat drinking it under the watchful eye of the policeman. 'You were lucky to get away wid dis,' he warned.

'Look,' said Murphy, 'I must have bin drunk.'

Garda Milligan eyed Murphy with great suspicion. He knew there was more to Murphy than met the eye, and more would certainly have met the eye had Murphy not kept his underpants on.

Meanwhile, Roy Coe, having dismantled the armour, was having some difficulty in reassembling it. The arms were now welded on backwards and the feet pointed in different directions. Murphy counted himself extremely lucky not to be still inside.

It was one of the few strokes of luck he had ever had. Maybe if he had had a bit more luck, he wouldn't have always been so poor.

'Yes,' thought Murphy, ''tis a terrible ting ter be poor . . . a terrible ting ter be poor . . .'

from Goodbye Soldier

Foreword

FIND A PLACE – STOP THE CLOCK

Sitting here at the typewriter, stop the clock. When I think of the kind of human being I was then, I can't believe that it was me. I was twenty-eight, with the best years of my life spent in the Army. I had found the transformation from civilian life painless: it allowed freedoms I hadn't had before. No longer did I have my mother's dictatorship about going to mass – we had unending rows over it, in fact I left home for a time. No longer did I have that voice on the landing when I came home at night, 'Is that you, Terry? What time do you call this?' type rows. I had always given my mother my entire wage packet, £5.00. In return, I got half-a-crown pocket money at the age of twenty-one. Now I kept *all* my pay, came in late and didn't have to go to mass. It was freedom! I was living for the moment. If there was any future, it was the next band job. I loved being there, playing the trumpet, me the music maker, me being asked by officers, 'I say, Milligan, can you play such and such a tune?', me singing, flirting with the girls. Now here I was in Italy on £10.00 a week with officer status, playing with a trio that I thought would bring us fame and fortune, and all this and a pretty ballerina. This was Italy, the sun shone, free of all responsibilities except the show, free all day. Oh, life was good! One day that would all end.

Spike Milligan
Monkenhurst

1 May 1986

Barbary Coast

Barbary Coast opened at the Argentina Theatre on Monday, 24 June. It was an immediate success and the Bill Hall Trio again the hit of the show. Wait till England heard about us, rich, rich, rich!!!

It's a busy show for me: I have to appear in sketches, in the Bowery Quartette singing 'Close the Shutters, Willy's Dead', play trumpet in the orchestra and the guitar in the Bill Hall Trio – all at no extra charge. Bornheim has a dastardly trick. During my solo in 'Close the Shutters', he drops a lone ping-pong ball that bounces slowly and repeatedly and faster into the orchestra pit, where he has arranged for a man to drop a brick into a bucket of water. It was a simple but funny idea.

Of others in the show, the lead comic was Jimmy Molloy, about forty, overweight, a cockney, very left-wing, his comedy all aggressive. After the war not a word was heard of him in the profession, so . . . There's one born every minute and we had one who was, Sergeant Chalky White, ex-Marine Para Commando. What he was doing in the entertainment world was as baffling as finding Adolf Eichmann in the Israeli government. His only claim to fame was he once leapt off Bari Bridge into the harbour with an umbrella – all very clever, but there's a limit to how many times. He was a bouncing all-noise cockney boy: if you were in a pub with him, you all *had* to sing and do 'Knees Up Mother Brown'. He had a brain that would have fitted into a thimble with room to spare. He was i/c transport and scenery, both of which strained his mental capacities to the limit. Yes, he was a nice bouncing thirty-year-old cockney lad who should have stayed on his barrow. However, he was turned on by the bright lights and birds of showbiz, so he wheedled his way into the show. He couldn't act, he couldn't sing, he couldn't dance, but he could fight . . . So, for no reason at all, in the middle of the show a mock fight breaks out and we all have to pretend to be floored by Sergeant White.

'Don't worry, I won't 'urt yer, I'll miss you by a whisker.'

This didn't work out. Every night he would mistime and render one of the cast unconscious. As I had boxed in the past, I rode his punches. Even then, to this day I have a chipped front tooth and a scarred inner lip. Finally, after we'd all been hit, Lieutenant Priest had to put a stop to the 'Fight'. White sulked off.

'It's professional jealousy,' he said.

White truly believed that after the war he would 'become someone'. He did, a dustman.

Maxie – just Maxie – was a short, squat mid-European. A huge head dwarfed his body and his neck didn't exist, so much so that he couldn't turn his head but had to revolve his whole body. He spoke very little English. His 'act' consisted of bending iron bars on his head and shoulders, concluding with his bending an iron bar on his forearm.

'Maxie has developed this special muscle that "no living human has developed". In this attempt, if he misses the muscle he could break his arm,' announced Molloy.

There followed great grunts and thwacks as the sweating strong man beat the shit out of himself, finally holding up the now bent bar and collapsing into the wings.

*

Time for the last show. We gather chattering in the foyer, then board the Charabong through the Roman cacophony of motor horns. Tonight our strong man, Maxie, will try and break his own weight-lifting record of umpteen pounds. We all watch from the wings as the dwarf-like strong man strains to get the weights above his head. The silence is broken by his grunts and strains, the veins stand out on his head. Finally, with a gasp, he gets them above his head. He takes the applause.

'What a way to make a bloody living,' says Hall. 'I bet one day 'e'll get a double rupture.'

There's a sense of sadness in the air. This company has been together every day for three months; it has become as familiar as a family. As the Trio are taking an encore, I think well that's it; the next time we play will be in England. Then what? I can still hear that applause on the last night . . .

The stage party is very good. Chalky White and his helpers erect trestle tables which are loaded with cheese, wine and biscuits. We help ourselves. Johnny Bornheim plays the piano. The Italians have invited members of their families, big fat mommas and kids. It's a very jolly affair. Before we finish, Lieutenant Priest thanks us for our efforts and says the show is the most successful one that Combined Services Entertainment have put on. We drink and eat our fill. We stand in circles, chatting and laughing, recalling moments that have highlighted our tour, and then the evening has run out. Time for home. Some of the Italian cast will be leaving us at Rome; there are tearful goodbyes, a lot of red eyes and red noses. Mulgrew's nose is going red for an entirely different reason. In dribs and drabs we board the old Charabong where patient Luigi waits. The engine is running, but no one else is. Finally, we set off for the hotel. We all start slightly inebri-ated singing: 'You are my sunshine, my only sunshine, you make me happy when skies are grey' echoes along the now empty Roman streets.

It's nearly 2 a.m. by the time we get back; yawning, stretching and farting we climb wearily into bed. I can't sleep, my mind starts to revolve around the things I have to do when we get back to naughty Napoli. I must collect all my kit from the CSE barracks, get a passport, an advance of money, presents to take home, fix the boat trip home – all this, and fix a week on Capri. Gradually I fall into fitful sleep to the sound of Mulgrew's snoring in Scottish, plus a few postern blasts.

from Peace Work

Home

Indeed, we won the war, but I lost five precious years. I was to mourn, and still do, the physical break-up of my family; it was a sort of time-warp Belsen. As my ship left Naples harbour – it was the cool end of autumn, the year 1946; time, like the ship, was slipping away – an azure twilight glazed the Campania, lights enumerated along that seemingly timeless shore, now lifeless, Vesuvius was turning into a faded amber silhouette. I stood aft on the promenade deck, seamen still fussed around the ship's limits, other passengers leaned out at the rail. I watched the oncoming pollution, as they tossed their cigarette ends in the sea.

Goodbye, here was I saying 'Goodbye to all that' though I was only twenty-eight, here I was saying goodbye, I hated goodbyes, they gave me the same haunting sadness every time. Wherever I had put down emotional roots, it was painful to bid it adieu; I am still haunted by all the homes I have had to leave. What was it like to live in a cottage in a village in the sixteenth century, and never say goodbye to it? Is the modern social pattern of unending change and movement the cause of two modern diseases, insecurity and dissatisfaction? How lucky Thomas Hood was to be able to write:

> I remember, I remember,
> The house where I was born.

I don't even know what mine looked like! I stayed on deck, smoked a Capstan 'full strength', one of my last NAAFI-issue cigarettes. On the portside, we passed what were then isles of magic memory, Capri and Ischia, scarlet and bronze in the sunset; the sea was turning to ink, our propellers churning up a Devonshire cream wake, the ship's siren sent out a long mournful departure note – it echoed across the bay.

from Treasure Island According to Spike Milligan

Prologue

HOW GROUCHO JOINED THE CREW

Q: Are you, Groucho Marx, willing to appear in 'TREASURE ISLAND'?

GROUCHO: Oh? What's in it for me, my good man?

Q: Fame and fortune!

GROUCHO: Never mind that, what about the money?

Q: Who's talking about money?

GROUCHO: No one. That's why I mentioned it.

Q: In this book no one gets paid.

GROUCHO: Well, I wish them luck and goodbye, suckers.

Q: Wait! In your case perhaps we can come to some special arrangement.

GROUCHO: In my case, my special arrangement is money.

Q: What do you want?

GROUCHO: Ten dollars a word.

Q: What if you don't speak?

GROUCHO: Then I'll get fuck all.

Q: Supposing we paid a dollar a word?

GROUCHO: Then I'd talk very fast.

Q: OK, you're on, a dollar a word.

GROUCHO: I agree. Yes I agree, yes I agree, I agree. That'll be sixty-two dollars.

Q: Have you change for a hundred?

GROUCHO: No, but I'll keep it till I do.

Q: Right, sign this agreement.

GROUCHO: I'll just sign it with a cross.

Q: A cross? Are you illiterate?

GROUCHO: Heavens no. I can spell cross.

Q: You are a difficult man to deal with.

GROUCHO: Sometimes if the date is right, I'm a difficult woman to deal with.

Bow! Wow! Wow!

GROUCHO. Whose dog is that?

* * *

from Peace Work

Yes, what did we do in the day? One time at the Windmill canteen, Harry introduced me to 'Jimmy Grafton who owns a pub'; he was to figure in my life in those immediate post-war years. He had served as an officer in the infantry and was at Arnhem. He was now serving behind the bar; he had, somehow or other, become a script-writer to Derek Roy, a would-be comic appearing on *Variety Bandbox*, so Jimmy had an 'in' into broadcasting.

Michael Bentine introduced Harry to Jimmy; as Harry recalls, 'Mike told me of this pub in Strutton Ground where I got a drink after hours, and somehow Jimmy became my manager and script-writer.' He started back to front by me telling him what bloody awful scripts Derek Roy had, and Jimmy said, 'Well, I write them'. A strange start to a forty-year relationship.

Hackney Empire

'I've got a week for you at the Hackney Empire', the words fell from the mellifluous lips of Leslie MacDonnell, our agent, sitting behind his desk at Piccadilly House, Piccadilly Circus.

We were overjoyed, I could see our name in lights. MacDonnell then added, 'I've arranged for Val Parnell to see you on the Monday performance.'

Val Parnell!!!! This was something. If Parnell was coming to see us, MacDonnell must have thought pretty highly of us; for giving us this break, Bill Hall proffered his thanks, 'Ta', he said.

I burst out laughing. 'Bill', I said, 'Ta? Ta? Excuse him, Mac-Donnell, Bill is a man of few words and that was one of them.' I then thanked MacDonnell more formally, 'Like this, Bill', I said. I knelt in the grovelling position, my head on MacDonnell's shoe, 'Oh a thousand thanks, oh great wise one.'

MacDonnell was highly amused. 'Is he always like this?' he said.

'Only when the money's right', said Mulgrew, pulling me away. 'There, there boy', he said, patting me on the head and feeding me pretend sugar lumps. So to the big time.

'Oh, we'll be there* son', said my dad when I told him. My parents, especially my father, were very proud, he having been a stage

---

* At home.

performer. 'I never knew you had it in you,' he said. I told him I myself had never had it in me, but I had had it in other people, the opposite sex, well that's where they were at the time.

That fateful Monday night, the night of 3 February 1947. Heavy snow had been falling, it was very cold – up to then it was the worst recorded winter in living memory. Our dressing room was on the fifth floor. 'They must think we're bloody eagles,' said Mulgrew, humping his double bass. Dressing room six feet by ten: a cracked mirror with dabs of greasepaint, a surround of forty watt bulbs, three fused, a leaking washhand basin – 'Warning, do not stand in the sink, one of the girls did and was TERRIBLY INJURED'. It must have been something to see. Before the show started we peeped through the front curtain. My God, there were only three people in and two of them were Val Parnell. Even by curtain-up there were only twelve customers. Serious. The pit band struck up. I strolled on the stage alone, started to tune my guitar, Bill Hall runs on backwards as though being cheered on – he collides with me – looking directly at me he places the hair of the bow over the string and with the bow underneath the violin saws through 'Organ Grinder's Swing', until then a popular tune, during which Mulgrew brings his bass on. The diminutive audience don't laugh, one person applauded, which made it sound even worse, in the box we could see the chair-oscuro figure of Val Parnell. We went through our repertoire, after each number there was the lone clapper. In desperation I ad-libbed, 'Please sir, you're spoiling it for the other people.' This got the only laugh of the evening, it would go on to be the only laugh of the month. We died the death. The pit band played us off with 'Where's That Tiger?'; if I'd have found it I would have shot it.

We stood there in the gloom. 'Never mind, lads,' said the Stage Manager, 'it's Monday, they'll be better by the middle of the week.'

'They're not staying here till then are they?' I said, always cheerful Spike.

We sat in our dressing room. In silence, in unison, we lit up a cigarette. 'Where the fuck did they get that audience?' 'It's the Nazi Party.' Never mind eh? Val Parnell had seen us, he knew a good act when he saw one. We never heard from the bastard again. Tuesday night only eighteen people in, the next night it snowed heavily. 'This'll kill the business,' said the manager. On the Saturday night we did well; why, oh why did Val Parnell come on a Monday? 'He's a perv, that's why,' said Mulgrew. 'I bet he feels little girls' bicycle saddles.' However, from that week we received £75! Who would have dreamed such wealth existed! It meant £25 each, but each of us had to pay £2.10.0 commission. Mulgrew rolled his wages into a tight roll then wedged it into his wallet with a rubber band around it; I think he was marinating it.

A Dream of Grandeur

The story that follows tells of the bitter experience of a bass player who basically had the arse out of his trousers, even someone else's trousers. This first week's wages went to Mulgrew's head. He had met a girl – Elsie, I remember was her name; she had enormous bosoms that promised pneumatic bliss, it appeared as though a giant hand had grabbed her bottom half and squeezed it all upwards. Mulgrew was besotted with all three of her. Every night after the show, she waited at the stage door, and he whipped her away from A to B – that is, stage door to bed. By the time I arrived back at 13 Linden Gardens, groans and steam were coming from under his bedroom door. I would send a prayer to help him through the night. On the Sunday I was up at the crack of one in the afternoon. Sunday was the one day we didn't get breakfast, so I made tea and toast on my gas ring and did my accounts for the week.

There was a faint tapping on my door; there after a good night's coitus stood the wreck of a man in the Robbie Burns manner. I sang at him as he tried to shush me.

> They were fucking in the hallway
> They were fucking on the stairs
> Yer could nae see the carpet
> For the xxxx and curly hairs.

'Ssh! She'll hear you,' said the wreck of a man whom I recognized as the remains of Johnny Mulgrew. 'Ha, you got any tea?' he said.

Ha – yes, so I boiled up a pot for him and his wee lassie. That night we repaired to the Coach and Horses (now alas demolished). Here Mulgrew's attempts at the grandiose failed. What he had done, the little Scottish nana, was to cut thirty strips of the *Daily Mirror* to the size of pound notes. These he rolled into a wad, then wrapped his twenty-five one-pound notes around them. This looked very impressive until the following Thursday when, at the same pub, well oiled, he forgetfully peeled off his last two pounds to reveal the *Daily Mirror*; it didn't stop there, he peeled off two *Daily Mirrors* – the barman said, 'I'm sorry, we only take the *Express*.'

My brother Desmond, like all males in a sexual trauma, is to get married; Pixie Roberts of Devon is the one to get it. I'm to be the best man, thank God I've got that new suit made by the tailor in the Circus Maximus in Rome – what a heritage for a suit!!! Why didn't I choose Royal Purple? The wedding took place at St Saviour's RC, Lewisham, with the reception at Chiesmans (now Army & Navy), where the entire Milligan family assembled.

5 *May 1947*

Phone for me from Leslie MacDonnell, thank God! 'Spike, I've got a few dates for you.'

Dates? Where is he, Arabia?

'We have a week's variety for the Trio!'

Oh boy! We're on our way. 'Thank you, Leslie. I'll tell the boys.' First week is in Beautiful Sunless Blackpool – Hollywood with flat 'ats.

So we proceeded to do the No. 1 dates, something my father would have given his right arm for. Why he wanted to do a one-armed act I'll never know. It seemed as though I personally was like a gramophone needle stuck in a groove. Life was like moving but standing still, 1939 was hard to recapture; on stage I wasn't crooning, or looking like Robert Taylor – no, I was in rags, with a grotesque make-up, and ridiculing the music we played. It was the liberties we took with the music that got us our applause – but 1939 it wasn't; it was digs like 356 Hagley Road, Birmingham – poached haddock in milk for breakfast, lunch in a café, dinner was Arrggg!!! Cold Collation!

One show a night, matinées Wednesday and Saturday. Friday night, the agents came in, Lew Lake, Joe Collins, to suss out the acts; from it a Joe Cohen got us some work after the show at working men's clubs. Everyone changed in the same room. We shared with a lady act. Cathy, the cowgirl (Will lasso your heart), say forty-one, but not in front of her. I watched fascinated as she put make-up to cover the varicose veins on her plump legs. 'I should have the operation, but I'd be laid up fer a month, I can't afford that.'

Bill Hall felt sorry for 'Poor Cowgirl', he said. He felt so sorry for her he took her back to her digs and screwed her. Bill! All those veins like snakes crawling up her legs. Don't worry, Spike, you couldn't see 'em, she had her elastic support stockings on. Ah, *l'amour*! It was in these very digs, 356 Hagley Road, the landlady had caught Sir Donald Wolfit at it on the marble washstand with his leading lady. 'It's all right, Mrs Cartwright,' said the steaming actor, 'it's . . . it's only my sister.'

The afternoons of those distant days were spent at a cinema. I remember seeing Danny Kaye in *The Kid From Brooklyn* and thinking, I should be doing that . . . that was me up there. I realize now that while I was young, vigorous, good-looking and a natural clown I should have gone just for that, it was the right time for my type of clowning – but fear of unemployment, inherited from my mother, kept me with the Trio, at £25 a week I could save, but what for? In any case I always felt I had no talent outside of music; I came from a family who were basically working-class, who had left the poverty of London's Poplar and Woolwich, then suddenly were with the Indian Army in India – servants, free quarters, free rations, horse riding, shikar, polo. Despite this, I remember my family thought of anyone above the rank of Sergeant as 'Superior'. I didn't think I could do *anything on my own* – because I was working-class. When

I think of the number of idiots I said Sir to because they had a posh accent. Oh, what did class do to me? I could have been a Scholar, University, hell . . .

Money can't buy you friends,
but it does get you
a better class of enemy.

– from 'Spike on Spike', *Memories of Milligan*

from Peace Work

During the week Secombe and I hang around Alan's Club and go to news theatres to see cartoons – we see the newsreel of a shark, its mouth held open. When it's dropped it looks like an idiot. We went into hysterics and stayed to see it round a second and third time.

We are the hit of the bill – Harry Foster and Leslie MacDonnell see us second house Saturday. 'We're very pleased, boys, we're managing to up your money to £100 a week.'

I phone my father at work and tell him. 'I'll come home right away,' he said.

I rode all the way to 3 Leathwell Road and told my mother, I stayed the night and slept in the room where the trains shunted. I still let jazz music run through my head – always had, always will. I turned on my little green Bakelite radio, it's Billy Ternent and his tinkly-poo band – no jazz, but what the hell, this is Deptford not Birdland.

Dizzy live at 3 Leathwell! Wow! Sing Dizzy, blues.
Hey there Dizzy playing at Leathwell Road!

Hey there Dizzy playing at Leathwell Road!
You play that music
A knighthood will be bestowed . . . oh, yeah!

I was listening to radio. *Men At Work* was one that grabbed me. It's forgotten now, but it was what put *The Goon Show* on the road. *Men At Work** were ignoring logic and for me it worked, but nobody seemed to notice it. I laughed at Derek Roy, a bit at ITMA, but things that really made me laugh were Groucho Marx, W. C. Fields, Beachcomber, Sid Fields – so there! I was writing things on paper with no object in mind; I'd joke a lot with Secombe, but with variety work, neither Bentine nor Sellers got together much – it was to come. Only when we had a week out or a weak heart (eh?) did we meet. I met Sellers at Hackney Empire where Secombe was appearing. Bentine introduced him to me in the bar; he was 'sprraunced' up, felt trilby, gloves, Dick Barton collar-up mackintosh. As usual, Mike did most of the talking. That's all I remember of the occasion.

Inside me I had no idea where I wanted to go. I'd stopped playing trumpet. Big bands were going out, *radio* was the thing, how could I get in? I had no confidence as a solo performer, and never had until Oblomov, so I was a maelstrom of complexities. I certainly admired Secombe, Sellers and Bentine – I'd hang around them.

A week out! The first week we're promised £100, we're out – don't worry boys, it's Bolton next week. Bolton – the Angel of Mons, Manna from Heaven. Bolton, the Promised Land. Bolton, an anagram of Notlob! Yes, Notlob, there was lots to do in Notlob – the pubs, the pictures – wait, it's been cancelled. Sod. Everything comes to he who waits, even unemployment.

Ally Pally

Incredible! We've been booked for the modern wonder, Television! At Alexandra Palace. So important is the occasion that Leslie

* Written by Max Kester.

MacDonnell has summoned us to his office to tell. 'Yes, boys, a Mr Richard Afton of the BBC.' The BBC, the words send the blood swirling in the swonnicles, the BBC. 'Yes,' says MacDonnell, 'the BBC,' he stands to say the majestic words, 'BBC – Tele-e-vision.' He could be Lincoln before Gettysburg, Antony at Actium! TELE-VISION!

Hall the Wretch explained the wonder. 'Television!' he said ecstatically. 'It will bring us into people's homes.'

Our parents had already warned me they would never have him in their homes. 'We don't want to catch it.'

The show was called *Rooftop Rendezvous*, the producer Richard Afton, like BBC producers, had delusions of grandeur; he had his name changed by deed poll to Lord Afton, oh yes, dear reader, there are plenty like him in the BBC, those who want weddings at dawn on Navaho Indian mountain tops. The fee! Leslie, the fee! 'Well boys, it's £150 before commission.'

My God, that would leave us each with £40.

'I'll nae ha to cut strips of *Daily Mirror* any mair,' said Mulgrew. At 13 Linden Gardens we informed flatmates Reg O'List, the singer from the Windmill, his girlfriend Jennifer with a forty-two inch bust (the unflattest flatmate).

'Let's have a party,' I said.

A fiesta, okay. That night we sat on beds eating chicken and drinking Chianti – memories of Italy were still strong. Reg O'List entertained with his guitar. He, Gracie Fields and Donald Peers should never have sung, but, there is Reg now, 'Over the plains, now I hear the Russian horsemen riddinggg.' Please God they're coming for him. I got very squiffy and sang Boo-Boo – 'Body and Soul'.

I woke up next morning with Blanche and her kipper at the door, 'God, I must hurry, Blanche – I'm on television tonight.'

'Oo-er,' she said. Yes, that's what people say when you become famous. 'Oo-er.' Mulgrew has already had his kipper and oo-er. We are lumbered with the props. Hall will meet us at Ally Pally. We get a taxi to the gig: Alexandra Palace is a warren of signs and BBC men with hats on who mindlessly point the way, 'Der lift to der turd floor,' said an Irish one. 'Oh yes,' said a clipboard girl, who had as much feel for showbiz as Mrs Higgs had for hunting basking sharks. 'I'm Penelope Mutts, I'm the floor manager.' Who manages the ceiling? 'You are the . . .' she consults her board, 'Marty Midge and Naylor.'

We are shown into a dressing room with several other performers; some are dressed as cowboys, they are Big Bill Campbell and his Bunkhouse group, all done up in stetsons and a Red Indian chief – all from East Acton. They were practising, 'There's an old covered wagon for sale.'

'If it goes, they'll have to walk back,' said Mulgrew.

A gay floor manager calls us for rehearsal with Eric Robinson and the Orchestra. 'Is this all you got?' he said, looking at our meagre band parts.

'Yes, just play them loud,' I said.

The orchestra applauded our rehearsal.

'Can I have your agent's number?' said Robinson.

'You gonna kill him?' I say.

'No, I might be able to use you, have you got a card?'

'No, just this bit of paper.'

'Make-up?' says a girl.

'Is that what you're wearing?'

'No, the make-up you have to wear is green,' she said. 'It comes off with water.'

Hall has arrived, I knew he comes off with water. I've got good news, he said; it *was* good news, he'd turned up. He'd got a gig immediately after the show at the Domino, a nightclub in Balham, the arsehole of London. The wretched appearance of Hall disturbs the make-up girl. 'I don't think you need any,' she says, backing away. The show centres on the Television Toppers, fifteen rather lovely girls, Argggghhh. Fifteen Arghhhs! The TV show is all very interesting, being live, it's split-second timing.

The set is a Parisian Cabaret with a maître d', an old broken actor with an awful French accent; he announced us, 'End nous, from ze Coco-nut Grover-er, Le Beel Hall Trio.' There's no real audience so a planted one acts insane with artificial applause. Our problem is we have no time afterwards to remove the green make-up, so that's how we appear at the Domino, green.

*

Alan Clare, a friend, superb ballad player, told me a story. A Sloane Ranger and her micromind came in and said, 'Oh dear, ha ha ha, I thought you were a recording, ha-ho-he-ha.' Alan said, 'Ha ha ha – that's funny, I thought you were one too, can they switch you off?' Another jolly chap said, 'I say pi-ano, do you play this thing?' Alan said, 'Yes.' 'Oh – do you play requests?' Alan says, 'Yes, what would you like?' 'Oh, anything.' He's possibly head PR for Harrods.

Playing my masterpieces at the Grafton after hours, I ignored everyone, and they ignored me. I like making sounds; my life was shattered by bone and spoon players, they didn't have a clue what you were playing and didn't care; that terrible clattering of some dead cow's ribs.

Of course, with Secombe and Bentine, they would play the idiot along – 'Were you taught, chum?'

'No, it's just natural like.'

'Yes, seems natural like.'

'Do you read music?'

'No need to, any tune comes easy.'

'Do you know Beethoven's Fifth?'

'Oh yer.' He bursts into the opening Victory Vs of the introduc-tion – on and on he rattled, off his elbows, off his knees, his arse (very funny). Finally, with a furious rattle he stopped.

'Was that it?'

'Yer.'

'Amazing.'

'Yer, I keep it all in my head.'

'That was a very short version of the Fifth.'

'Ah well, I go fast and I leave out bits I don't like.'

I abandon the piano and join in joking and ad-libbing with Secombe and Bentine – with Jimmy adding drinks; he was a shrewd man and he sensed we had something – like rabies.

BENTINE: I arrest you for nose.

ME: My nose is innocent – who are you?

SECOMBE: Just a minute. I'm Inspector Thuds of Scotland Yard.

ME: This man's nose is on undercover service.

BENTINE: On or under, make up your mind.

ME: Then where's its secret cover?

SECOMBE: He's off duty.

BENTINE: Not so fast – Secombe.

SECOMBE: All right, I'll speak slower.

BENTINE: I happen to be chief nose cover inspector to the Sûreté – *où est cover du nez*?

SECOMBE: It's in 10 Downing Street – with Mrs Clement Attlee's plumber.

BENTINE: Her plumber?

SECOMBE: Who would look for it there?

ME: Narkington Quench Esq.

BENTINE: Then all is lost – the only escape is in this match-box. Etc, etc.

We pulled a lot of grimaces during our clowning.

ME: Sir, this finger will never make it on its own.

SECOMBE: Hold it on your other hand and purse your lips.

This was all after hours, with just a few late drinkers. One man said, 'Two years in the army would do you wastrels good.'

'We've just done five,' we said.

'Then do five more, you're not better yet.'

It was the late Kenneth More who was fascinated by our humour, as were Norman Castle, Michael Howard, Dick Scrongle, Tim Gritts, Len Trock, and many other people with names.

One night Sellers said: 'I have just eaten the Elfin Oak.'

ME: Did anybody see you?

SELLERS: Yes.

ME: Then you're a marked man.

SELLERS: I haven't got any mark, only a brown spot on my knee – it's a birthmark.

ME: How long have you had that?

There were miles of that.

So the week prior to Zurich, I spent the days hanging around with Bentine, Secombe, for ever watching newsreels, cartoons, ribald laughter, mad ideas. In the *Telegraph* it says an atomic paper had gone missing. Bentine and I spent the night drawing up a bogus formula; he knew all the mathematics, I just went along for the ride. It ended by scraping the luminous dials off our watches, which contain radium; we leave it all in a phone box, it all looked very authentic – it had taken all night. We kept watch on the booth. Someone threw it on the floor.

PENNIES FROM HEAVEN

I put 10p in my Piggy Bank
To save for a rainy day.
It rained the *very next morning*!
Three cheers, Hip Hip Hooray!

– from *Unspun Socks from a Chicken's Laundry*

from Peace Work

I get home to 3 Leathwell Road and go to bed. It's almost the end of the Bill Hall Trio – though we don't know it. My mum is worried; I've been in bed five days, unshaven. 'Get up, son, have a wash and a shave, you'll feel better.' Perhaps. I try a hot bath in front of the fire. Mum adds another bucket of hot water. Had I caught something when I was in Germany, did I sit on any dirty lavatory seats, or eat any German food? No, I didn't eat any lavatories or sit on dirty food. The doctor comes (yes, in those days). He wants to know when I was in Germany, etc. No, he says I haven't got German measles or rabies. My temperature is normal, my pulse rate is fast. He writes a prescription. My dear mother goes out in the rain to the local chemist. 'It's a good tonic,' he tells my mother. My mother tells me, 'It's a good tonic.' It gives me the shits.

I went to tell Bill and Johnny I wanted to finish with the Trio; Bill took it badly. 'You'll never work again, you bastard,' were his parting words. The Trio went on with a new guitarist, Bart Norman, once of the Three Admirals. The Trio went on working for another thirty years doing the same act. When Johnny died six years ago, it finally stopped.

Ann Lenner Trio

The Bill Hall Trio was not the last trio I would appear in. No, Jimmy Grafton has found me work – Ann Lenner, one-time lead vocalist with Carol Gibbons at the Savoy, wants to break away. So she wants to form a trio but finds it hard on her own. I am introduced to her at the Grafton Arms, which is becoming for me what Berlin was for Isherwood. Ann is a petite lady in her late thirties. 'Hello, pleased to meet you, Miss Lenner – I hope I'm suitable.'

She smiles. 'Well, you look suitable.'

We are joined by the third member of the Trio, my old friend Reg O'List, late of the Windmill Revue. 'Super, super,' he said, so now, the act.

'Mostly vocal with a little light comedy,' says Ann.

Jimmy Grafton is to write the act for us, Reg and I will accompany Ann on guitars. Reg has a straight, shivery, light baritone, Ann is a soprano with a very good range, I'm – well, light Bing Crosby baritone. So, the act is on. Our first job is in an Army Welfare Show, *Swinging Along*, with the comic Eddy Molloy. He's never made the big time, he's a summer season or pantomime comic – in America called a second banana. I can't imagine what a fourteenth banana's act must be – it must be so bad you're not allowed on. We rehearse the show over the Irish Club in Eaton Square. My God, the fug that arose from the bar below! You got pissed inhaling it.

The Ann Lenner Trio goes like this: I spring from the side of the stage singing 'Flat Foot Floogie' with the Floy Floy. To cut me off, Reg O'List comes from the other side singing 'The Cossack Patrol' – then Ann Lenner enters centre singing 'I'll Capture Your Heart Singing'. Light patter – who do you think you are? I think I'm me, who did you think I was? Etc. Then 'A Quiet Town in Crossbone County', made popular by Danny Kaye; during the number I clowned a lot, and I became aware during rehearsals people in the cast were laughing out loud, the best way   I can't remember all that act but we ended on a sing-along – your favourite tune, but not mine. For a briefing on the show, the whole cast assemble at the rehearsals on the Friday before we leave, and, wow, there's eight girl dancers. Captain Richard Leche tells us we will play Hamburg, Munich, Lüneburg and Vienna. I spot one of the chorus girls, Dorita Smith, another redhead with green eyes. She is Head Girl. We do a complete run-through of the show – I have to appear in some of the Eddy Molloy sketches, which I think are as funny as a baby with cancer, but it's work, money and, perhaps, fame.

'Well, looking forward to the trip?' says Reg.

'Yes, it would be silly to look backward to it, even sideways at it – no, it's best to look forward, it's a jolly good direction. In the dictionary it says, Forward: at or near the forepart of anything. Well, that's where I wanted to be, Reg – at or near the forepart of anything. How proud my mother would be when she saw me on stage. "That boy there near the forepart of anything is my son."'

Poor Reg got three weeks of this. 'Spike, my boy, I will do my best to understand you, I am older than you in years (even minutes!) so I'm a patient man.'

'Yes, Reg, with your complexion, you look like a patient, if you lie on the floor I'll call the ambulance.'

Reg smiles. He hasn't got the mind that can handle my ravings. Reg is just lovely, kind, solid but square. Reg and I compare wages, well rather *I* compare wages. I say, I'm on £30 a week, anyone want to swop? 'No, Spike, I too am on that princely sum; it'll suffice, it'll be hard to save, I tell 'ee lad.'

No, I said, if he didn't save it, the sum would stay at £30, no matter what. You could transfer it from your back to your breast pocket provided, in between, you didn't spend any, it would end up £30. I didn't have £30 at the time, I only had one, and I showed Reg how I transferred it from my back to my breast pocket, then slowly I returned it to my back pocket, then I triumphantly showed the pound safe and sound.

'Very good, Spike, very impressive, as soon as I get my £30, I'll sit up nights practising that very valuable financial move.'

I said, 'I must warn you, in time the money will start to fray, and that's when to spend.'

'Yes, that's enough for today,' says Reg, 'I'm wearing thin.'

'Are you all packed?' says Ann – all this while the chorus are going through the routines.

'Yes, I'm all packed, Ann, and most of it is in this suit – well, half of my underwear is; I always travel light, that's why I leave my mother and father behind.'

'You won't bugger the act, will you Spike?' she said.

'You'll see, I'm a good pro, as good as £30 can make.'

In the rehearsal break, I go down to the Irish bar for some cigarettes. 'Twenty Players, please.'

'Oh no, sir,' says the Irish barman. ''Tis only Sweet Afton we have.'

What in God's name was Sweet Afton?

''Tis an Irish cigarette.'

Irish cigarettes? Like saying Irish bananas. So I smoke Sweet Afton; where, when and how in Ireland were they growing tobacco? I felt so proud, yes, I felt my knee, elbow and wrists and they all felt proud. I wondered where the tobacco plantations were.

As she danced, all flashing, cherubic limbs, I watched Dorita Smith. God, she was luscious – but I was luscious too, me and my nine-stone Belsen body.

Here I was, really standing still; I was in a Trio that was mediocre compared with the Bill Hall Trio, so where was I headed? I could clown, tell jokes, sing, play the guitar and it was in the style of Danny Kaye who was now wowing audiences. I'd done all the continental touring I wanted; I needed another tour of Germany like a drowning man needed a piano. Somehow, there just might have been a drowning man who needed a piano – take the *Titanic*: the lifeboats were full, those drowning would have been very grateful for a piano floating by. There is a story of the *Titanic*'s band, a quartet; as the ship sank they played on, the violin leader said 'Keep playing', but as the ship tilted, the drummer slid away, then the piano, next the cello – to avoid the water, the leader stood on a chair – finally, he too slid into the Atlantic with a cry of 'Fuck show business'.

*

I go over to the Grafton Arms and Jimmy is happy that I continue writing part-time with him for Derek Roy. 'I don't want to be rude, Jimmy.'

'Then don't be,' he interrupted with a giggle.

'I was going to say that I don't think Derek Roy is very funny.'

Jimmy agrees, then says perhaps the scripts are bad? Not so, I had seen Derek Roy perform at the Gaumont State, Kilburn; he was a nice unfunny fellow with a jolly singing voice.

'Well, it's up to us to make him funny, there's money in it.'

I suggest he should wear a Harpo Marx wig and a red nose. *Variety Bandbox* on BBC is the biggest entertainment show of the week; Roy alternates with Frankie Howerd, who is much funnier.

At the same time as writing, Jimmy is trying to progress the career of one Harry Secombe, our perambulating, chattering Welshman; also in the pipeline is a possible series for Roy. As Jimmy's writing times are erratic, he works in the cracks between running the pub. He has also put himself up as a Conservative Councillor, so usually we work at nights on the living-room table when his wife, Dorothy (long-suffering), and two children James and Sally, along as I say with Buller the bulldog, Minty the cat, and Jacko the monkey, are abed. By the time we've finished writing, it's too late to catch a train home, so I sleep on a mattress in Jimmy's attic using one blanket and overcoats. In rush hours I sometimes help behind the bar.

Jimmy, now with no movement from the Ann Lenner Trio, tries to get me odd dates. He gets me one at the Nuffield Services Club; first I have to meet Mary Cook to vet me. With my affair with Dorita going like a piston the last thing I needed was a vet. Mary Cook is a well-educated, terribly well-spoken lady with enormous hips; it looks like a thin person has been slid into someone else's bottom half. 'Now, Mr Milligan, or do they all call you Spike?'

No, she can call me Spike, normally I'm called 'Hey you' or on bad days 'Stop thief'.

Is my act clean, yes, that means I'll have to drop the joke about the monkey, the elephant and the sore arse. So on the Friday night, wearing a velvet jacket I've knocked off from Army Welfare Service Wardrobe, I do an act doing imitations of wallpaper and end up singing 'Body and Soul' as a coloured girl. I go down okay, but nothing to write home about. But a singer, David Hughes, goes and sings 'The Desert Song'; he gets an ovation, so fuck him.

So back to the attic and scriptwriting. Margaret Lockwood is to be Derek Roy's guest – now his gimmick is to be billed as 'The Laughter Doctor', opening his act with 'hello patients', they all were by the end of his act – so we have to write a script with her as the nurse. We work all night on the script, in fact, I haven't shaved for three, then there's a panic: Miss Lockwood must see the scripts right away, so first thing in the morning I shave at speed, cut myself to pieces. Off I go to somewhere on the outskirts of London to a posh block of flats. ''Ere, where you goin'?' said a grotty hall porter.

'I'm going to see Miss Lockwood.'

He savages me with his crust-edged eyes. 'No, you're bloody not,' he said. He picked up the phone, 'Miss Lockwood, there's a man here says he's got a script for you from the . . .' He looks at me, 'Where is it?'

'The BBC – Derek Roy.'

He repeats it down the phone. 'Okay. Second floor, room 118, the lift's not working,' he said gleefully.

The RAF? I thud up the stairs two at a time. I'm in fine fettle, in fact I've never been fettler. I press a polished, polished bell on a gleaming white door. Wow, Miss Lockwood opens it with her beauty spot.

'Oh,' I said surprised. 'No coloured footman.'

She gave me a Rank Charm School smile, took the script, said a Rank Charm School thank you and shut the door; it was all of one-minute fifty.

'Oh Jimmy,' I say, 'is it worth £10 scriptwriting for Derek Roy, the man who kills 99 per cent of all known jokes?'

Jimmy said, 'Patience, it can lead to bigger things.'

I tell him I don't need bigger things, mine are big enough, ask any heavy plant operator.

'There could be a series,' says Jimmy.

'What, of disasters? Roy is *not* funny.'

'It'll put money in your shatteringly hollow account,' he says.

So when he's in the bar serving I bang away at the jokes. I remember an early one: Man says to doctor, 'My wife thinks I'm mad because I prefer brown boots to black.' Doctor says, 'How silly, I myself prefer brown boots to black.' Man says, 'How do you like them, boiled or fried?' Now that's how a normal joke would end; not me, with me the Doctor says, 'I like mine boiled, my wife thinks I'm mad too.'

Jimmy organizes a night with the Goons, as we have decided to call ourselves. So one evening, after hours, we have an ad-lib session. Bentine starts the ball rolling, 'Gentlemen, now you know why I've called you here?'

'No, we don't,' we murmur.

'Very well, we've been besieged in this fort for, does anybody know?'

'Forty days,' says one.

'Fifty,' says another.

Any advance on fifty – ?

Seventy.

'Right, we've been besieged forty, fifty and seventy days. Gentlemen, you will synchronize watches.'

They all adjust their watches, but never say a word, the phone supposedly rings, Secombe answers, 'Hello, Fort Agra, hello? Just a minute.' He holds his hand over the phone, 'Does a Mrs Gladys Stokes live here?' No, sorry Mrs Stokes doesn't live here.

SELLERS: Someone has got to go and get reinforcements.

ME: Yes, someone has to.

BENTINE: Yes someone has to.

SECOMBE: Yes gentlemen, someone has to go and get reinforcements.

(Pause)

SELLERS: Good, well that's settled.

ME: Run up the Union Jack.

SELLERS: Right, sir.

ME: Wait, that flag should be red, white and blue.

SELLERS: Yes, I thought I'd run up the white part first.

BENTINE: It's these night attacks that worry me, one more night attack and I'll have to change the sheets.

It went on for an hour, with all four of us crawling on our stomachs in the desert dying of thirst.

ME: Water.

BENTINE: Water, for God's sake.

SECOMBE: Yes, water –

SELLERS *(drunk)*: Scotch and Soda.

I suppose it would only be a matter of time before someone in the BBC might use us. There was one enlightened producer streets ahead in perspicacity, Pat Dixon, totally unrevered by the BBC but directly responsible for giving us the break. Already we had introduced the first comedy show on the new Third Programme (for unknown reason now called Radio 3, they can't leave alone can they), using Harry Secombe, Peter Sellers, Benny Hill. It was the first comedy show without an audience, I used to go and listen through the studio door, I was desperate to be given a break as such on the media; it never did, the three, Secombe, Sellers, Bentine are all working and earning. If I hadn't written myself into *The Goon Show*, I'd never have been heard of.

*

At last, another breakthrough! The BBC have commissioned Jimmy Grafton to write a series for Derek Roy – Jimmy asked me to write it with him, I really wasn't up to it yet, I could drum up a few one-liners but a whole half hour was behind me. But in we go, we both work long hours, split with Jimmy in the bar, then he's running as a Conservative Councillor and he gets me going round putting his election leaflets in letterboxes, all this and writing with visits from the monkey. At night Jacko was locked in the attic next to me. Out of curiosity I wondered what he was doing and I looked through the keyhole only to see his eye looking at me. To keep himself going Jimmy took pep-up pills, consequently he could stay awake when I was falling asleep. The show was very well received.

Well, folks, that's where I was at on Wednesday, 5 October 1949. I went on writing for the series, which was far from being a success when it ended. I was back where I started, though I had been paid £30 a week and I'd saved nearly all of it, except I bought my very first radio, hoping one day I would be on it with my own show.

Napoleon's Piano

from The Goon Show Scripts, Woburn Press 1972

The Goon Show, no. 129 (6th Series, no. 4)
*Transmission: Tuesday, 11 October 1955: 8.30–9.00 p.m. Home
    Service*
Studio: The Camden Theatre, London

THE MAIN CHARACTERS

Ned Seagoon	Harry Secombe
Grytpype-Thynne	Peter Sellers
Moriarty	Spike Milligan
Mr Henry Crun	Peter Sellers
Miss Minnie Bannister	Spike Milligan
Eccles	Spike Milligan
Major Denis Bloodnok	Peter Sellers
Justin Eidelburger	Peter Sellers
Throat	Spike Milligan
Yakamoto	Spike Milligan
Bluebottle	Peter Sellers

The Ray Ellington Quartet
Max Geldray
Orchestra conducted by Wally Stott
Announcer: Wallace Greenslade
Script by Spike Milligan
Production by Peter Eton

Tricked into signing a contract to bring over to England the very
piano that Napoleon played at Waterloo, Neddie Seagoon stows
away on a boat to France. A chance meeting in the disreputable
Café Tom with piano robbery specialist Justin Eidelburger seems

to solve all Neddie's problems – but others, too, are after Napoleon's piano. With £10,000 at stake, the only solution is to sail the instrument back to England – a voyage fraught with peril . . .

BILL: This is the BBC Home Service.

GRAMS: OUTBREAK OF PEOPLE SIGHING.

BILL: Oh come, come, dear listeners – it's not that bad –

HARRY: Of course not – come, Mr Greenslade, tell them the good news.

BILL: Ladies and gentlemen, we now have the extraordinary talking-type wireless 'Goon Show'.

GRAMS: SCREAMS OF ANGUISH. PEOPLE RUNNING AWAY.

HARRY: Mmm – is the popularity waning? Ahemm.

SPIKE: Ho ho ho, fear not, Neddie lad – we'll jolly them up with a merry laughing-type joke show. Stand prepared for the story of 'Napoleon's Piano'.

GRAMS: VERY OLD RECORD OF A PIANO SOLO (MARSEILLAISE).

SEAGOON: Napoleon's piano – the story starts in the bad old days, back in April 1955. It was early one morning. Breakfast had just been served at Beauleigh Manor – I was standing at the window, looking in. With the aid of a telescope, I was reading the paper on the breakfast table – when suddenly an advertisement caught my eye. It said –

GRYTPYPE-THYNNE: *(Distort)* Will pay anybody five pounds to remove piano from one room to another. Apply, The Bladders, Harpyapipe, Quants.

SEAGOON: In needle nardle noo time I was at the address and with the aid of a piece of iron and a lump of wood – I made this sound.

F.X.: THREE KNOCKS WITH IRON KNOCKER ON SOLID OAK DOOR.

MORIARTY: Sapristi Knockoes – when I heard that sound I ran down the stairs and with the aid of a door knob and two hinges I made *this* sound.

F.X.: DOOR KNOB BEING HEAVILY AGITATED FOLLOWED BY FAST SQUEAKY HINGES AS DOOR OPENS.

SEAGOON: Ah, good morning.

MORIARTY: Good morning? Just a moment.

F.X.: FURIOUS DIALLING.

MORIARTY: Hello, Air Ministry Roof? Weather report. Yes? Yes, thank you.

F.X.: PHONE DOWN.

MORIARTY: You're perfectly right – it *is* a good morning.

SEAGOON: Thanks. My name is Neddie Seagoon.

MORIARTY: What a memory you have.

SEAGOON: Needle nardle noo. I've come to move the piano.

MORIARTY: *(Insane laugh)* Come in.

SEAGOON: *(Insane laugh)* Thanks.

MORIARTY: You must excuse the mess but we've got the Socialists in.

GRYTPYPE-THYNNE: *(Approach)* Oh Moriarty, can I borrow a shoe? Mine's worn out – oh, you have company.

MORIARTY: Ahh ah – these three men are called Neddie Seagoon. He's come in answer to our ad.

GRYTPYPE-THYNNE: Ohhhh – come in – sit down. Have a gorilla.

SEAGOON: No thanks, I'm trying to give them up.

GRYTPYPE-THYNNE: Splendid. Now, Neddie, here's the money for moving the piano – there, five pounds in fivers.

SEAGOON: Five pounds for moving a piano? Ha ha – this is money for old rope.

GRYTPYPE-THYNNE: Is it? I'd have thought you'd have bought something more useful.

SEAGOON: Oh no – I have simple tastes. Now, where's this piano?

GRYTPYPE-THYNNE: Just a moment. First, would you sign this contract in which you guarantee to move the piano from one room to another for five pounds.

SEAGOON: Of course I'll sign – have you any ink?

GRYTPYPE-THYNNE: Here's a fresh bottle.

SEAGOON: *(Drinks)* . . . ahhhhhhhh. Gad, I was thirsty.

MORIARTY: Sapristi Nuckoes – do you always drink ink?

SEAGOON: Only in the mating season.

MORIARTY: Shall we dance?

GRAMS: OLD 1929 SCRATCHY GUY LOMBARDO RECORD OF 'LOVER' WALTZ.

SEAGOON: You dance divinely.

GRYTPYPE-THYNNE: Next dance please! Now, Neddie, just sign the contract on the side of this horse.

SEAGOON: Certainly.

F.X.: SCRATCHING OF PEN UNDER SEAGOON AS HE SPEAKS NEXT LINE.

SEAGOON: Neddie – Seagoon – A.G.G.

MORIARTY: What's A.G.G. for?

SEAGOON: For the kiddies to ride on . . . get it? A gee-gee – ha ha ha ha –

(Agonized silence)

GRYTPYPE-THYNNE: You're *sure* you won't have a gorilla?

SEAGOON: No thanks, I've just put one out. Now, which room is this piano in?

GRYTPYPE-THYNNE: Ahemm. It's in the Louvre.

SEAGOON: Strange place to put a piano.

GRYTPYPE-THYNNE: We refer to the Louvre Museum, Paris.

SEAGOON: What what what what what? Ahhhh, I've been tricked – ahhhh.

F.X.: THUD OF UNCONSCIOUS BODY HITTING GROUND.

MORIARTY: For the benefit of people without television – he's fainted.

GRYTPYPE-THYNNE: Don't waste time – just open his jacket – get the weight of his cruel wallet off his chest – mmm – found anything in his pockets?

MORIARTY: Yes – a signed photograph of Neddie Seagoon, a press cutting from the Theatre, Bolton, a gramophone record of Gigli mowing the lawn, a photo of Gigli singing, and a half share in Kim Novak.

GRYTPYPE-THYNNE: He's still out cold – see if *this* brings him round.

F.X.: PENNY THROWN ON CONCRETE FLOOR.

SEAGOON: Thank you, lady. *(Sings)* Comrades comrades – ever since – oh – where – where am I?

GRYTPYPE-THYNNE: England!

SEAGOON: What number?

GRYTPYPE-THYNNE: Seven A. Have a gorilla.

SEAGOON: No, they hurt my throat. Wait! *Now* I remember! You've trapped me into bringing back a piano from France for only five pounds.

GRYTPYPE-THYNNE: *You* signed the contract, Neddie – now, get that piano or we sue you for breach of contract.

SEAGOON: Ahhhhhhhh. *(Going off)*

F.X.: DOOR SLAMS.

GRYTPYPE-THYNNE: Gad, Moriarty, if he brings that piano back we'll be in the money. That piano is worth ten thousand pounds.

MORIARTY: How do you know?

GRYTPYPE-THYNNE: I've seen its bank book. Do you know, that's the very piano Napoleon played at Waterloo. With the moolah we get on that we can have a holiday. *(Sings)*

BOTH: April in Paris – we've found a Charlie.

BILL: I say – poor Neddie must have been at his wits' end! Faced with the dilemma of having to bring Napoleon's piano back from Paris, he went to the Foreign Office for advice on passports and visas.

F.X.: BITS AND PIECES DROPPING DOWN.

CRUN & MINNIE: *(Nattering away)*

CRUN: Ohh dee deee – dee, X9?

MINNIE: *(Off)* X9 answering – who's that calling, buddy?

CRUN: It's me – the Foreign Secretary. Do you know where the key to the secret documents safe is?

MINNIE: Yes – it's with the charlady.

CRUN: Do you think that's wise – she has access to all the vital British secret documents.

MINNIE: She can't read them, buddy, she only speaks Russian.

CRUN: That's a bit of luck –

F.X.: KNOCKS ON DOOR.

CRUN: Ohh, that might be one of England's strolling Prime Ministers of no fixed abode.

MINNIE: Coming, Anthonyyy – coming . . .

CRUN: Tell him we're very sorry.

MINNIE: Sorry for what?

CRUN: Oh, mmm – make something up.

F.X.: DOOR OPENS.

MINNIE: Ahh, we're very sorry, Anthony, we – ohh, you're not the Prime Minister.

SEAGOON: Not yet, but it's just a matter of time. My name is Neddie Seagoon.

CRUN: Want to buy a white paper –

SEAGOON: No thanks, I'm trying to give them up.

CRUN: So are we –

SEAGOON: I want a few particulars. You see, I want to leave the country . . .

CRUN: He's going to Russia! Stop him, Min – get him!

MINNIE: Hit him, Hen . . .

GRAMS: MIX IN GREAT BATTLE. ALL STOPS SUDDENLY.

CRUN: There! Let that be a lesson to you – get out.

SEAGOON: I will, but not before I hear musical saboteur Max Geldray.

MAX & ORCHESTRA: 'AIN'T MISBEHAVIN'.

(Applause)

BILL: Seagoon was confused – it seems that the cheapest method of getting to Paris was to stow away to France on board a Channel steamer.

GRAMS: SHIP'S TELEGRAPH RINGING. SEAGULLS – WASH OF SHIP'S WAKE.

SEAGOON: Down in the dark hold I lay – alone – so I thought . . .

ECCLES: *(Off – sings)* I talk to der trees – dat's why they put me away . . .

SEAGOON: The singer was a tall ragged idiot – he carried a plasticine gramophone, and wore a metal trilby.

ECCLES: Hello, shipmate. Where you goin'?

SEAGOON: Nowhere. I think it's safer to stay on the ship until we reach Calais.

ECCLES: You going to Calais?

SEAGOON: Yes.

ECCLES: What a coincidence. Dat's where the ship's going – ain't you lucky.

SEAGOON: Here – have a gorilla.

ECCLES: Oh, thanks!

GRAMS: GORILLA FIGHTING ANOTHER GORILLA (IF YOU CAN'T GET THE RIGHT SOUND TRY TWO LIONS). ALL STOPS ABRUPTLY.

ECCLES: Hey – dese gorillas are strong. Have one of my monkeys – they're milder.

SEAGOON: And so for the rest of the voyage we sat quietly smoking our monkeys. At Calais I left the idiot singer. By sliding down the ship's rope in French I avoided detection. Late that night I checked into a French hotel. Next morning I sat in my room eating my breakfast when suddenly through the window a fork on the end of a long pole appeared – it tried to spear my kipper.

BLOODNOK: *(Off)* Strained. Aeiough.

SEAGOON: Who the blazes are you, sir?

BLOODNOK: Aeioughhh – oh, oh, I'm sorry, I was fishing.

SEAGOON: Fishing? This is the thirty-fourth floor.

BLOODNOK: Oh, the river must have dropped.

SEAGOON: Who are you, sir?

BLOODNOK: I've got it on a bit of paper here – ah yes – Major Denis Bloodnok, late of the Third Disgusting Fusiliers – OBE, MT, MT, MT, MT and MT.

SEAGOON: What are all those MTs for?

BLOODNOK: I get tuppence on each of 'em – aeioughhhh.

SEAGOON: You're acting suspiciously suspicious – I've a good mind to call the manager.

BLOODNOK: Call him – I am unafraid!

SEAGOON: Mmmm – no! Why should *I* call him?

BLOODNOK: Then *I* will – manager?

F.X.: DOOR OPENS.

SPIKE: *(French)* Oui, Monsieur?

BLOODNOK: Throw this man out.

SEAGOON: Ahhhhh. *(Thrown out)*

F.X.: DOOR SLAMS.

BLOODNOK: Now for breakfast – see, kippers – toast de da dee deeee. What's this coming through the window – flatten me krurker and nosh me schlappers – it's a fork, on a pole, and its trying to take the kipper off me plate – I say, who's that?

SEAGOON: I'm sorry, I was just fishing.

BLOODNOK: What, you! I've a good mind to call the manager.

SEAGOON: Go on then, call him.

BLOODNOK: No, why should I?

SEAGOON: Then I'll call him. (Watch me turn the tables, listeners.) Manager?

F.X.: DOOR OPENS.

SPIKE: Oui, Monsieur?

BLOODNOK: Throw this man out of my room.

SEAGOON: Ahhhh. *(Thrown out)*

F.X.: DOOR SLAMS.

SEAGOON: Alone in Paris – I went down the notorious Café Tom. Proprietor: Maurice Ponk.

GRAMS: 'SOUS LES TOITS DE PARIS'.

SEAGOON: Inside, the air was filled with gorilla smoke – I was looking for a man who might specialize in piano robberies from the Louvre.

F.X.: WHOOSH.

EIDELBURGER: Gute evenung. You are looking for a man who might specialize in piano robberies from the Louvre?

SEAGOON: How do you know?

EIDELBURGER: I was listening on the radio and I heard you say it.

SEAGOON: Good – pull up a chair. Sit down.

EIDELBURGER: No thanks – I'd rather stand.

SEAGOON: Very well, stand on a chair. Garçon!

THROAT: Oui?

SEAGOON: Two glasses of English port-type cooking sherry, and vite.

THROAT: Two glasses of sherry and vite coming up.

SEAGOON: Now – name?

EIDELBURGER: I am Justin Eidelburger.

SEAGOON: Oh. Have a gorilla.

EIDELBURGER: No zanks – I only smoke baboons.

SEAGOON: This piano we must steal, it's the one Napoleon played at Waterloo.

EIDELBURGER: That will be a very sticky job.

SEAGOON: Why?

EIDELBURGER: It's just been varnished – he ha, zer German joke.

SEAGOON: Zer English silence.

EIDELBURGER: Now, Mr Snzeegroon – meet me outside the Louvre at midnight on the stroke of two.

SEAGOON: Right.

SEAGOON: True to my word, I was there dead on three.

EIDELBURGER: You're late.

SEAGOON: I'm sorry – my legs were slow.

EIDELBURGER: You must buy another pair. Zis here is my oriental assistant, Yakamoto.

YAKAMOTO: I am very honoured to meet you. Oh boy.

SEAGOON: What does this oriental creep know about piano thieving?

EIDELBURGER: Nothing – he's just here to lend colour to the scene. Now, Neddie, this is a map-plan of the Louvre and the surrounding streets.

F.X.: LONG UNFOLDING.

SEAGOON: You take one end.

F.X.: UNFOLDING. THE MAP BEING UNFOLDED CONTINUES FOR A WHOLE MINUTE.

SEAGOON: It's big, isn't it?

EIDELBURGER: *(In the distance)* Yes, it is! This bit here shows the Rue de la Paix.

SEAGOON: Good heavens, you're miles away – walk straight up that street – take the second on the left – I'll be waiting for you.

F.X.: TAXI PULLS UP.

EIDELBURGER: I took a taxi – it was too far. Now – we disperse and meet again in the Hall of Mirrors, when the clock strikes twinge. At midnight we strike.

F.X.: BIG BEN STRIKES TWELVE – AT VARYING SPEEDS.

SEAGOON: Shhhhhh.

EIDELBURGER: Is that you, Seagoon?

SEAGOON: Yes.

EIDELBURGER: Good.

F.X.: HAND BELL.

BILL: *(French)* Every bodee out, closing time – everyone back to zere own bed.

SEAGOON: Quick, hide behind this pane of glass.

EIDELBURGER: But you can see through it.

SEAGOON: Not if you close your eyes.

EIDELBURGER: Gerblunden, you're right – are all your family clever?

SEAGOON: Only the Crustaceans.

BILL: Everybody out – and that goes for you idiots with your eyes shut behind that sheet of glass.

SEAGOON: You fool, you can't see us.

BILL: Yes, I can – get out or I'll call the police.

EIDELBURGER: Why, you anti-Bismarck swine, I shoot you.

SEAGOON: No, not through the glass – you'll break it. First I'll make a hole in it.

F.X.: PANE OF GLASS SHATTERING TO PIECES.

SEAGOON: *Now* shoot through that.

F.X.: PISTOL SHOT.

BILL: You've killed me – now I'll get the sack. Ooooooo – ohhhh – ohhhhh – I die – I fall to the ground – ahhh meee – ahh my – ohhh ohhh I die, killed by death!

SEAGOON: Never mind – swallow this tin of Lifo guaranteed to return you to life – recommended by all corpses and Wilfred Pickles. Forward, Ray Ellington and his music!

QUARTET: 'BLOODSHOT EYES'.

(Applause)

BILL: Part Two – in which our heroes are discovered creeping up to the piano.

EIDELBURGER: Shhh, Neddie – there's someone under Napoleon's piano, trying to lift it by himself.

SEAGOON: He must be mad.

ECCLES: *(Sings)* I talk to der trees . . .

SEAGOON: I was right. Eccles, what are you doing out after feeding time?

ECCLES: I signed a contract that fooled me into taking dis piano back to England.

SEAGOON: What? You must be an idiot to sign a contract like that – now, help me get this piano back to England. Together, lift!

OMNES: *(Grunts, groans)*

SEAGOON: No, no, it's too heavy – put it down.

ECCLES: Here, it's lighter when you let go.

SEAGOON: I have an idea – we'll saw the legs off. Eccles, give me that special piano leg saw that you just happen to be carrying. Now . . .

F.X.: SAWING.

ECCLES: *(Sings over sawing)* I talk to der trees – dat's why dey put me away –

SEAGOON: There! I've sawn all four legs off.

EIDELBURGER: Strange – first time I've known of a piano with four legs.

ECCLES: Hey – I keep falling down – ohhhhhhh.

SEAGOON: Sorry, Eccles – here, swallow this tin of Leggo, the wonder leg-grower recommended by all good centipedes.

BILL: Sweating and struggling, they managed to get Napoleon's piano into the cobbled court.

SEAGOON: *(Dry)* Which was more than Napoleon ever did.

BLOODNOK: Halt – hand over le piano in the name of France!

SEAGOON: Bloodnok, take off that kilt, we know you're not French.

BLOODNOK: One step nearer and I'll strike with this fork on the end of a pole.

SEAGOON: You do, and I'll attack with this kipper.

BLOODNOK: I've a good mind to call the manager.

SEAGOON: Call the manager.

BLOODNOK: No, why should I –

SEAGOON: Very well, I'll call him (I'll get him this time). Manager?

F.X.: DOOR OPENS.

SPIKE: Oui, Monsieur?

SEAGOON: Throw this man out.

SPIKE: *(Raspberry)*

F.X.: DOOR SHUTS.

SEAGOON: Nurse? Put the screens around that bed.

BLOODNOK: Seagoon, you must let me have that piano – you see, I foolishly signed a contract that forces me to –

SEAGOON: Yes, yes, we know – we're all in the same boat. We have no money, so the only way to get the piano back to England is to float it back. All together into the English Channel – hurl.

F.X.: PAUSE – SPLASH.

SEAGOON: All aboard – cast off.

ORCHESTRA: SEASCAPE MUSIC.

GRAMS: HEAVY SEAS. GULLS.

SEAGOON: The log of Napoleon's Piano. December the third – Second week in English Channel. Very seasick – no food – no water. Bloodnok down with the lurgi. Eccles up with the lark.

BLOODNOK: Ohhh – Seagoon – take over the keyboard, I can't steer any more.

SEAGOON: Eccles? Take over the keyboard.

ECCLES: I can't. I haven't brought my music.

SEAGOON: You'll have to busk for the next three miles.

BLOODNOK: Wait! Great galloping crabs, look in the sky.

GRAMS: HELICOPTER.

BLOODNOK: It's a recording of a helicopter – saved!

SEAGOON: By St George – saved – yes. For those of you who haven't got television, they're lowering a man on a rope.

BLUEBOTTLE: Yes, it is I, Sea Ranger Blunebontle. Signals applause.

GRAMS: APPLAUSE.

BLUEBOTTLE: Cease – I have drunk my fill of the clapping.

SEAGOON: Little stinking Admiral, you have arrived in the nick of time.

BLUEBOTTLE: Silence – I must do my duty – hurriedly runs up cardboard Union Jack. I now claim this island for the British Empire and Lord Beaverbrook, the British patriot – thinks, I wonder why he lives in France. Three cheers for the Empire – hip hip hooray – hip hip . . .

SEAGOON: Have you come to save us?

BLUEBOTTLE: Hooray! Rockall is now British – cements in brass plate – steps back to salute.

GRAMS: SPLASH.

BLUEBOTTLE: Help! I'm in the dreaded drowning-type water.

SEAGOON: Here, grab this fork on the end of a pole.

BLUEBOTTLE: It's got a kipper on it.

SEAGOON: Yes, you *must* keep your strength up.

BLUEBOTTLE: But I'm drowning.

SEAGOON: There's no need to go hungry as well. Take my hand.

BLUEBOTTLE: Why? Are you a stranger in paradise?

SEAGOON: Heave . . . for those without television, I've pulled him back on the piano.

BLUEBOTTLE: Piano? This is not a piano – this is Rockall.

SEAGOON: This is Napoleon's piano.

BLUEBOTTLE: No, no – this is Rockall – we have tooked it because it is in the area of the rocket testing range.

SEAGOON: I've never heard . . .

F.X.: ROCKET WHOOSH. EXPLOSION.

BILL: What do you think, dear listeners – were they standing on Rockall or was it Napoleon's piano? Send your suggestions to anybody but us. For those who would have preferred a happy ending, here it is.

F.X.: DOOR OPENS.

HARRY: Gwendeloine?? Gwendoline.

PETER: John, John darling –

HARRY: I've found work, darling. I've got a job.

PETER: Oh John, I'm so glad for you – what is it?

HARRY: All I've got to do is to move a piano from one room to another.

MORIARTY: *(Mad laugh)*

ORCHESTRA: SIGNATURE TUNE: UP AND DOWN FOR:

BILL: That was The Goon Show – a BBC recorded programme featuring Peter Sellers, Harry Secombe and Spike Milligan with the Ray Ellington Quartet and Max Geldray. The Orchestra was conducted by Wally Stott. Script by Spike Milligan. Announcer: Wallace Greenslade. The programme produced by Peter Eton.

ORCHESTRA: SIGNATURE TUNE UP TO END.

(Applause)

MAX & ORCHESTRA: 'CRAZY RHYTHM' PLAYOUT.

from Depression and How to Survive It

The best scripts I wrote were when I was ill. I've just recalled this – the ones that I wrote best were when I was ill – a mad desire to be better than anybody else at comedy, and if I couldn't do it in the given time of eight hours a day I used to work twelve, thirteen and fourteen. I did, I was determined. There was a time when I was positively manic. I was four feet above the ground at times, talking twice as fast as normal people. Working on this with great fervour to write this stuff and to hear them do it every Sunday. I couldn't wait for them to do it, to hear how it sounded, because it would be acclaimed when it went out. 'I've done it, I've done it' – and then I had to go and start all over again, that was the awful part of it.

When I look back at it, I think, 'Was that really me, was I ten feet off the ground all the time?' I was – I was terribly manic.

I once did write 10,000 words in one day, like Balzac! I was pressured inside. I couldn't sleep. I just wrote and wrote. I couldn't stop, couldn't control it. I did stop. In all, the state lasted about forty-eight hours. All I could think of was the book. I didn't think of time. I may have been manic once or twice since but I haven't noticed it.

I was so ill when I wrote those scripts, particularly at the beginning, that now, when I think back, that is what I remember. Of course I take pleasure in the fact that I made people laugh and the scripts still do. But it was at a terrible price for me. If I could choose now, which of course I cannot, I think I would choose to be free of the illness and not to have written the Goons. It took that much out of me. It caused me that much pain – and pain to my wife and children too.

[Michael Mills was Head of Light Entertainment at the BBC. He wanted Spike to become involved with a project on Lear. He tried for several months until finally Spike said yes. This is Spike's letter explaining how he saw the Lear programme.]

9 Orme Court
London W 2

4 February 1970

Michael Mills Esq.
British Broadcasting Corporation
Television Centre
Wood Lane
London W12

Dear Michael,

Lear. Okay. When you say ten to fifteen poems, I presume you mean some of the limericks, in which case here goes:

1) 'The Cummerbund'
2) 'The Quangle Wangle's Hat'
3) 'The Duck and the Kangaroo'
4) 'The Jumblies'
5) 'The Owl and the Pussycat'
6) 'The Dong with a Luminous Nose'

The above are six quite long poems. Find attached a separate sheet with the limericks. You will notice I have added an additional fourth line in brackets which are my own personal idea of how the limericks should end. I did this not in an attempt to better Mr Lear, but merely as an exercise. Basically, I think it's much droller to repeat the first line as the last, and it is also much more in keeping with the thinking of that time.

Music can also be included in the programme. The 'Yonghy Bonghy Bo' has been set to music, as has 'The Pelicans'.

I thought that some enchantment could be added to the programme, by the use of commissioned cartoonists, to help ride out long poems like the 'Duck and the Kangaroo'. I also envisaged some bizarre locations for some of the limericks. For instance, a great general falls dying at a great Napoleonic Battle. He pulls his ADC to his ear, and then dies with the limerick:

> There was an Old Man with a beard,
> Who sat on a horse when he reared;
> But they said, 'Never mind! you will fall off behind,
> You propitious Old Man with a beard!'

Leave the ADC with a baffled look.
Likewise, a Constable suddenly stops a man in the street, and goes on:

> There was an Old Man in a Tree,
> Who was horribly bored by a Bee;
> When they said, 'Does it buzz?' He replied, 'Yes it does!'
> 'It's a regular brute of a Bee!'

There could also be an 'on the spot artist' who could draw the subject matter, and one of the limericks as it is spoken.

There are also his nonsense alphabets, which with more imagination could be choreographed; and again his nonsense botany; such as the 'Knutmigrata Simplice' which the design boys could have fun with, and with other of his botany specimens make a brief spot with a nonsense 'horticultural lecture'.

Anyhow, I have done your bidding. I hope it might provide some ideas for Eleanor Fazan. I was only thinking in terms of this being one programme. It could, with ingenuity, last forty-five minutes.

Another idea has occurred to me:

LEAR SEEN AT LECTERN OR WRITING DESK

LEAR: 'There was an Old Man who said . . .'

(Cut to Old Man)

OLD MAN: 'Hush – I perceive a young bird in this bush'

LEAR: 'When they said . . .'

(Cut to SMALL GROUP OF PEOPLE)

SMALL GROUP OF PEOPLE: 'Is it small?'

LEAR: 'He replied'

(Cut to Old Man)

OLD MAN: 'Not at all, it's four times as big as the bush!'

As the Old Man speaks the line, on the words 'four times as big as the bush', B.P. behind shows a thrush which grows in size on each syllable.

   (Cut to Lear. Sits back, drops pen, having finished the limerick.)

   I must leave you now, as I smell something burning. I think it's my overdraft.

   Regards
     Spike

1) There was an Old Man of the West,
   Who wore a pale plum-coloured vest;
   When they said 'Does it fit?' he replied 'Not a bit!'
   That uneasy Old Man of the West.
   (Can't you see I'm exposing my chest?)

2) There was an Old Man who supposed,
   That the street door was partially closed;
   But some very large rats, ate his coats and his hats,
   While that futile old gentleman dozed.

3) There was an Old Man of Corfu,
   Who never knew what he should do;
   So he rushed up and down, till the sun made him brown,
   That bewildered Old Man of Corfu.
   (And the moon turned him red white and blue.)

4) There was an Old Man of the Dee,
   Who was sadly annoyed by a flea;
   When he said 'I will scratch it' – they gave him a hatchet,
   Which grieved that Old Man of the Dee.
   (So he chopped the poor flea in the threa.)

5) There was an Old Man of Jamaica,
   Who suddenly married a Quaker!
   But she cried out – 'O lack! I have married a black!'
   Which distressed that Old Man of Jamaica
   (What a terrible, terrible mistaica!)

6) There was an Old Man of the Coast,
   Who placidly sat on a post,
   But when it was cold, he relinquished his hold,
   And called for some hot buttered toast.

7) There was an Old Man at a casement,
   Who held up his hands in amazement;
   When they said 'Sir! you'll fall!' he replied 'Not at all!'
   That incipient Old Man at a casement.
   (But he did wallop thud on the pavement.)

8) There was an Old Man of Peru,
   Who never knew what he should do;
   So he tore off his hair, and behaved like a bear,
   That intrinsic Old Man of Peru.
   (And now the poor sod's in a zoo.)

[The Boulting Brothers, John and Roy, were head of British Lion Films. They produced all the Ealing Comedy classics such as Peter Sellers's *I'm All Right Jack* and *Heavens Above!*]

9 Orme Court
London W2

21 December 1970

Messrs John & Roy Boulting
British Lion Films
Broadwick House
Broadwick Street
London W1

Dear John and Roy,

According to my diary and the number of employer's stamps on my card, you have not employed me for six years.

 Now, I don't want to have to resurrect the Irish Rebellion of 1916 so I am going to give you an alternative.

 In case you have doubts about my acting, repeat acting, ability would you like to watch the following programmes and see the diversification of characters that I do:

HANDSOMEST HALL IN TOWN	26 December 1970
FOLLIES OF THE WISE	31 December 1970

After watching these, if you fail to recognize my talents I can only presume it's the hang over from the days your ancestors made porcelain ware for toilets, and because I don't appear as one of your customers, you are holding it against me.

 I will give you the year 1971 to make up for your shortcomings.

*After which, I will invite you to lunch and beat you lightly to death
with a surfeit of iron lampreys 17' 0" long.*

> *Love, light and peace, and employment*
> *for talented actors lying in the wilderness*
>   *Spike Milligan*

9 *Orme Court*
London W2

30 December 1970

Messrs John & Roy Boulting
British Lion Films
Broadwick House
Broadwick Street
London W1

Dear Boultings,

*Thank you for your circular. So, it's coming to this. You think
you can buy off the Prince of Eire, dripping with Gaelic talent,
by a grotty lunch on some sausage stall, somewhere in vile Soho.*
    *Very well, owing to certain financial difficulties with Messrs
Coutts & Co. (branches in the Strand) I am forced to accept your
meagre fare (a plate of meagre for Mr Milligan, please).*
    *My, my, didn't we get edgy at the mention of the family's connection
with early English water easences. Let's face it lads, when the Englishman John Carze invented one it was through sheer necessity. There was
shit everywhere, so don't be too cock-a-hoop; face it lads, the Boulting
dynasty was launched on the sea of commerce by shit, and in this
respect my family have been helping the business ever since, without
ever once asking for a seat on the board. It was not for nothing that I
cried out to the amassed aborting Milligans 'Gentlemen, be seated.'*
    I trust this letter will receive a reply in the Times, *where we can
further discourse the humble beginnings of the Boulting family.*

All right, if you insist, I accept your good wishes from you and your brother for the coming year. After consulting my solicitor he has given me an all clear to wish you and your brother a Happy New Year from me.

I would like to point out that this does not constitute a contract.

Yes, my exotic secretary will ring your beautiful secretary and fix things up.

I must warn you that my exotic secretary has lesbian tendencies and wears an appliance.

Love, light and peace
Spike

Don't forget, watch me in Follies of the Wise *on BBC1 at 6.45 p.m. on 31 December.*

[Spike was on a tour of Australia and New Zealand with his 'One Man Show'. He had been grumpy for months (a delaying tactic to avoid getting down and writing Volume 5 of his War Memoirs). This letter was to lay the blame on everyone else. When he finally finished the book, it became *Where Have All the Bullets Gone?*]

9 Orme Court
London W2

28 February 1983

Ms Norma Farnes
Ms Shelagh Sinclair
Jack Hobbs Esq.
Pat O'Neill Esq.

Dear All,

This is a forewarning as to what I would like to do in June, 1983, on my return from Australia.

I would like to be given total freedom to write Vol. 5 of my War Memoirs, so far I have delayed it for my One Man Show, and my television series.

I have been given an advance of £20,000 in various stages, therefore, unless somebody can come up with a higher offer, this is what I want to do.

I am giving due warning, so that I am not approached at the last minute because I would find it very hard to put aside all the work I had done on it.

Otherwise I am well, and the proud possessor of six damaged pairs of underpants, ranging between the ages of six and seven, a pair of socks I do believe have marks of the Blitz, and a pair of shoes which are so thin in the soles, they could be warn as frog masks for deep sea diving.

Sincerely,
Spike

[David Clark was the Producer/Director of *Give Us a Clue*, a game show for Thames Television. Spike was very fond of him, hence the warmth in his letters.]

9 Orme Court
London W2

12 April 1984

David Clark Esq.
Thames Television Limited
Brook Road
Teddington
Middlesex

Dear David,

Listen, I have never got over that terrible clue you gave me in which I had to mime Zorba the Greek. I mean how do you mime

Zorba, and how do you mime Greek, I had never seen the film.
   It's time you did it again to me, I await your reply. Please find enclosed £1.00 as a bribe, current value 27.8p.

  Love, light and peace
    Spike Milligan, and his Manager, Norma Farnes,
    who desperately needs the commission

                           ⌒

                                  Teddington Studios
                                  Teddington Lock,
                                  Teddington
                                Middlesex TW11 9NT

                                  19 April 1984

Spike Milligan Esq.
9 Orme Court
London W2

Dear Spike,

Thanks for your letter. You have obviously forgotten that you redeemed yourself admirably with 'I was a Teenage Werewolf' and 'Inka Dinka Doo' a couple of series ago.
  I was thinking of asking you if you would like to come on again during the next series, but your 'green Queen' tells me that I definitely should. We are recording on 9 and 17 June, 1, 8, 15 and 29 July – so take your pick. Incidentally, Michael Parkinson is taking over as Chairman and I hope this doesn't make you change your mind.
  It's good to hear from you, and your bribe will find its way to the nearest children's charity box.

  Look forward to seeing you,
  Best wishes
   David Clark

PS. We're repeating your 'redemption' next Tuesday – purely coincidental, I assure you!

9 *Orme Court*
London W2

24 April 1984

David Clark Esq.
Thames Television Limited
Teddington Studios
Teddington Lock
Teddington
Middlesex TW11 9NT

Dear David,

Obviously money talks, who knows with a £1 here and a £1 there I could be in Dynasty next year, screwing Joan Collins, wearing a wig.

Listen regarding the £1 'to the nearest children's charity', the nearest children's charity is possibly yours, give it to them; the next nearest children's charity is mine, so send it back.

Out of the plethora of dates, I have chosen the 9th June. I had been invited to have tea on that day by Barbara Cartland, and this is the greatest out I've ever had.

Love, light and peace
Spike Milligan

⌒

[Virginia McKenna and her husband Bill Travers were instrumental in founding the Born Free Foundation. Spike admired and respected her for her undying devotion to animal rights campaigns.]

The Oast House
Hazelhurst Farm
Ticehurst
East Sussex TN5 7LF

18 April 1988

Ms Virginia McKenna
Zoocheck
24 Tempo House
17–27 Falcon Road
London SW11 2BJ

Dear Ginny,

I have unwittingly made a boob. My Manager telephoned me and said 'I've got a very easy commercial for you to do, all you have to say is "Come alive, come to Whipsnade Wild Animal Park" – without thinking I did it, and I am sending you part of my fee so that some good comes out of it. I won't do it again.

Love, light and peace
Spike Milligan

~

['Esther' here is better known as Esther Rantzen, whom Spike admired for what she achieved in her campaign to set up Childline.]

9 Orme Court
London W2

9 June 1989

Mr & Mrs Desmond Wilcox
Blood Oaks Farm
Bramshaw
Hampshire

My dear Esther & Desmond

Thank you for your wonderfully worded invitation. I see you have tea by the pool, normally I have it by the cup, and that you are serving lunch on the grass, haven't you any plates?

Alas on that day I will be sunning my skinny white body on some distant Mediterranean beach. I got it on the NHS, my doctor said 'I must warn you you are too white to live, either you get into a microwave for 30 seconds or use the Mediterranean NHS.'

Love, light and peace
Spike Milligan

~

[Susan Watt was the managing director of Michael Joseph. Spike had tremendous respect for her, but not for her female editors, who he thought had no sense of humour. They didn't think the seven volumes of his War Memoirs were funny. It was down to the marketing director, Dick Douglas Boyd, to tell them how funny they were and to 'publish'.

In an interview I did with Dick he said 'a phone call would come

down from the women editors saying they had got a new manu-
script from Spike and would I look at it because they didn't think
it was funny.'

That's why Spike called them the Vestal Virgins.]

Susan Watt
Michael Joseph Publishing
27 Wrights Lane
London
W8 5TZ

28 June 1993

Dear Susan,

I have just completed a comic version of Lady Chatterley's Lover
and rather than give it to one of your virgins to read I realized this
book needed somebody with balls to read it and therefore I have
given it to a friend of mine Jack Clarke to read and he has said it
is, and I quote, 'hysterically funny'. I am not given to accepting
lavish praise but I wanted you to know that it is a genuinely funny
book. Please tell the wise virgins this.

  Warm regards
    Spike Milligan

PS. I am just off on the road to Damascus to see Jesus.

[The documentary that Jonathan James-Moore refers to here was
about the *Goon Shows* and how they had survived for forty years. It
culminated in the airing of two *Goon Shows*. Spike fought the BBC
for years to have the *Goon Shows* repeated. He failed; so this was a
bonus for him. 'They repeat a *Goon Show* once a year on Boxing
Day. They take me off the shelf and dust me down for Christmas.'

Thank God for Mary Kalemkarian, and Radio 7. They play the

Goon Show tapes every week. Alas, Spike never heard them. Mary launched the channel in December 2002.

Spike was asked to write 150 words for the cover of his cassette. He did just that: exactly 150 words, none of them related.]

British Broadcasting Corporation
Broadcasting House
London W1A 1AA

4 June 1991

S. Milligan Esq.
9 Orme Court
Bayswater
London W2

Dear Spike,

I hope you enjoyed the documentary. At the weekly meeting of BBC initials it was deemed to have been a thoroughly good thing.

By careful timing I found myself on a week's holiday in Italy. I didn't feel too guilty because I had enjoyed reading of your escapades there. However, I have now listened to the tape which I thought was terrific: a good pacey mix of fun, insight and information.

I expect Norma has told you that the documentary is to be repeated along with two of the selected shows on Radio 4: Thursday 12.25, August 29th and September 5th with the 'Go On' programme on Saturday 31st August 10.02am.

There is no doubt that the glorious fun of the shows will last as long as the tapes survive and the ears that hear them.

Thank you for giving time for the interview and I hope this little festival has given you pleasure.

Best wishes
Jonathan James-Moore
Head of Light Entertainment Radio

PS. I enjoyed many of your 150 words on the cassette!

9 Orme Court
Bayswater
London W2 4RL

11 June 1991

Jonathan James-Moore Esq.
BBC
Broadcasting House
London W1A 1AA

Dear Jonathan,

It is we the beggars on the outside of the Corporation who are still remembering the Goon Shows *and are very grateful to get letters praising some of the things we did half a century ago, it just goes to show that the waiting game pays off. I am currently trying to sell 150* Goon Show *tapes to Ethiopia whom I am encouraging to eat them, at least they can die laughing.*

   I look forward to another fifty years anniversary with great anticipation. I am having my body deep frozen in case I die before that occasion. I am going to have an audio cassette tombstone in which visitors can buy a Goon Show *and insert them and play them over my dead body.*

   Yours ever most humble
     Spike Milligan
     Ex BBC Employee

PS. I mean there are people still laying flowers on the tombstone of Charlie Kunz.

4

Taking One's Place in Society

Chopsticks are one of the reasons the Chinese never invented custard.

– 'Spike on Spike', *Memories of Milligan*

After the success of that innovative show, *The Goons*, Spike found his place in society. It was at this point that he started to write books, beginning one of the most successful writing careers of any twentieth-century comedian, or any writer for that matter . . .

His first published work came in 1959. It was a poetry book, *Silly Verse for Kids*. After that he started on a novel.

Puckoon was published in 1963. He had started writing it in 1958. (This was all before I came to work with him at Orme Court.) It was a traumatic time for him. In 1959, while he was writing *Puckoon*, his wife left him. She waited until Spike was in Australia and sent him a telegram to say it was over and that she'd taken the children with her. He attempted suicide by taking an overdose of sleeping tablets. And yet, in 'the worst time of my life', he continued to write what I consider to be his funniest book. When it was published in 1963, he said, 'It nearly drove me mad, and I vowed I'd never write another novel.'

But now that he was up and running, the books came pouring out of him: plenty of poetry as well as the seven famous volumes of his War Memoirs. The first in 1971, *Adolf Hitler: My Part in His Downfall* – the prologue read, 'After *Puckoon* I swore I would never write another novel. This is it' – and the last of them, twenty years later, called *Peace Work*.

Throughout this time he wrote and appeared in his television series Q5, a sketch-comedy show that ran and ran, until the last series, Q10, *There's a Lot of It About*.

The writings, the television and radio appearances were his 'work', but the love of his life was the theatre. He toured England, South Africa, New Zealand and Australia over a period of twenty years with his 'One Man Show', a (for him) gruelling two hours, apart from a fifteen-minute interval, of reading poetry, doing impressions, audience reaction and playing his beloved trumpet.

Enough? No, there was also his involvement in numerous char-
ities, saving the planet and the now endless political demonstrations
– not to mention his correspondence with the great and the good
(and the not so good), which I've included in this chapter. The
boundless energy. How did he do it? And how did I keep up?

~

from Scunthorpe Revisited, Added Articles
and Instant Relatives

My Home

It was 1951. I was young and green in my years and I sang in my chains like the sea. The flat my wife and I occupied suddenly started to shrink; this was caused by the unexpected appearance of two children, a dog and a stray cat – the last two I don't know about, the children were apparently mine.

'We must get a bigger place,' said wife.

'Infanticide is cheaper,' I said.

A house. We started what all Britons will know as the most agonizing time of one's life. For the next year we scanned the columns for a home. We visited house agents – their names became more familiar than Hollywood stars, names like Benham & Reeves, Knight, Frank & Rutley, and Chestertons.

Those who answered the phones in these establishments became gods – they all sounded like Battle of Britain pilots in between scrambles. 'You'll go to what? – £3,900 (He made it sound like you were a Mega-Scrooge) and that is your final offer.'

'Yes.'

Then, in tones in which doctors tell of a terminal illness, he'd say 'Oh dear.' He would conclude with that old favourite: 'I must warn you' (like a boxer with a low blow) 'that there are several offers already in the pipeline.'

'Are they higher?' you drivel. No, he's not at liberty to say, breach of etiquette. You wait a day, two – three – four – five – after a week you can't stand it.

'Hello, remember me.'

'Who? Oh, you want Mr Gibbs-White. He's on holiday, can I help you?'

You go carefully through the whole sombre story.

'Ah, yes – 29 Clens Avenue – I'm afraid it's gone.'

'Gone!? You – he – never told us.'

There follows a standard apology. New Secretary – phone out of order – World War 3 pending. So passes six months. We are now well and truly on the books – circulars cascade through our letter-box arriving on a Saturday morning. We race around north London to see 'Delightful Edwardian Home: 3 bed. 2 sit. Kit. Bt. Gr. Gdn. In need of decoration'.

The outside is peeling, and not just the paint – the bricks – the front garden was once, I suppose, a garden – weeds – vestiges of a pebble path – caravan – a jacked-up Ford Zephyr – and dog shit – several ageing 'For Sale' signs almost invisible with weathering (two of the Companies have gone into liquidation).

'It might be better inside,' says wife.

'I'll top that,' I said. 'It's *got* to be better inside.'

Monday 9.00 a.m. 'Hello, 127 Holden Road – could we make an appointment?'

The agent with all the enthusiasm of a rabbi at a Nuremberg Rally says: 'I think that can be arranged.' I want to say, would you feel better if I knelt down?

We saw the home. It was terrible – but it was better than this continued enslavement to house agents and – *ah!* SURVEYORS – 'It's not worth buying – it's got dry rot – damp rot – damp course gone – needs re-wiring – re-roofing.'

'You forgot leprosy,' I said.

The grovelling, cringing, paying and signing of documents went on for months. In mid-contract the owner died of a stroke – a stroke of luck for his wife. He left her £50,000. She now wanted the price of the house raised. I was now on tranquillizers, and would sign anything – money didn't matter – one had to escape from the enslavement of the system. I put the deposit down in 1951. I was in the house for twenty years; nineteen of those it was still the building society's. I called the home 'The Millstone'. In February 1971 I paid the last instalment – now, it was *mine*.

Despite the surveyor's report condemning the house – he didn't know (or find out) the house was built on a spring. One day the floor in the cellar burst and filled to four feet. The children loved it. To cap the spring would cost £2,000 – or as the builder said, 'We can contain it by digging a well, but you'll have to bail out with a bucket when it floods.' I re-christened the house 'The Titanic'. I sued the surveyor, but he was too clever for me – he died.

The roof. In 1957 there was an incredible gale. The whole roof tiling fell apart. The insurance policy, yes, there it was, full cover for storm damage. The assessor arrives. 'Ah yes, you need a new roof,' he said. 'Have you had a builder in?'

'Yes, and rain.'

'Ah – £1,500 for re-roofing, I'll go over this at the office and let you know.'

A week passed – two – three – rain poured in – we slept in a tent in the bedroom. I couldn't wait; I told the builder, Ernie Stevens, to go ahead. He started by putting waterproof sheeting in the attic. The dripping stopped. It was quite something to hear an approaching scream from above – and for a workman to hurtle through the bedroom ceiling and crash to the floor by the bed. It was Ernie's mate Ted. He was unconscious. We had the ambulance. It rained that night, especially through the new hole.

'I need a couple of hundred up front for more scaffolding.'

I never saw Ernie again. I got another builder, Mr Dick Soames, but his price would be £300 more. I phoned the Samaritans six times that week. Dick Soames mended the roof. He took six months, during which the insurance company joker said they would meet a *fifth* of the cost. A fifth? But it says storm damage. Ah yes, but that's only for buildings built after (in small print) 1932, provided the roof gables were double-latticed, dove-tailed, one made by a Chinaman during the Equinox of the moon only visible in the Easter Islands.

I'll sue! I brief my solicitor.

'Don't do it, Mr Millington, you'll lose the case, it would cost a lot in legal fees – like this advice, £35.00. Yours etc. Jim Solicitor.'

I was now forty. I *owned* my own home, on eight Tryptazol a day, three Secanol at night. As I write, my wife is bailing out the cellar. Tomorrow I'm registering the house as a ship.

~

Carpenters Meadows
Dumbwoman's Lane
Udimore
Rye
East Sussex TN31 6AD

11 October 1988

HRH The Prince of Wales KGKT
Buckingham Palace
London

Dear Prince Charles,

I have just received an invitation to your Birthday Ball. Of course I will come but can I have the first waltz with you? It's 1–2–3 1–2–3. If you do 1–2–3–4 it means you get there first.
I will see you at the snacks counter.

Love, light and peace
Spike Milligan

9 *Orme Court*
London W2

11 April 1984

D. Vaux Esq.
Lloyds Bank Limited
85 High Street
Barnet
Herts

Dear Mr Vaux,

My wife went to cash a cheque for £3,000 at your bank, and they said they did not have enough money, and to come back the next day. Can you tell me how much money you carry so that, in future, I will know whether a cheque should be no more than £5.00 or £10.00 or whatever.

I can't believe a giant bank like Lloyds could not cash a cheque for £3,000.

I mean, the adverts they put out on television and newspapers must cost more, so really the adverts are a total contradiction of the actual material merchandised. When it comes to the crunch – don't bank at Lloyds if you want to cash a cheque for £3,000.

Tell you what, supposing I deposit £3,000 in your bank, do you think if I came back in a year you could cash that cheque for me.

That giant horse I keep seeing prancing up and down – does one have to own one of these before one can get a cheque cashed.

With Barnet Lloyds in such a terrible plight, I shudder to think what it's like at Lloyds in Potters Bar; as for St Albans, no wonder the Romans left, obviously Lloyds could not cash their cheques.

Sincerely
  Spike Milligan

from Indefinite Articles and Scunthorpe

One Man's Week

Monday. Arise at 7.30. Open the window and scream. Put telephone back on hook. London Broadcasting, where news comes first (also second, third, fourth and fifth), is telling us the latest. 'Belfast 3 bomb explosions, London 2. Belfast still lead by 311 . . .' the news is all bad, but does the announcer have to sound as if he is personally involved in it? Even the most trivial news is read in a hard-driving the-world-is-ending-tomorrow-voice, i.e. 'Today the Queen Mother opened a Flower Show at Bournemouth', but when he says it, you feel as though the Queen Mother has broken into a Bournemouth flower shop wearing a stocking mask and shot the proprietor.

Why, why, why do they all create an atmosphere of tension? Likewise sports reports: 'Manchester United smashed to defeat today etc. etc. Leeds pulverize Villa in savage five-goal attack. Tottenham destroyed in three devastating minutes.' We complain about soccer hooliganism, yet all the matches are described in violent terms . . . The news continues. Moslems and Christians are slaughtering each other in . . . Basques and Spaniards . . . In Ulster Protestants and Catholics . . . Portugal Left against Right on the verge of Civil War . . . I suppose what it all boils down to is man's never really quite happy unless he's killing himself. And it's still only Monday.

Another day. I've got to go to the Prince of Wales (Theatre), a post-show presentation to Harry Secombe. I go backstage in the interval – we have a laugh. After the show it was intended that Peter Sellers, Michael Bentine and I were to give Secombe the Variety Club award for his one-hundreth year in show business. Alas, Bentine is confined to bed with a severe overdraft, and Sellers is in America studying the plans of his next wife, so I have to clod on the stage at the end and say: 'Harry Seacrune, apparently you haven't been found out yet, so on behalf of someone or other here is something or other Value £2.50 VAT 37p.' He then looked at me and said: 'Who is this man? The play isn't over yet. Throw him in the general direction of out.' It was a thick first-night audience. One had the feeling that once they had established they could afford the £25 seat, they left. Back in his dressing room, Secombe consumes so much brandy that he convinces me he has weaned himself off food.

Monday continues. The story of man's follies continues. An Air India flight arrives at Heathrow. From it step 100 well fed, well tanked up, tired but healthy people – 'Air India looks after you.' In the hold of the plane are 171 little dead birds; in two following flights the number of dead birds total 2,000. I phone Mr Whitaker, the Manager, RSPCA Heathrow. Like me, he is morally decimated at the needless killing of these small creatures. I ask him who's responsible; they won't tell him. He does, however, find the name of one home importer, and I print their name large: LADY DELL of Worthing. I write to Fred Peart, Minister of Agriculture, and ask him does he intend putting an end to this outrageous trade. If so, what? I have my hackles up and I decide to do something positive. To my way of thinking, a law that imposed massive fines on airlines would stop the trade dead in its tracks. With that in mind I write to people asking them to become patrons of my cause. I write to Prince Charles and say if he becomes *the* Patron, I will let him off the hook for fox-hunting. Lady Dowding promises support, so does Michael Foot . . . Good heavens, it's still Monday!

Monday. I watch a bureaucratic charade on TV. The Hounslow Council have spoken. Women's Aid under Erin Pizzey are the only organization who give immediate safe refuge to battered wives and children. Needless to say, they are overcrowded. 'Unless you evict half the women and children, we will withhold our financial aid.' The reason is there is a health and fire hazard. The latest inmate, Mrs Gwen X (I can't print her name for fear of reprisals by her husband) arrived with six broken ribs, a swollen face, and scalds between her thighs – and all done by her husband in full view of their six-year-old little girl. Alderman A. King says: 'If they go to their local social worker they will help.' Well, we then see Mrs Gwen X who had gone to her social worker who told her: 'Go back to your husband.'

I cannot see the reasoning of the Hounslow Council. I decided to help. We will put on a poetry and jazz concert on Sunday 2 November at 8.30 p.m. at Ronnie Scott's, who has given the hall free for Women's Aid. Sir Bernard Miles says: 'Of course I'll do something, Spike.' Likewise Christopher Logue, Bill Kerr, the Stan Tracey Quartet. There's no shortage of volunteers . . . This wife-battering is a terrible thing. I wish I could do more.

Still Monday, Bloody Monday. I am thinking about the Blackpool Conference. Old hat by the time you read this, but the aftermath still lingers on. What I thought was a monumental piece of walking backwards was the rejection of the chance of electoral reform. OK, it's democracy, but the *reason* for rejecting it, to quote the prime mover against, Mr Angus Maude, was: 'Why should we make it possible to let in another 100 Liberals, when the most they can ever muster is twenty?' My God, the nerve!!! He's not interested in the electorate, only the fear of letting in Liberals!!! He concluded with: 'Why should we have electoral reform when we have no idea of the consequences?' Thank God Jenner didn't think like that, or the entire Conservative Party would be pox-marked.

My God, it's still Monday. I'm rehearsing my new TV series, *Q6* (why *Q6*? Why not?). We have an hour to go to recording time and we have a disaster. One of the sketches is about a Day in the Life of an Ordinary Pakistani Dalek (eh?), in which we use the original Daleks, but NO! The agent for the copyright refuses to let us 'make fun of the Daleks'. What to do? I phone the inventor, Terry Nation. He's heard about the trouble and says: 'Listen Spike, I've been waiting to repay a favour. Remember when I first came to London twenty-three years ago, broke, you lent me twenty quid to tide me over?'

'Did you pay it back?'

'No.'

'Well, the interest on that will keep me for life.'

'Listen. I'll let you use the Daleks and we'll call it square.'

'OK.'

It is the last show of the series, so I take the entire cast and technical crew to the Kalamaris restaurant. I awake next morning face downwards on the office floor fully clothed. What went wrong? Curse, it's Monday again.

Monday. Midday concert for the women of Holloway Prison. I can't understand – you can only give them one and a half hours' entertainment. If I had gone over time, would they have let me out?

The fourth Monday in a row, it's got to stop.

My continuing battle with food additives is reagitated by a sticker on a packet of jam tarts: 'These tarts *must* be eaten before 7 November.' Why? What exactly happens to them on the 8th? I mean, if you put them in the fridge and forget to eat them before the 9th, when you open the fridge does a green hairy arm covered in jam reach out and pull you in? I can't believe that man has got to the state where he is swallowing millions of tons of chemical additives a year, and has never ever been asked if he agreed to them being put in his food. Who's in charge?

The last Monday. The end of the week, and one thing looms large in my mind. Someone is spending a lot of money on publicity for Mrs Thatcher . . . Who?

Yet another Monday, 19 October. To dinner at Michael Foot's home. When I entered the room Tom Driberg stood up. Has my time come at last? On my left hand was Paul Foot. Had a wonderful dinner, which terminated with the table opening in two, and those at each end having to keep their knees at fourteen inches above normal to keep the table stable for the cheese and biscuits. Yes, Michael is a great man, so am I, so is Tom Driberg, so is Paul Foot, and so is Mrs Jill Foot. It took eighteen bottles to reach that stage. Take a little wine for thy stomach's sake – well, I also took it for my legs, arms, teeth, ankles and the abdominal ridge.

I must fly now, I feel an attack of British Railways coming on.

Carpenters Meadows
Dumbwoman's Lane
Udimore
Rye
East Sussex TN31 6AD

7 December 1988

The Listener
BBC Television
199 Old Marylebone Road
London NW1

Dear Sir,

Milligan's Ongoing Revelations of the BBC

I put up a record programme idea to a producer who thought it 'too good an idea to waste', and he put it up to some unknown, nameless committee who took eight months to say no, whereupon I phoned Capital Radio and in one phone call they said yes.

The BBC used to be called Auntie – I think it's time to call it Grandma.

Sincerely
Spike Milligan

~

BBC Television Centre
London W12 7RJ

25 October 1988

Mr Spike Milligan
c/o Norma Farnes
9 Orme Court
London W2

Dear Spike,

Re: 'The Royal Variety Performance 1988'
Monday 21 November 1988
The London Palladium

It is with much regret, that I have to inform you that our proposed comedy quick fire gag sequence, in the opening spot of this year's 'Royal Variety Performance', has now had to be withdrawn from the show.

   As I explained, the item was based upon the participation of the top British Comedy Stars. To be successful, this sequence had to be a star-studded 'tour-de-force', but, unfortunately, as so many artists were unavailable we have been unable to achieve the required number of Stars.

   I do apologise for this cancellation, but I'm sure you will understand that it is because of circumstances beyond _my_ control. I do hope that this has not inconvenienced you; but, once again, thank you, in advance, for your kind understanding.

   Yours sincerely
      Michael

Michael Hurll
Executive Producer and Director

c.c. Norma Farnes

9 Orme Court
London W2

28 October 1988

Michael Hurll Esq.
The Royal Variety Performance
British Broadcasting Corporation
Television Centre
London W12 7RJ

Dear Michael,

Your grovelling circular to hand – 'the best laid schemes o' mice an' men gang aft agley', but in your case it's a fuck up.

Warm regards
  Spike Milligan

PS. I am going to tell the Queen Mother.

from Indefinite Articles and Scunthorpe

Read All About It!

Let me take you back to India circa 1924. (Try dialling it, you get put through right away.) It was a period when a khaki copy of *The Times* flew alongside the Union Jack at Government House. I was seven at the time. Every morning at Reveille a Coggage Wallah* delivered the

* Paper boy.

Poona Times, which I dutifully took to my bedridden, dying grand-father. In those early years I thought a newspaper was something you gave to dying grandfathers. Having just read the entire range of morning papers, I am still of the opinion it is something you give to dying grandfathers. Hindu editors never quite got the hang of our language, for example the headline: 'GANDHI SENT TO YERO-DAH GAOL. SERVES HIM JOLLY WELL RIGHT.' And again the same week: 'GANDHI THREATENS HUNGER STRIKE: KING GEORGE VERY ANGRY GOD BLESS HIM.'

I still retain cuttings of my father's theatrical exploits in India. The *Bangalore Cantonment Gazette*: 'Bombadier and Mrs Leo Milli-gan, the married couple, were the hitting of the night' and, further on, 'Mr Bertram Kettleband did very fine readings from Charles Dickens' *Great Expectorations*.' Once a month we would receive the Overseas *Daily Mirror*, in its gamboge cover.

My early knowledge of England then was through the headlines. I thought an ordinary day in England was 'Heavy Snow in Cots-wolds. Villagers cut off. Sheep Starving. Jimmy Wilde Champion of the World. King George Gravely Ill. Desperate Unemployment in Wales. Gracie Fields Mobbed. Fol de Rols break all records in Eastbourne. Beheaded Nude Body of Woman found on Brighton Beach.' The only normal thing in the paper was Pip, Squeak and Wilfred. It was a shock when I arrived in England to find that people in the street were not penguins, dogs or rabbits. This made me sad, as I was a member of the Gugnunk Club. I was thirteen at the time. Sitting on the train from Tilbury to London I saw the headline: 'DOCKS. RAMSAY MACDONALD STEPS IN.'

My own father went to work for the Associated Press of Amer-ica off Fleet Street, and was soon on the bottle and murmuring: 'There's a nasty rumour going around Fleet Street and his name is Lord Northcliffe!' During his delirium he made up headlines. 'Titanic arrives safe at Southampton. "I overslept," says Captain,' or 'Archduke Ferdinand still alive! World War 1 a Mistake! Sorry says Kaiser.' He told me that every night news editors knelt naked in front of a statue of Beaverbrook, crossed themselves with print-ers' ink and said, 'Please God may something terrible happen in the world tonight preferably to (a) the King, (b) the Pope, or (c) Jack Buchanan, and please in time for the next edition, eh?'

I was fourteen at the time. It's on record that the old editor of the now dead *News Chronicle* was without a morning headline and lay face down on the floor chewing the carpet. The phone rang. 'Hello Dad? Brace yourself. Mother's just been killed by a coloured Chinese Jew who plays the trombone in Harry Roy's band.' 'Thank God,' said the editor, 'I'll have a photographer round in a flash.'

In those days newspapers did straightforward reporting, i.e. a football match was reported on the merits of the game. Not so today. The reporter concentrates on the player-manager-dressing-room-boardroom conflicts. You don't report goals, you report punch-ups. A Rangers–Celtic match is now reported: 'Rangers: 3 dead, 20 injured. Celtic: 7 injured, 1 dead.' The unruly player gets the news. Let's take George Best. He arrives ten minutes late for practice; 'GEORGE BEST MISSING! "I don't know where he is," says sexy 23-year-old Pop Star Sandra O'Toole, son of Peter O'Toole, who is also missing from his grave in Highgate Old Cemetery where is making *Carry on Up Your Dracula*.' When Best arrives ten minutes later: 'BEST GIVES HIMSELF UP!' says the midday edition. 'Under questioning from hard-hitting team manager Jim "Socks" Scrackle, "Best broke down and confessed that he was 10 minutes late."' 'BEST CONFESSES! "Ten Minutes That Nearly Ruined My Life." Read all about it in the *News of the World*. The newspaper with its heart in your knickers.'

There is a surfeit of news in England, unlike my parents' bush town in Australia, Woy Woy. Nothing happens in Woy Woy. Some headlines are desperate: 'TODAY IS THE 3RD OF APRIL. OFFI-CIAL.' Cub reporters try and turn minutiae into leaders. 'Woy Woy. April 10. This morning during Woy Woy's rush hour, a Mrs Glenda Scrock, 64-year-old housewife, was standing at the corner of Kitch-ener Avenue and Bindi Bindi Crescent when she saw a broken pencil lying on the pavement. She picked it up. It was a 2B. She threw the pencil in the gutter. The police have ruled out foul play.' The fact that Harry Secombe arrived at Woy Woy station with a banner saying 'I AM HARRY SECOMBE' and went unrecognized is by the way.

Let's look at the character of each British newspaper each covering the same story. Let us imagine that Princess Anne, like Sir Stafford Cripps' daughter, married a coloured man, say an African goat herder.

Morning Star

MARRIAGE OF CONVENIENCE.
CUNNING MOVE BY
HEATH
GOVERNMENT TO PLACATE
BLACK RHODESIANS

Daily Telegraph

COLOURFUL ROYAL
WEDDING

It was announced from the Palace today that Her Royal Highness is to marry Mr N'galu N'Goolie, a foreign gentleman with farming connections in Africa, his dark skin no doubt the result of long hours in the tropical sun supervising his herds.

Financial Times

SOUND FINANCIAL
MOVE BY
ROYAL FAMILY

The forthcoming marriage of Princess Anne to a PAYE native Rhodesian commoner will entitle her to £100,000 from the privy purse as a married woman. Her husband's goat herd will be put in her name. The Goats will go public next year as Royal Goat Herd (Holdings) Limited.

[John Stonehouse was the MP who famously faked his own death in 1974. He'd got into financial difficulties and apparently disappeared into the sea at Brighton, leaving behind a pile of clothes on the beach. He turned up in Australia (he hadn't swum there!). He was eventually found, deported to the UK and convicted of fraud, reducing Harold Wilson's Labour government to a minority.]

9 Orme Court
London W2

28 April 1988

Ms Linda Lee Potter
Daily Mail
Northcliffe House
London EC4

Dear Linda,

How nice of you to be so kind about John Stonehouse in your column. The acrid part of it, of course, was the complete non-appearance of any of his old political colleagues.

It doesn't speak much for compassion from the Mother of Parliaments.

Love, light and peace
Spike Milligan

⌒

10 Downing Street
London SW1A 2AA

12 September 1990

Spike Milligan Esq.

Dear Mr Milligan,

Thank you for your further letter of 8 August about the future of College Farm which is occupied by Mr Chris Ower.

I have made enquiries at the Department of Transport. I do realize the difficulties which the delay has posed for Mr Ower; and as I have previously mentioned the rent which he is paying does appear to reflect the uncertainty of his position. Nonetheless I can understand his frustration that it is taking so long to reach a decision upon the road scheme.

I very much hope that it will not be too long before a decision on the scheme, which initially gave rise to the purchase of the farm, can be made. As soon as a decision on the scheme is announced, immediate consideration will be given to the future of the farm.

I am copying this letter to Cecil Parkinson: I know that he will make every effort to expedite matters as soon as possible.

Kind regards,
Yours sincerely
    Margaret Thatcher

9 Orme Court
Bayswater
London W2 4RL

26 September 1990

The Prime Minister
10 Downing Street
London SW1A 2AA

My dear Mrs Thatcher,

It's very heartening to get such an extended letter from such a busy woman as yourself, re College Farm.

I hope you do not mind I have sent a copy of your letter to Chris Ower as it might sound encouraging to him.

You are a good lass.

My warm regards
Spike Milligan

9 Orme Court
Bayswater
London W2 4RL

2 June 1993

Rt Hon Norman Lamont MP
House of Commons
London
SW1A 0AA

Dear Norman Lamont,

Despite all the condemnation I would like to say that as Chancellor of the Exchequer you did the very best you could. Alas you were not just facing a recession in England, you were facing one which was world wide. I really think you did your best but I thought you were a bit naive when you kept announcing the economy was recovering, it wasn't recovering and it still isn't and it will go on for sometime.

Anyhow just to let you know that I thought you were a good Chancellor.

Sincerely
Spike Milligan

Carpenters Meadows
Dumbwoman's Lane
Udimore
Rye
East Sussex TN31 6AD

20 March 1997

John Gummer MP
Secretary of State for Environment
Room 6/0
Eland House
Bressenden Place
London SW1E 5DU

Dear Mr Gummer,

I live in Dumbwoman's Lane Udimore and in the Spring it is a riot of wild flowers. The Rye council cutting machine comes down the lane and literally exterminates all the wild flowers. I think the statute book states that there is a fine of £1,000 for destroying wild flowers.

I have twice telephoned the town clerk and asked if they could delay the cutting machine for just three weeks which will enable these flowers to proliferate. Over to you chum.

Sincerely
Spike Milligan. Ace Naturalist.

South Asia Educational Fellowship
2 Eaton Gate
London SW1W 9BL

14 July 1983

Spike Milligan Esq.
Spike Milligan Productions Ltd
9 Orme Court
London W2

Dear Mr Milligan,

Recently I had a private lunch at the Institute of Directors for the South Asia Educational Fellowship to launch a national appeal of £500,000 to further the need for English medium teaching in the Indian subcontinent – the philosophy of SAEF being leadership through education.

In writing to you I would hope that you would consider being a Patron for this Appeal. I have accepted the role as Chairman of the Appeal Committee which consists of many leading figures in the business community and others.

The monies from the Appeal will be used to further increase the facilities for education in poor rural areas, aimed at young people to obtain appropriate qualifications that will enable them to enter medicine, teaching and the business, academic and civil service worlds as well as agriculture.

Recognizing that India is short of some two million teachers with a 64% illiteracy index and a population growth of one million a month, the urgency is self evident.

As you will see in the attached Boardroom Brief, Dr Alka Peter from Nagpur, north India, received a grant from SAEF that has enabled her to finish her medical training and return to India with the appropriate qualifications.

My dear Robert,

Your letter to hand, which I will set about 'decoding' later, but in the same post came a letter from Emilia, eight explosive pages which one could almost 'hear' the writing., she managed to get nailed on a narcotics charge, (all a mistake of course) spent time in some lousy jail in Mexico, but all ended well. Very busy. Will write again. Fed up with England

As Ever

Spike

CROSS WORD FOR IDIOTS
1 Down. The indefinate article
1. Acros. 1st letter of Alphabet

When I asked Spike the date of this letter to Robert Graves he said, 'Somewhere, sometime.' This is the original of the crossword joke, now a greetings card.

Charges to pay

Tariff £

V.A.T. £

Total £

RECEIVED

From

By

No.
OFFICE STAMP

Her dear ...... Birthday with out ...... Telegram birthday card.

Office of origin and Service Instructions. Words

T/4 1430 ST JAMES ST BO 37 =

SPIKE MILLIGAN

BIRTHDAYS COME AND BIRTHDAYS GO
WE'RE GOVERNED BY LIFE'S EBB AND FLO
BUT AS I FACE THE NACKERS YARDS
I THANK YOU FOR YOUR KIND REGARDS =
LOVE NED THE DISAPPEARING TENOR +

CPD MN 930 4124

For free repetition of doubtful words telephone "TELEGRAMS ENQUIRY" or call, with this form at office of delivery. Other enquiries should be accompanied by this form and, if possible, the envelope

(*above*) 8 September 1974. A telegram from Harry Secombe thanking Spike for his birthday card.

(*left*) 1978. Signing copies of *Mussolini*; while promoting Friends of the Earth with his T-shirt and animal rights on his cap.

Telegram content:

```
M
  298111 PO PD G
  299992 PO TS G
N91 1212 LONDON T 65

  MR SPIKE MILLIGAN [ ]
  V2

  DEAR SPIKE I AM DESPERATE TO HAVE SOME REAL FUN AGAIN WITH YOU AND
  HARRY . PLEASE CAN WE GET TOGETHER AND WRITV SOME MORE GOON SHOWS ?
  WE COULD PLACE THEM ANYWHERE I DONT WANT ANY MONEY I WILL WORK JUST
  FOR THE SHEER JOY OF BEING WITH YOU BOTH AGAIN AS WE WERE .
  LOVE
       PETER

  COL 5 72 . ? WRITE SOME MORE .

  299992 PO TS G
  298111 PO PD G
```

1980. Telegram from Peter Sellers. How apt that Spike should have said, 'We were all happy then.' Peter trying to recapture the happiness. He died two months later.

1981. One of the guests at Prince Charles and Lady Diana's wedding – but who?

1984. Now wearing his Great Ormond Street jumper, pictured here with his hero.

Dear Norma

Happy Birthday
from your burden
Spike Milligan

1985. My birthday card, but why 'Spike Milligan'? He got carried away with his calligraphic signature.

Spike Milligan.

The Oast,
Hazelhurst Farm,
Ticehurst,
East Sussex.
TN5 7LF

Tel. (0580) 200514

NORMA

HELP!

JRRY POSTMAN . BANKRUPTCY LETTER

N. Farnes
9 Orme Court
Saudi- Bayswater
London
W2 . . . . . .

from Spike !

Norma Farnes
9 Orme Court
(Saudi) Bayswater
London
W2

1⁰ Class
Norma Farnes
9 Orme Court
Bayswater
London
W.2

N. Farnes,
9, Orme Court,
Bayswater,
London,
W2

½ a Queen is →
better than none

FIRST CLASS MAIL.

SAY
HELLO TO
THE POSTMAN
DEAR.

NORMA FARNES.
9 ORME COURT.
LONDON W.2.

Good morning
Postman.

N. Farnes
9 Orme Court
Bayswater
London
W2

Spike's love affair with the postmen – and they loved it too. 'Another letter from Spike,' they'd say.

(*top*) 1988. In those famous red braces, with his Irish friend Terry Wogan. He drove Terry mad, but he loved him.

(*centre*) 1990. *The Harry Secombe Show*. Spike came back after the shoot and said, 'I know now that that's what I should have been all my life – a busker.'

(*right*) Spike on hard times? This photo was sent from New York and addressed to the *News of the World*, asking if it was really Spike. Spike's response: 'Bring on the clones …'

With John Paul Getty. 'Taking his place in society'?
You could say he'd arrived. They were great friends.

1992. Well, that's a lie.

1995. His sweetheart, the love of his life: Maria Antoinetta Fontana, aka Mrs Toni Pontani,
on *This Is Your Life*.

1990. He had to cancel this performance.
He was too ill to appear. Note: Natalie the
Neighbours star!

1998. His last performance at
the Palladium with his one-man
show.

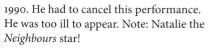

1999. The last photograph of two old mates.

2008. A Spike Milligan bridge and Spike Milligan room in Woy Woy library. Perhaps he did take his place in society after all.

I very much look forward to hearing from you in the hope that you will agree to be a patron.

Yours sincerely
  The Viscount Slim

⌒

9 Orme Court,
London W2

22 July 1983

The Viscount Slim
South Asia Educational Fellowship
2 Eaton Gate
London SW1W 9BL

Dear Viscount Slim,

How can I ever refuse anything from a man like you. Of course, any project to help humanity.

I beg you to bear in mind though, my own particular work which most people are ignoring, that is the desperate need for first a population stabilization, and then a reduction of population to a level whereby which the produce of their own country can match their own fertility.

This is the big problem of our time, we have a limited size Globe, and yet our leaders seem unaware that limitless numbers are trying to live off it, hence starvation, malnutrition, disease, squalor and filth.

Good luck to the project.

Love, light and peace
  Spike Milligan

Carpenters Meadows
Dumbwoman's Lane
Udimore
Rye
East Sussex TN31 6AD

27 February 1989

Mr Christopher Patten
Minister of State
Overseas Development Administration
Eland House
Stag Place
London SW1E 5DH

Dear Christopher,

I write to you pleading with you to cease supplying funds for this monstrous dam in South America. What we are doing, Chris, is destroying reality for something artificial and along with that we Christians are going to dispose two primitive tribes of their homeland where they have lived since the beginning of time. Do look deep into your conscience, not as Minister of State but as an ordinary person and say to yourself, 'What am I doing to these people?' What is happening, Chris, is the system is running the people and the people are not running the system.

Love, light and peace
  Spike Milligan

⌒

from Indefinite Articles and Scunthorpe

Honesty

The Editor of *Punch*, slobbering white, comes tippy toe to me, Spike Milligna the well-known typing error, and whines 'Will you write an article on Honesty?' Of course I will, anything to stop the closure of the magazine. There was the usual hand to hand struggle with pangas to agree the fee. Honesty? Of course I knew all about it, wasn't it growing in my garden under the name of *Lunaria biennis*?

It wasn't until I had finished the third volume that Silly Willy Davis pointed out the mistake. 'You silly twit, you've made a cock-up.' I accepted the apology and a cheque for eighty new pence in lieu of a court case. He went on 'You really are a sillypoo, what we want is the moral connotation. Write one thousand two hundred words.' *One thousand two hundred words?* On Honesty? Nobody was that HONEST. Twenty-seven words was enough for anyone, even Jesus, and he's a bit suspect – it's strange, *he never put anything in writing!*

HONESTY. I went to the British Museum, where they kept the word under lock and key. The word has been on loan to Mr Jack Jones, but the moment he mentioned 'HONEST day's work' he was floored by a docker. The keeper of the word HONESTY took me into its cage. 'It's getting a bit old and worn. We've tried to get a new one but it's very rare, in fact it's in the World Wildlife Fund Red Book as endangered. I think myself it's 'ad it. I sometimes take it for a walk on a lead, but nobody seemed to recognize it, some children patted it but that's all.'

'What is your opinion of the word HONEST?'

'It can't live in twentieth-century environment sir, so she's dyin', we try matin' it wiv the word PAYS, and get a sort of cross-breed called HONESTY-PAYS. We flew it in!'

'In? Where from?'

'Russia, they has this word PAYS on its own in a cage, it was a male, because the Male always PAYS.'

'Did it work?'

'No.'

In the Reading Room I looked it up. There it was. HONEST: Upright, fair, trustworthy in dealings, frank. Open. Honest to goodness, to turn an honest penny, to seize opportunity to make a profit, to make an honest woman of a seduced woman . . . so, an honest man had a military bearing (upright). Blond hair (fair). Plays cards (trustworthy dealings). Christian name Frank (frank). Doorman (open). Welsh (honest to goodness). Robs weak old ladies (seizes opportunity to make a profit). Makes single women pregnant and then marries them (To make an honest woman of a seduced woman).

Next on the list of Silly Willy's questions was:

QUESTION 1: 'Have there been times in your life when you were totally honest, and regretted it?'

ANSWER: 'Yes. I once said to a 6 ft 3 in Canadian soldier "I'll punch your bloody head in."'

QUESTION 2: 'Are there times when you wished you *had* been totally honest?'

ANSWER: 'Yes. My first marriage. I said "I do."'

QUESTION 3: 'What sort of things on the national scene, etc. do you think we should be totally honest about?'

ANSWER: 'All those faceless bastards called "Spokesman Said" should be forced to give their names i.e. "A Spokesman Said called the Hon. Startling-Grope OBE said, etc. etc."'

And who cares about honesty in this day and age? Diogenes walked the streets of Athens in daylight holding aloft a lamp to help him find an honest man. Imagine that in Piccadilly.

POLICEMAN: 'I saw the accused, Diogenes, at midday in Piccadilly carrying a hurricane lamp, which he held up in the face of oncoming men.'

JUDGE: 'Is that true?'

DIOGENES: 'Yes. I was looking for an honest man.'

JUDGE: 'In London?'
DIOGENES: 'Yes.'
JUDGE: 'Remanded for a psychiatric report.'

And take the first American President. There he is as a lad, a fresh felled cherry tree lies at his feet, he is clutching a hot axe, not another person for miles when a man asks:

MAN: 'Son, who chopped down the cherry tree?'
GEORGE: 'I cannot tell a lie, I did.'

I mean, what *else* could he say? And because of that he's called honest? And why is it that those in dodgy professions use the word? The bookie 'Honest' Bill Hampton? A glance down shows him to be wearing running shoes. Why not extend the idea? . . .

BBC TV ANNOUNCER: 'And now a partially political broadcast by Honest Reginald Maudling . . .'

Or 'And now our annual company report by Honest Sir Val Duncan.' Why should the word only apply to homo sapiens? Why not, 'Look out here comes HONEST Tiger,' or 'Help, I am being strangled by HONEST Gorilla'? Let's break the word down into units. Take H, Hitler, Hum-drum, Hack, Horrible, or HO, Ho Ho Ho, mocking laughter, three letters HON, the HON Edward Heath, see? It leads to a twit.

No, we need a new word. I suggest Eileen. 'That man's one of the most EILEEN men in the world', or 'He's never done an EILEEN day's work in his life.'

Well, that should keep Silly Willy quiet for a while. And I say to you all, try and live an EILEEN life. That's the best I can do, Willy. EILEEN it is.

⌒

Carpenters Meadows
Dumbwoman's Lane
Udimore
Rye
East Sussex
TN31 6AD

17 January 1989

The Officer Commanding
Regimental Headquarters
The Coldstream Guards
Wellington Barracks
Birdcage Walk
London SW1

Dear Sir,

I really must unburden my conscience. On the night of 5 Novem-
ber 1943 Lieutenant Walker MC and myself, Lance Bombardier
Milligan, were in an OP trench on the slopes overlooking the
village of Cala Britto. It was an appalling night made slightly
humorous by a report on my OP phone that there was a position
near called Bare Ass Ridge. That said during the evening the
position was heavily stonked by 88mm guns firing air bursts over
our trenches. Somewhere about 3.00 in the morning it was my
duty to crawl out of this trench and go to a collection point where
we were to gather our rations, in this case some hot stew in a
container. In the darkness and the gloom there were many units
collecting various rations and then, and this is where I must have
brought the wrath of the Guards Brigade on me, in the darkness a
voice called out, 'Coldstream Guards rum ration,' and in that split
moment I shouted out, 'Here,' and I was given a glass/carton
container with rum in it. I got safely back to my OP trench where

Lieutenant Walker and I drank it all the while toasting the Brigade of Guards. Apparently during the night we both became stupified with the alcohol because at dawn the next day when we were relieved the relief party officer said, 'That was a nasty German attack last night,' whereupon I replied in all innocence, 'What attack?'

What I am trying to do is to arrange an occasion when I can present a case of twelve bottles of rum to any particular unit of the Coldstream Guards that are in need of that rum ration.

I remain, sir,
repentant but now sober
  Spike Milligan

⌒

9 *Orme Court,*
Bayswater
London W2

8 *March 1989*

Lt Col. E.B.L. Armitstead
1st Battalion
Coldstream Guards
Wellington Barracks
Birdcage Walk
London SW1E 6HQ

Dear Lt Col. Armitstead,

Alas, owing to other commitments I will be unable to accept your very kind offer to lunch on Thursday 6 April. However, I would still like to have the dozen bottles of rum delivered. As I have no phone number for you I will phone Major Cazenove and ask him the best place to have it delivered.

I hope this meets with your approval.

It is over forty years since I drank the Coldstream Guards rum and now my conscience will be salved.

Sincerely
Spike Milligan

⌒

Archbishop's House
Westminster
London SW1P 1QJ

29 August 1990

Mr Spike Milligan

Dear Mr Milligan,

Please kindly forgive this way of writing to you!

I am trying to collect texts for a possible book on the theme of HEAVEN/PARADISE to be called I WILL MEET YOU IN HEAVEN. *The book will be ecumenical.*

I would be honoured if you would contribute one page to this work. This could be expressed in a personal way or through: SCRIP-TURE, HYMN, POEM, PROSE, SPIRITUAL OR GENERAL WRITING, YOUR OWN WORDS (published or other).

I hope and pray that you will answer this request and that people will be helped by your words as a source of hope and strength.

On a very practical note, if you give a quote, please kindly give the TITLE, PAGE, PUBLISHER AND DATE or the translation of a Bible used, etc. May I also have your permission to use the text and to give your name (all proper copyright would be fully respected).

You might simply mail me a Xerox copy of any material or if a Bible quote please just give Chapter and Verse. I would like very much for it to be near a page in length.

I would appreciate very much a quick reply, knowing just how very very busy you are.

God bless and keep you.

With my sincere and warm thanks.

Affectionately,

   Fr. Michael, SA

Father Michael Seed, SA
Ecumenical Adviser

PS. Forgive this way of writing to you – do hope you can help.

9 Orme Court
Bayswater
London W2 4RL

27 September 1990

Father Michael Seed
Archbishop's House
Westminster
London SW1P 1QJ

Dear Father Michael Seed,

Forgive the delay in replying to your letter of August 29th it arrived when I was on holiday.

Yes of course I would like to help and I am enclosing herewith my text.

I do hope this is what you wanted.

Love, light and peace
  Spike Milligan

I have a problem, I would like to believe in heaven and an afterlife but I can find no evidence of it. There is much spoken about the after-life and the glories that it contains but personally I cannot feel that such a place exists; that does not stop me living a life of a good Christian whose philosophy, through the teachings of Jesus Christ, I try to observe closely mixed with a touch of Buddhism on the environmental side.

Shall I put it this way I find heaven is on earth I am stunned by the beauty of a blade of grass, can I say more.

If there is a heaven then I will consider it a bonus.

———

[Knowing he was a supporter of their cause, the Hunt Saboteurs Association wrote to Spike asking for a quote for their newsletter.]

9 Orme Court
London W2

4 August 1988

Chris Bishop Esq.
Hunt Saboteurs Association
PO Box No. 87
Exeter EX4 3TX

Dear Chris Bishop,

Here is my quote, in answer to your letter of the 24th July.

'I like birds in the sky
Not in the pie.'

Sincerely
Spike Milligan

⌒

from Indefinite Articles and Scunthorpe

The Hell of Flying

There was a time when Canopus and Solent flying boats, complete with beds, cabins, lounges, etc., would fly one to Australia, but – ha ha – since then we've made that bloody pardon-me-howling-with-laughter-word 'Progress'. Let me recount that progress, if at all, amounts to 300 mph faster, and 20,000 feet higher; the rest is sheer agony. When I pay BA or Qantas or South African or TWA airlines hundreds and hundreds of pounds to travel first class, the word 'first' should have a meaning beyond more grog, grovelling and grub. One needs most of all on a long journey to, say, Australia, relaxation, tranquillity and rest – and do we get it? My God we don't! Let me carry out a blow-by-blow account of the punishment from the moment we board.

First that terrible sound-swill is playing, that unbearable Muzak. Even more terrible, the sound control is with, not a musician or a passenger, but a member of the cabin staff, and the degree of blasting you get depends on exactly how thick or deaf he is. He has no idea what is on the Muzak tape – one is fed absolute absurdities. Board a BA 747 on a snow-bound day at Heathrow, and the idiot machine will be playing 'Springtime in Vienna'. It is mindless. No one listens to it. It is a waste of time, money and energy and is IMPOSED upon the traveller irrespective of whether he wants it or not.

I show my boarding pass to a young thing who by her slightly dazed reaction shows she has not been on the plane much longer than I have. 'Now see, in a Trident the As are there and on a 747 there.' She shows me my seat.

'I asked for, and was told, I would be in a non-smoking area. This is a smoker.'

'Oh, we'll see what we can do after we take off,' she says.

Great, I wish I could say that when I was buying my ticket: 'I'll see what I can do about paying you.'

'Paper, sir,' says a sweet young thing.

'Yes, I'd like the *Guardian*.'

'Sorry, there's only the *Financial Times* and the *Sun*.' I see, it's money or tits. I opt for the money rag. As I'm excitedly reading about the variability of the equity market, I am offered a glass of champagne.

'No, thanks. I don't drink at 10.30 of a morning.'

'Orange juice?'

'No, thanks. I had some for breakfast.'

All my answers are received with a commutability. It's either yes or no and, like the milkman's horse, she moves on at the word 'no'. All the other regular travelling slobs are downing the stuff so they can forget who they are. I'm looking for some news in the *Financial* –

'Canapés before lunch, sir?'

'It's a bit early for lunch.'

'Oh, it's not yet.'

'When?'

'As soon as we take off.'

'When is that?'

'There's been a delay so we can't say.' (Note the Royal We.)

'No lunch for me then.'

The word 'no' sends her on her way. I am looking for news in the *Financial Ti* –

'Writing paper and postcards, sir?'

I accept them. I note the smoking lunatics are clenching and unclenching their fists waiting for the NO SMOKING signs to disappear. Some of the loonies are sitting with a cigarette in their mouth, match in one hand and matchbox in the other. The Muzak grinds endlessly on. I am looking for news in the *Financial Ti* –

'Headphones, sir.'

'What for?'

'The music channels, sir.'

'Music? I can hear it playing quite clearly.'

'No. These are other music channels.'

'I'll think about it.'

'It's one pound for the headset.'

I am looking for news in the *Financial Ti* –

'Programme, sir.'

'What for?'

'The music channel.' She sticks it in my hand.

I am looking for news in the *Financial Ti* –

'Hot towels?'

'No, thank you. I can't eat another thing.'

I am looking –

'Socks and eye masks?'

I'm handed another envelope with the stuff in. When in Christ is it going to stop? Almost immediately I am given the lunch menu. A bowl of peanuts is put beside me (YOU'VE GOT TO HAVE THEM).

'More champagne, sir?'

I have given up trying to read. I sit back, look blankly ahead, listening to the Muzak gunge pour out.

An announcement: 'Will cabin crew check all doors for take-off.'

Hooray, that actually stopped the Muzak. Wait. No, it's back again.

Announcement: 'Good morning, this is your captain speaking. I'm sorry about this delay, it's to do with the rain, but we should be taking off shortly.' Muzak.

'Will you fasten your safety belt, please.'

Ah! the Muzak has stopped. 'Hello, hello. Ladies and gentlemen, under your seat you will find a life jacket. In the event of an emergency, etc. etc.' The girl stewardess does the cabaret, and we all cheer at the end. Muzak.

Hoping that the interruptions are over, I start to read *Twenty-four Hours in Entebbe*, and wish I was there and not on this bloody plane.

'This is your flight deck steward. For your information, the stewards or stewardesses [and there's very little difference] can be called by pulling the button in your arm rest. Thank you.'

We're moving!!

'Hello, ladies and gentlemen, this is your captain speaking. We've had a clear for take-off, so we should be airborne in about twelve minutes. Thank you.'

There is hardly a pinpoint between the announcement and the interruptions. You realize we are all on one great conveyor belt. We taxi to the runway.

'I must apologize for this further delay, but we should be off in about five minutes.'

The restrained smokers are now sitting with bulging eyes, pouring alcohol down themselves to neutralize their craving for the weed. We are actually taking off!!! Fortunately the whine of the engines has partially drowned the Muzak. We are up. Off goes the NO SMOKING sign, the nicotine lunatic next to me is off in a cloud of smoke, and that awful job of me having to inhale some of it for him is on. I remind the hostess of her promise of a non-smoker. Luckily there is a vacant non-smoking seat in which I now take up residence. Outside is a beautiful, silent, clean, aired world. Inside the Muzak is grinding my mind to pulp.

'Hello, this is your captain speaking. Just to fill you in, we shall be flying at . . .' Here we all join in the chorus '500 mph', '. . . and we will be flying at . . .' All together! '30,000 feet . . .'

Muzak again. I pull the call button. Sweet thing arrives.

'Can you turn off this Muzak, please? I've heard it round three times.'

'I'll speak to the chief steward.' She really doesn't understand. Why? No other passengers have ever asked for it to be turned off.

I carried out a minor psychological experiment. I asked each one of the stewardesses if they could remember any tune of the tape. No. I even asked several passengers if they remembered any. Answer. No. So will someone tell me what it's on for?

It's switched off, and a little girl in the seat behind says, 'Mummy, they've switched off the don't-be-frightened-we're-not-going-to-crash-on-take-off music', and that summed it up.

~

Concept Public Relations
4 Cupar Road
Battersea
London SW11 4JW

13 September 1986

Spike Milligan
Spike Milligan Productions Ltd
9 Orme Court
London W2

Dear Spike,

Please accept this complimentary sample of Braun's latest electrical appliance.

It has been specially designed for men who like to keep their beards in trim.

Braun hope you enjoy using this to keep your World famous beard in trim.

Kind regards
Yours sincerely
pp. A. Heath

Lyndon Evans
Shaver Product Manager
Braun UK Ltd

9 Orme Court
London W2

23 September 1986

Lyndon Evans
Concept Public Relations
4 Cupar Road
Battersea
London SW11 4JW

Dear Lyndon Evans Shaver Product Manager Braun UK Ltd,

Thank you for your magnificent gift of the Braun Beard Trimmer, alas I haven't a beard, can we swop one for an electric razor; this is, of course, if you intended it to be a useful present. If it is intended to be a useless one, then thank you I will keep it.

Love, light and peace
Spike Milligan

~

Concept Public Relations
4 Cupar Road
Battersea
London SW11 4JW

30 September 1986

Spike Milligan
9 Orme Court
London W2

Dear Spike,

Thank you very much for your letter in response to our apparently not very appropriate gift. What ever happened to your beard!!?
Enclosed, please find our swopsy, a Braun 3512 electric Shaver, I hope that you will find this a lot more useful.

Many thanks
Kind regards
Abby Heath
Concept Public Relations

9 Orme Court
London W2

13 October 1986

Ms Abby Heath
Concept Public Relations
4 Cupar Road
Battersea
London SW11 4JW

Dear Abby,

What a magnificent gift; my legs look magnificent now, in fact, I have given up wearing trousers. Clean and smooth, white and spotless, with dimpled knees, wearing fishnet stockings I can be seen any day on the tube between Queensway and Leicester Square and my importuning licence is up to date.

You asked what became of my beard, for services to the nation it now lies buried in a time capsule at Runnymede where it will be captured by Martians.

Give my love to your mother she knows what this is all about. Let's get married, I love you. A picture of you standing naked outside Buckingham Palace would suffice.

Love, light and peace
Spike Milligan

⌒

from Scunthorpe Revisited, Added Articles
and Instant Relatives

Holiday Package

There was a honeyed time when through the impoverished eyes of
my early post-war years, the nearest I got to the exotic holiday was
through a Travelogue at the local flea pit, or the glossy travel
brochures that were starting to proliferate with the coming tourist
boom. One day, I thought, I will make enough money to go to a
sun-scorched beach, and splash in turquoise waters. Well, what do
you know? It all came true. I worked hard, money was shovelled
into my coffers, and the world was my oyster.

Wrong! Had I only gone on dreaming. Alas, I found the conditions in the glossy brochure better than reality. I first settled for
'Historic, sunladen, land of the Lotus Eaters'. So said the brochure.

I arrived at Goulette Airport Tunis, destination Skanes Palace
Monastir. The Glossy Brochure Car – 'Will meet you at the airport
and waft (yes, waft!) you to your destination' – did not materialize.
What did materialize was one hour of argument with the tour rep,
during which a Tunisian customs officer tried to confiscate my
radio/cassette player believing that the reason for my trip was to
sell it!

Finally a taxi turned up, who, having us by the shorts, charges
us double for the trip. The 'Delightful bungalow on to the sea' had
delightful non-functioning air-conditioners, so we slept with every
window, and door, closed at night to avoid malarial mosquitoes. It
was like sleeping in a sauna. I won't warn tourists of the minor
irritations, but we made a visit to Ras Domas (Roman Thapsus). I
and my wife were looking over the ruins, when three Arab youths
with spear-guns threatened us with violence. It was very frighten-
ing. I wrote to President Bourgiba, and despite a second letter, I
was ignored.

Had enough Milligan? No, this was just a one-off. Next glossy brochure holiday – 'Greek villas in historical Lindos'. This turned out to be a cupboard with a fridge. At dawn it was a rat race for three-wheeled motor vehicles to awaken you. Every afternoon during siesta it was noisy. Greek men sat under our window and spoke as though conversing with the deaf. At night, across the bay, four discos blared out appalling Quadrophonic music which continued until 4 a.m. We searched out isolated beaches, only to find them so fouled as to be unbearable. I prayed for the day I flew home.

What's that jolly British Airways tune? 'We'll take good care of you.' Well, something must have gone wrong. From the roof of the plane water kept dripping, the carpet underfoot was soaked.

'It's the condensation,' explained the helpful air hostess.

Surely this was just a run of bad luck? One more time. Comes 1980, year of hope, and this time it's gotta be good. My auntie has recommended us a villa in Corfu. The brochure looks good; I speak with the agents, all charming, helpful, quiet, yes, isolated, yes, own catering, etc. fine. There's the usual cattle round-up flight, OK Corfu. Most dangerous airport in the Med, says helpful fellow passenger. Hire car OK. Off we drive to Kassiopi. Our villa is isolated, the views are superb, Albania. Villa a converted farmhouse, no luxury but comfortable.

Shortcomings occur as time passes. Half the light bulbs are dead; 'Sorry no replacements, we have to get them from England.' (Then why don't they?) Water pressure not very good. Why? Water is from well, well is nearly empty.

'I'll get a water wagon to fill it up.'

'Daddy, Daddy, the toilet won't flush.'

Daddy can get it to flush, no he can't. What Daddy can do is fight a burst pipe which is flooding the house, and he only succeeds because he brought (a) a kit of tools, and (b) adhesive waterproof tape.

Eating out in Kassiopi, very nice if you can stand appalling Western Rock music, full blast, not one tune mind you, but five tavernas, cheek by jowl, each with a different tune.

Conversation is impossible. The tourists don't seem to mind as they appear to be pissed out of their minds. Young trainee rapists with tattoos from their ankles up to their teeth shout, 'Whey oop, Spike, can I have your autograph on this fag packet?'

So, meals at home for Daddy. Never mind, there are those glossy 'Golden Beaches', but, not apparently on Corfu. There was every kind of filth on the beach except dying lepers. A fortnight's holiday in the Gents' Urinal at Victoria Station would be preferable. There were, of course, the intermittent electrical blackouts. The best surprise was the electrical shocks from the water taps. Nothing like 200 volts in the bath with a wet body. A search revealed an earth wire wound round the water pipes. It was hell having to bath in rubber gloves and plimsolls.

～

9 Orme Court,
London W2

10 June 1985

Miss D. Harman
Rostrum
Christie's
85 Old Brompton Road
London SW7 3JS

Dear Debbie,

I wont say it was an appalling piece of editing, but it must have been a total puzzle to people who read my article (did you edit it), when suddenly at the end of the whole article it said 'For the anxious, the two Elizabethan chairs were copies of English ones, made in Goa, India in about 1850, inlaid with bone and ivory.' Whereas there is absolutely no mention of this previously in the article, it made no sense at all.

 Yours baffled
  Spike Milligan

            GGK London Ltd
            76 Dean Street
          London W1V 5HA

             17 June 1985

S. Milligan Esq.
9 Orme Court
London W2

Dear Mr Milligan,

Re: CHRISTIE'S

Following a conversation I have had with Debbie Harman at Christie's South Kensington, she has asked me to write to you in her absence this week.

 It is, of course, in respect of your article that appeared incorrectly in Rostrum magazine. As the producer of Rostrum, can I apologize for what is a mistake of considerable proportions. It is somewhat academic how the mistake occurred, though perhaps it is relevant to say that it was not a case of crass editing, but a failure in the system between typesetting and make up, and ultimately proof reading.

 I very much appreciate the considerable effort that goes into producing such articles and I can well understand the anger felt when such a mistake as this occurs. I hope that the episode has not caused you too much embarrassment and I am sure, should you wish, that a suitable piece could be published in the next issue of *Rostrum*, to correct matters.

Finally, may I say that your article was a much valued contribution and there is considerable embarrassment over what has occurred. I hope our sincere apologies will go some way towards repairing the situation.

Yours sincerely

Paul Silvester
Client Services Director

C.C. Debbie Harman, Christie's South Kensington

⌒

9 Orme Court
London W2

19 June 1985

Paul Silvester Esq.
GGK London Ltd
76 Dean Street
London W1V 5HA

Dear Paul,

What's this terrifying, grovelling, eating humble pie letter. I was just pointing out to the poor reader, suddenly we were being told about these two chairs, that were not mentioned in the article – that's all, don't worry too much about it, continue on your way, be happy, take tranquillizers, massage your body with palmolive oil, keep your face in the fridge, you will look younger, in all these things I wish you well.

Love, light and peace
Spike Milligan

PS. A bit on the side does you good.

⌒

Norma

The enclosed is the correct way my books should be listed –

Love
   Spike

Yes Spike. But I ought to point out. That there are four titles miss-ing. And two titles which are incorrect.

Love Norma

AUTOBIOGRAPHY

1971 Adolf Hitler – My Part in His Downfall
1974 'Rommel?' 'Gunner Who?'
1976 Monty – His Part in My Victory
1978 Mussolini – His Part in My Downfall

FICTION

1963 Puckoon

DRAMA

1970 The Bedsitting Room (with John Antrobus)

POETRY

1959 Values
1972 Small Dreams of a Scorpion
1979 Open Heart University

MISCELLANEOUS PROSE

1977 The Spike Milligan Letters, edited by Norma Farnes
1981 Indefinite Articles & Scunthorpe

CHILDREN'S BOOKS

1959 Silly Verse for Kids
1968 Milliganimals & the Bald-twit Lion
1973 Badjelly the Witch
1974 Dip the Puppy
1981 Unspun Socks from a Chicken's Laundry

HUMOUR

1961 A Dustbin of Milligan
1963 The Little Pot Boiler
1965 A Book of Bits, or a Bit of a Book
1969 The Bedside Milligan
1972 Goon Show Scripts
1973 More Goon Show Scripts
1971 Milligans Ark
1975 The Milligan Book of Records
1976 William McGonagall: the Truth at Last
1978 Goblins
1979 The Q Annual
1980 The Q Annual
1982 101 Best Limericks

Book of the Goons
Transports of Delight
Great McGonagall Scrapbook
Sir Nobonk and the Dragon

Incorrect Titles:
Get in the Q Annual
101 Best and Only Limericks

5
Tender(ish) Moments

My love is like a red, red rose,
but my underwear is off-white.

> – Spike Milligan to Norma Farnes,
> accompanied by a large bouquet of flowers

I think the tender(ish) moments in Spike's life were the times spent with his families. He loved his children and the joy they brought him, particularly when they were young. He had a wonderful childlike quality, which he shared with not only his own children but other children through his poetry books.

In June 1946 came his first great love affair: he met Maria Antoinetta Fontana, an Italian ballerina. She was appearing at the Bellini Theatre in Rome with the Italian *corps de ballet*. He was appearing with the Bill Hall Trio at the same theatre.

In January 1952 he married June Marlow. June was friends with Anne Howe, at that time Peter Sellers's girlfriend. They made up a foursome, and their first date was at the Edgwarebury club. Spike and June had three children: Laura Theresa, born November 1952, Sean Patrick, born September 1954, and Sile Javotte, born December 1957. The marriage ended in divorce. Spike claimed: 'The strain of writing a *Goon Show* every week would tear us apart.'

In April 1962, Spike married Patricia (Paddy) Ridgeway. They met on the set of *Muckinese Battlehorn*. Paddy was an extra. She was also appearing as a nun in *The Sound of Music*, and Spike went to see the show. Spike and Paddy had one daughter, Jane Fionnuala, in May 1966. Paddy died in February 1978.

In July 1983, he married Shelagh Sinclair. The marriage was childless, and he was married to Shelagh when he died.

Throughout his life, though, Spike had many girlfriends. He loved the company of women. One 'tender moment' in 1972 resulted in an illegitimate daughter, Romany Anne Jocelyn, whose mother was Roberta Watt, a wonderful Canadian journalist who was in love with Spike all her life. Tragically, she died when she was only thirty-six years old. And yet another tenderish moment and yet another result: an illegitimate son, born in 1976.

⌒

HAMLET

Said Hamlet to Ophelia,
'I'll do a sketch of thee.
What kind of Pencil shall I use,
2B or not 2B?'

Perth, WA
March 1980

– from *Unspun Socks from a Chicken's Laundry*

⌒

from Goodbye Soldier

So far Bornheim has passed the journey immersed in the *Union Jack* newspaper. He walks down the Charabong, swaying and bumping. He makes reference to my new amour.

'Is there something going on?' he said, nodding towards my Toni.

I told him most certainly there was a lot going on. I had met her, according to my new watch, at ten-thirty precisely. Yes, there was a lot going on but as conditions improved I'd hoped for a lot coming off. He grins like a fiend.

'The poor girl,' he said. 'You'd better not show it to her all at once.'

He slunk away chuckling, the swine! This was not *that* kind of affair, this was *true* romance. No tawdry thoughts entered my head, but they were entering other areas. South of Rome we lumber through hot dusty villages, the grapes are heavy on the vine and on sale are large luscious red bunches for a few lire. But I don't have eyes for the delights of the Campagna, only Toni's glances and the squeeze of her little hand.

Late evening and the dusty chugging Charabong enters Rome through the Porta Maggiore. It's a Sunday evening and the sunlight is turning to rose-petal pink. The streets are full of the populace taking their evening strolls – elegant Romans are *really* elegant, they wear clothes well. But! None of them are wearing sensible brown English shoes like me . . . The Charabong comes to rest outside the Albergo Universo. *I'll* help Toni with her luggage to her bedroom. Her mother wants her to go home, but, because she wants to be near me, lies, and tells Momma the company rules insist she stays at the hotel. Ha! Ha! Love finds a way.

LOVE SONG

If I could write words
Like leaves on an Autumn Forest floor
What a bonfire my letters would make.
If I could speak words of water
You would drown when I said
'I love you'.

– from *Small Dreams of a Scorpion*

~~~

from Goodbye Soldier

We pile on the Charabong which threads its way up a mountain, or was it a hill? That's a point: at what height does a hill become a mountain? The sun is shining ferociously, even after we reach the snow line. We are met by a sergeant ski instructor. He fixes us up with skis and leaves us to it. So, it's fun on the slopes. There must be a world record for falling over, and I hold it. I strip to the waist – even in the snow, I'm perspiring. I rub my body with snow and feel exhilarated. The sergeant makes some tea for us in the out-of-season café. I notice lying among the trees spent cartridge shells. The sergeant tells us that this used to be a training depot for German ski troops. 'The lot that done Narvik trained here,' he says.

The afternoon passes with us falling down. Finally the sergeant lends us a two-man sleigh. 'This is more like it,' says Bornheim. The afternoon passes with us sliding down the mountain. No ski lift here, you have to schlep back up on foot. Plenty of tumbles on the overloaded sleigh.

'It was never meant for so many,' shouts Angove as five of us hurtle down into a tree. Great flurries of snow and tumbling bodies – sun, snow, sleigh, wonderful!

At six o'clock, Lieutenant Priest reminds us there's a show to do. I keep forgetting the show is the reason we are having all this fun. We arrive back sunburnt and shagged out, not looking forward to the show. A quick tea and a slice of cake, I collect my guitar and hurry to the waiting Charabong.

'Terr-ee! You all sunburn,' says Toni. I told her that all day I'd missed her and longed for her on skis next to me with the wind blowing through our hair as we raced down the mountain.

I stand up in the bus and start to declaim for all to hear, 'What a fool I was to leave you, darling, to do the laundry, while I, a young Celtic god, was coursing down the white mountain in a rapture of speed, wind and other things.' I kneel down and start kissing her arm. 'Oh, forgive me, my beloved, my little laundress. It will never happen again.' Toni is laughing with embarrassment and the cast give me a round of applause. Greta Weingarten is saying have we noticed how clean Austria is after Italy. I agree with her. 'I'll say this for Hitler: I bet before he shot himself he put on clean underpants!'

In the dressing room, Hall and Mulgrew get into an argument about women.

'I look for women with experience,' says Hall. 'I choose women who make the act of love last.'

Mulgrew guffaws. 'Bloody hell,' he says. 'Some of the old boilers I've seen you with don't look like they'd last the walk home.'

'Looks aren't everything,' intones Hall. 'I mean, most of these young tarts – show 'em a prick and they'd faint.'

Mulgrew is laughing. 'No wonder. When I saw yours, *I* nearly fainted. For a start, it's got a bend in it.'

'It's not a bend. It's a slight curve,' says Hall.

'Curve?' laughs Mulgrew, 'it nearly goes round corners.'

I was crying with laughter. Barrack-room humour, there's nothing quite like it.

After the show Major Hardacre, the Town Major, comes backstage with two young officers. They congratulate us over the show. 'It was jolly good.' They seem interested in the girls whom the Major has a slight tendency to handle. He's very interested in Toni, *my* Toni. He shakes her hand and holds it overlong. He'd better watch out or I'll have his Hardacre on a slab, sliced up like salami and stuffed up his married quarters! God, I was jealous! In love and jealous, it was like being on the rack.

After dinner, that night, we have a dance. The trio, plus Bornheim on the accordion, supply the music. Toni dances with Maxie. He dances splay-legged, as though he has messed himself. Toni, she was so doll-like. Strange – when I was a boy in India, up to the age of eight I liked dolls. My father was a worried man. Was it Toni's doll-like image that attracted me to her? Forward the resident analyst. I have the last waltz with Toni. Bornheim plays the 'Valzer di Candele'. He knows that it's 'our tune'. I hold Toni close and the room seems to go round and round – very difficult for a square room.

By midnight, the dance had broken up. Toni and I went and sat on a bench in the neglected rose garden. (Today's Special, Neglected Roses five shillings a bunch.) We talked about each other. Were we sure we were in love? The answer seemed to be yes. So, what to do? Do we get engaged? I think if I had asked her, she would have said yes. You see, I'd never thought about marriage. I was a day-by-day person. If at the end of day everything was OK, then we were set fair for tomorrow. Why ruin it by planning, say, six months ahead? I tell you, whoever planned my head should have *got* six months. I was a woolly thinker. Toni and I would go on for ever; there was no end to the tour, we would ride in the Charabong eternally and never grow old . . .

Bloody Awful

Next day, after breakfast, it's a real hot day. I tell Toni we must try and get a swim in the Wörthersee. We take our costumes and make for the lake. But everywhere it's reeds, reeds, reeds and where there is access, it's mud, mud, mud. So, we settle for a sunbathe. Oh, the heat. Toni so close, covered in oil – it's almost frying her. 'Terr-ee, some more oil on my back, please.' So Terree obliges, taking his time to rub the oil on her satin skin. Ohhhh, the heat. Ohhhh, the oil. God, we all need a button on us that says SEX ON–OFF. Right now, I'm fumbling for the off switch. Through the lazy afternoon we talk with our eyes closed, sweet nothings that would bore any but us. Being in love, everything seems important. Small things. God, why did I have a small thing?

'What's going on here?' I open one eye to see Bornheim and Mulgrew; the latter, who hasn't learned his lesson, is holding a fishing rod. 'You know there's no mixed bathing allowed in the long grass,' he says.

'Go away, Mulgrew. Weren't you ever young?'

'Yes,' he says. 'It was on a Thursday.'

It is tea-time, so we give in and the four of us head back to the guest house. I need a shower to get the oil off and a cold one to reduce the swelling. Toni came down to tea in an all-white dress to show off her suntan, and lovely she looked.

The show that night was pretty hysterical. A lone drunk in the middle of the hall started to shout out, 'It's bloody awful, bloody awful.' It took a time to evict him. Then, in the second half he obviously somehow got back in because he shouted from the gallery, 'It's still bloody awful, bloody awful.' Again he was thrown out, only to reappear through a front row fire exit direct from the street. 'It's bloody awful from here, as well,' he shouted, before doing a bunk. It caused great laughter in the audience and the cast. It wasn't the last of him, my God. As we were about to drive back to the billets, he was thumping on the sides of the Charabong, 'You're all bloody awful, bloody awful.' Bill Hall rolled down a window and blew a thunderous saliva-draped raspberry at him, causing howls of glee in the truck.

'Perhaps we *are* bloody awful,' said Bornheim. 'I mean, how many of us would a West End audience come to see?' he went on. 'I mean, they'd pay to see the Bill Hall Trio. But the rest of us?'

This started a real row till we got to the hotel. Everybody was suddenly in star class. *Of course* the West End audiences would pay to see Chalky White hitting people, etc., etc. There was a lot of laughter as each artiste defended himself against the 'bloody awful' label. The fact is none of them were ever heard of again.

At dinner, the argument breaks out again. When Bornheim plays the piano, a shout of 'Bloody awful' goes up. From then on, no one could make a move without a shout of 'Here comes bloody awful'. The Italian artistes couldn't get the gist of it. But when they did, they too took up the cry. Toni asked me with a perfectly straight face, 'Tell me, Terree. We are bludy awful, yes?'

The next morning broke sunny and warm. Across the road from us was a little Austrian beerhouse, so at lunchtime Bornheim and I toddled over and sat outside. We ordered a bottle of white wine and some cheese, then another bottle of white wine. Two Austrians in lederhosen with overmuscled legs and blue staring eyes asked us to join them for a 'drink of zer Schnapps' and my God we got pie-eyed. We wobbled back to our chalets. I was sick and crashed out groaning on the bed. Toni is horrified, I've never been drunk before. She sees the drunken wretch and says, 'Terr-ee, you, you, bludy awful,' bursts into tears and runs out. I stumbled after her and crashed to the floor where I was sick yet again. I now looked like a walking Irish stew on legs. By evening I was coming to and drank a lot of black coffee, brought in by faithful Mulgrew who knew drunkenness. That night on stage I *was* bloody awful. I muffed the announcements, got the wrong intros and generally buggered up the act. But we still went down well.

'Just bloody luck,' said Bill Hall.

'What did you get pissed for?' said Lieutenant Priest. 'About thirty Schillings,' I said. 'We were very economical.'

The weather stays divine. Up the road at the Wörthersee riviera Toni and I hire a rowboat and take a packed lunch. I row to the middle of the lake. It's one of those boats with a lounging double seat in the stern, so we snog while the boat drifts and drifts and drifts . . . Let it drift for ever, for we are lovers and the hands of the clock stopped the moment we met. We live in a time capsule called now. We can only think of each other. It is young and true love. The waters lapped the sides, lake birds flew hither and thither to their secret places and the day lay on us like a diaphanous dream . . .

Wake up, wake up! The boat is leaking. Blast, yes, there's three inches of water in the bottom. So I row the love wagon back to the boathouse and point out to the Austrian man what has happened. He just laughed and gave us half our money back. We walked back down the dusty road and arrived home for tea. Toni is giggling because somehow I have managed to wet the seat of my trousers, which looks like a giant ink stain. I hang my shirt out to cover it but that's wet as well. The hell with it! Wild poppies grow by the wayside. I pick some for Toni. Alas, the poor things start to die within a few minutes. Why can't we leave nature alone? Toni takes a photo of me. She wants me to turn my back to the camera. I refuse.

⌒

WHEN I SUSPECTED

There will be a time when it will end.
Be it parting
Be it death
So each passing minute with you
               pendulumned with sadness.
So many times
I looked long into your face.
           I could hear the clock ticking.

On a plane over Java
November 1977

– from *Open Heart University*

⌒

from Goodbye Soldier

Yes, *Madam Butterfly* was at the Rome Royal Opera House. Toni has two free tickets that her mother had given to her by a customer at the CIT travel agency. What a treat to look forward to! But it was a night of suppressed hysterical laughter. The whole opera was financed and cast by black marketeers. I couldn't believe it. When first I saw Madam Butterfly, she was *huge*, with a heaving bosom. I thought, out of this frame will come a most powerful voice. When she opened her mouth to sing, you could hardly hear anything. To accentuate the shortcoming, she overacted, throwing her arms in the air, clasping her hands together, falling on her knees with a groan, running across the stage with loud, thudding feet – all to thunderous applause from an obvious claque. Then we wait for Lieutenant Pinkerton: my God, he's half her size! He can't be more than five foot five inches and so thin that when he stood behind her, he vanished. He has a piercing tenor voice, high up in the nose, with a tremendous wobbly *vibrato* that fluctuates above and below the real note. He is obviously wearing lifts in his shoes that make him bend forward from the ankles as though walking in the teeth of a gale. If that isn't all bad enough, he is wearing what must be the worst toupee I've seen. It appears to be nailed down, the front coming too far forward on the forehead with a slight curl all round where it joins his hair.

Trying to laugh silently, I'm almost doubled up in pain. All around me are Mafia-like creatures – one wrong move and I'll be knifed. So be it, no comedy could exceed this. We notice that when Pinkerton tries for a high note, he shoots up on his toes, putting him at an even more alarming angle. When he and she embrace, she envelopes him completely, his little red face appearing above her massive arms as though he's been decapitated. I'm carried on the tide of enthusiasm. When the claque jump up applauding, so do I. 'Bravo, *encore*,' I shout. It was a night I can never forget.

At the little restaurant after the show, I keep breaking into fits of laughter as I recall it all. Toni is split down the middle, both halves being equal to the whole. She's ashamed that something so bad should go on at the Royal Opera House. '*Disgrazia*,' she says, but continues to laugh through it.

I remember that, as we sat outside eating, for no reason it started to rain. We retreat inside while a waiter rescues our food. The waiter is amusing; he apologizes for the rain and says even though some has settled on the food, there'll be no extra charge.

Seated inside, Toni suddenly says to me, 'You know, in two day you leave me.'

My mood changed, was it that soon? I was so impervious to days that each one came as a shock. Why wasn't time timeless?

'Toni,' I said, 'I'll come back as soon as I can and I'll write as much as I can.'

That's followed by us just looking at each other in silence.

'I miss you very much, Terr-ee.'

She looks so small and helpless; I *feel* so small and helpless.

'I tell you what, we have some champagne, yes?'

She pauses reflectively. 'OK,' she says.

The restaurant hasn't any champagne. '*Tedeschi hanno bevuto tutto,*' says the waiter. Would we like Asti Spumante? Yes, when in Rome.

When midnight strikes in some campanile, we toast each other. We'd done it so often before, but this time it's a little more meaningful – our sand is running out. In the taxi back, I sit with my arm around her, her head on my shoulder (sounds like a transplant). I hum her favourite tune, 'Valzer di Candele' . . . We tiptoe into the apartment and I instinctively wait for my mother's voice, 'Where have you been at this time of night.' No, it's Signora Fontana asking is that Toni. Yes, so goodnight.

The day is suit-fitting day. When we arrive at the tailor's, a man is leaving wearing a terrible suit that appears to have been made by a blind man. No, no, no, says the little tailor, he didn't make that. It's only his father-in-law visiting to collect the alimony. My suit is all ready on a hanger. Will I step into the cubicle and change? The suit is a great success; I can't wait to get outside for a photograph.

Oh, yes, this is a Robert Taylor suit. Quick! I must be seen walking about the town. What's the best street? Ah, yes, driver, the Via Veneto and step on it. When we arrive it's midday and the morning promenade is coming to an end. Nevertheless Toni and I and the suit walk up and down, then down and up. Toni and I and the suit sit at a restaurant and Toni and I and my suit have an ice-cream. All Rome must be talking about me. My suit is now smoking a cigarette. Toni is totally bemused: is this a man or a little boy she's going out with, or is it a suit? If only they could see me in Brockley now, standing outside the Rialto Cinema waiting for Lily Dunford. My picture would be in the *Kent Messenger*.

By mid-afternoon I think Rome has seen enough of the suit, so we return to the apartment. Gioia opens the door to my suit, *she doesn't seem to notice it*!!!! She'll *have* to be killed. I have a good reason to take my suit off: Gioia has to go out shopping. It's the last chance of Toni and I being alone. I draw Miss Toni's attention to this by making her take her clothes off and getting into bed, where we foreclose on the world. There *is* a Father Christmas. He was early this year. However, though it was divine making love to her, it lost a bit by Toni breathlessly telling me all the time to 'hurry up' as Gioia was due back. I did my best, finishing in under twenty-three minutes – beating Gioia by five and my own record by ten. With Gioia fiddling at the door with the keys, I rush madly back to my room, just slamming the door on my bare bum in time. Worn out by pressurized love-making, I have a siesta. It's a warm after-noon but nice and cool in the room. I can hear Gioia clinking and clanking in the kitchen . . .

I awake in the evening to the sounds of Signora Fontana and Lily talking. As this is my last evening here, they want me to have dinner 'a casa'. They know my love of pasta and have prepared spaghetti Neapolitan. Toni wants her mother to see 'the suit', so I put it on and do an 'entrance' into the sitting-room. Oh, yes, her mother thinks it's very smart. But should the flies be undone? Oh, dear. Today is Signora Fontana's wedding anniversary. She shows me a photo album: that's her as a young woman on holiday with her mother and father in Savona. Did I know her mother was French? No? Well, I did now. I see grinning photos, from her mother-in-law grinning in Ravenna to her husband grinning outside his soap factory in Abyssinia in 1936. It was possibly one of the best records of grinning I had seen.

We dine to a mixed conversation about the world: things aren't getting any better. I agree, I know my thing isn't getting any better. Shoes are very expensive, '*Troppo caro*,' says Signora Fontana. Has she thought of bare feet? They must be economical. The Communist leader Togliatti is a very dangerous man. 'He want revolution in Italy,' says Toni. So a ragbag of conversation. Gradually, I'm left out of it altogether as they all jabber heatedly in Italian. As the conver-sation swung from Toni at one end and her mother at the other, I must have looked like a spectator at a tennis match. I call out the score: 'Fifteen, love . . . thirty, fifteen . . .' They ignore me, but it's fun.

Dinner over, they listen to the news in Italian on the radio as I sip a glass of white wine. After the news comes Italy's premier dance band led by Angelini. Lily wants to know if I can 'jitter bugger'. Try me. We move back the chairs a little and Lily and I 'cut a rug'. She's very good, I am not. Toni and Mother watch on with amusement. Gioia looks on in amazement. The phone rings, Lily hurls herself at it: it's *him*! She is running her finger up and down the wall. The evening ends with us playing snap. How delightfully simple it was, the simplest of all was me . . .

*

I put through a phone call to Toni. After a delay it comes through.

'Hello, Toni.'

'Terr-ee,' she gasps, 'my Terr-ee, you go all right Napoli?'

'Yes, I go all right in Napoli.'

''Ow lovelee 'ear your voice, *mio tesoro*. I miss you much already. Why you go away?'

'What are you doing?'

'Just now we have dinner. Tell me you love me.'

'I love you.'

A little more of that type of chat and we finish. Yes, I promise I'll phone tomorrow. No, I won't go out getting drunk with Mulgrew. No, I won't go near other girls. Now, where is that man Hall. I buzz his room.

''Oos that?'

'Me, Spike. Are there any gigs going? I'm at a loose end till the boat sails.'

No, no gigs tonight. There's one tomorrow. Do I mind playing in a sergeants' mess? Well, as long as it isn't too big a mess.

'Wot you doing tonight?'

'I'm not doing anything tonight.'

'Well, good luck with it,' he says.

I met him in the dining-hall for dinner. Has he seen Mulgrew or Bornheim lately? Yes, he's done a couple of gigs with them. What about the *Dominion Monarch* and the sailing date? That's all fixed, I have to collect my ticket from Major Ridgeway. So the end is in sight: it's goodbye Italy and hello Deptford.

The remaining days were very very boring. So I won't bore the reader. I do a couple of band gigs on guitar with Hall, Bornheim and Mulgrew at military establishments. I collect my boat ticket and passport and I buy a few trinkets for my mother and father. Most days I spend in my room reading books from the hotel library. The very last one was the story of San Michele by Axel Munthe, a most moving story about Capri.

The night before I sail, Jimmy Molloy checks into the hotel. He's booked on the same ship as me. He wants to have a night out; he knows a good officers' nightclub on the seafront. OK, I'll come with him and wear the suit. It's the Club Marina, 'Officers Only'. We show our CSE passes. Down a corridor to a large room with a central dance floor, where a good Italian band are playing the music of our time. There are hostesses at the bar: no, Jimmy, I'm not interested. Well, he is. He goes over and chats to one and brings her back to our table. Ah, good, wait till she sees my suit. She is pretty stunning, small, petite, saturnine-dark with a pair of giant olive eyes.

'This is Francesca,' says Molloy.

'*Piacera*,' I say.

She throws me a dazzling white-toothed smile. More than that, as the evening progresses I realize that she fancies me and my suit. 'I fink I've picked a loser here,' chuckled Molloy. Do I want to take her over? No no no, Jimmy, I am promised to another. He gives me a disbelieving look. 'Come on, a bit on the side won't hurt.' I told him I had no bits on my side, all my bits were at the front, so I'd be the wrong fit for her. However it's nice flirting with her.

The lights go down: a spotlight on the stage illuminates an Italian MC in a white jacket. 'Laddies and Gintilmin, nower oura starer of thee cabareter, Gina Escoldi.' He points left, the band strikes up and a ballerina on points pirouettes on the floor and sings 'a hubba hubba hubba' with red-hot accompaniment. She has a coarse croaky voice, loaded with sex – all the while standing on points. It was a head-on collision between jazz and ballet, but very successful. She goes down big with what is, in the majority, an American officer audience.

At the end of the evening Molloy says, 'You takin' this bird or not.' I decline, cursing the fact that I have a conscience. 'One day,' he laughs, 'you'll regret this decision!' What did he mean 'one day', I was regretting it *now*. While he offs with her, I off to the hotel and bed. While I lay there, my mind was going through the long years away from home. Had I really been in action in North Africa? Had I really taken part in the Tunis Victory Parade? Did I land at Salerno? It all seemed unreal, like a distant dream ending up in the most distant dream of all – Toni and me on Capri. Would the sun ever shine like that again?

On departure morning I awake and, first thing, put in a call to Toni. We say our final goodbyes – tears on the phone from Rome. At breakfast, I meet Jimmy Molloy. 'That bird last night, what a con. When we get to 'er place, she just kisses me goodnight then pisses off. I think it was all your bloody fault, Milligan.' Smugly, I say, yes, it undoubtedly was.

Our ship sails at midday. We have to start boarding at 10.30. We take a taxi to the quay where the *Dominion Monarch* awaits. We both have first-class passages – I'm nominated a cabin on the port side. A young English steward carries my bag and calls me sir. It's a fine, single-berth cabin with a porthole for looking out – or, if you hang on the outside, for looking in. 'If there's anything you want, sir, just ring the service button.' I locate the Purser's Office where a grim-faced staff change my lire into sterling, which looks much less. Up on the promenade deck I find Molloy and I get him to take my photo.

The ship is alive with bustle, with sailors shouting yo ho ho and pouring hot tar down the hatches. At midday the gangplank is removed, the ship gives a long mournful blast on the hooter and a tug starts to manoeuvre us out to sea. Molloy and I stand at the rail. Slowly, the great ship puts on speed, the Italian mainland recedes into the distance, finally lost in a haze. It's over: it's goodbye Italy, goodbye Toni and goodbye soldier.

~

from Spike Milligan: The Family Album –
An Illustrated Autobiography

1952

On 26 January June Marlow and I were married. We were very happy together, but eventually the strain I was under in writing *The Goon Show* would tear us apart.

There were constant battles with the BBC. We did a whole spectrum of voices on the show. Peter could do anything from a dustman to the Queen, but the BBC didn't like us doing voices like General Montgomery, Churchill or the Queen. They only wanted jokes like, 'I used to play the Palladium.' 'Yes, I've never heard it played better.'

I was writing at our flat in Shepard Hill Road but when my daughter, Laura, came along, she distracted me so much I found an office at 137 Shepherd's Bush Road. I would take the Underground from Archway and change at Camden for Shepherd's Bush. It was a short walk to the office which I shared with Eric Sykes. I had bought a Letra 22 typewriter (I still have it) and I worked a long day, leaving home at 9 a.m. in the morning and working until ten or eleven at night; sometimes I worked through the night. I had to work long hours to make the scripts as good as I could. When I got home, June would have left out a meal for me to warm up. I had difficulty sleeping and I was seen by a stupid doctor who kept giving me sleeping pills – you name 'em, I've taken 'em.

This life put a great strain on me and my marriage with a wonderful wife, June. I must have behaved impossibly – it was all leading up to a breakdown.

In December I was writing the third series of *Goon Shows* when I finally broke down. If anybody wants to know what down is, ask me – I've been there. The doctor who was treating me realized that

I was too much for him to handle and had me taken to St Luke's Psychiatric Hospital in Muswell Hill in London. As I got out of the ambulance, there was a cat sitting on the doorstep. I stroked it. The contact with its fur was soothing. They put me in a room next to a noisy bloody kitchen. I screamed, 'Get me out of here!' A doctor gave me a jab of something and in ten seconds I was unconscious. I lay there in a deep sleep for fourteen days.

They brought me round occasionally to drink some liquid food. I grew a dark brown beard and I remember one nurse saying, 'He looks like Our Lord.' When I was half awake I had hallucinations. Hanging from the ceiling were halves of coat hangers. Then there was a live lion on top of the cupboard. There came a stream of silver, materializing in the doorway opposite into a lady with black ribbon round her hair, which hung down to her shoulders.

The trauma of my childhood bed-wetting haunted me and even though I couldn't pass any urine, I'd keep on trying, still unconscious.

The result, a prolapse. One good thing came from all this. I was a heavy smoker and being unconscious for two weeks had abated the craving. A nurse would sit with me all night. She smoked, I smelled it. Deep down I wanted to give up and now was the chance. I took it – I've never really smoked since.

June came to visit. She looked terrible with worrying about the breadwinner having come to a sudden halt.

1953

By February I was well enough to leave hospital, but still very shaky. I went back to the slog of writing which I faithfully did, although the payment was very small. For my acting part in the show I think I got £12 and for writing I got £25. As Sellers and Secombe were big names they got £100 a week. Ultimately, I was paid £100 as well and, with repeats, £200 – a lot of money. £200 – that must have hurt them!

By now Michael Bentine had left *The Goons*. He was an extraordinary character who told the most extraordinary stories. He once told me that his mother had levitated from the ground, across the dining room table and settled on the other side. One night when we were appearing in a show in Birmingham, I asked him, as he claimed to be a mathematician, could he give me the formula for the atomic bomb? He took out a lipstick and covered the mirror in the dressing room with Pythagoras, finishing off at the bottom on the right hand side with, 'There! That is the formula for the atomic bomb!' Unfortunately, there was a Professor Penny in the audience that night. I happened to know him and he came into the dressing room and looked at the mirror. I asked him what it was and he said, 'That's a load of bollocks!' I told Michael and he said, 'Of course it is! You don't think I would give away the secret of the atom bomb to you in a dressing room in Birmingham, do you?'

1954

On 17 September we had a second child, Sean Patrick. Joy, a boy! At least one successor to my name!

We bought a Maltese puppy and called him Baggage. He was scruffy but cute. Also scruffy but cute was the 1929 Austin soft-top tourer which I bought from Peter Sellers for £300.

1955

We bought, on a mortgage, 127 Holden Road, Finchley. It had a large garden with a stream at the bottom. That summer June took Laura and Sean on holiday in the car, by now named 'Little Min'. I couldn't go as I was still working hard to deliver a complete *Goon Show* script once a week.

~

from Indefinite Articles and Scunthorpe

Christmas Comes Once Too Much a Year

Christmas – the word strikes fear in every Christian adult. A time of good cheer – yes – but what does it add up to? So far mine adds up to £182. Is there any more spine-chilling remark than the wife saying, 'About the presents this year, dear'? That simple remark, that was once delivered about three weeks prior to the happy day, is now mentioned in November; one starts buying fireworks with holly on.

When *I* was a child my presents were two boxes of lead soldiers – but now my children's list starts thus:

Jane (8) – Honda motor bike.
Sile (16) – Quadrophonic hi-fi sound kit.

I tell you, there should be a Minister of Christmases! Laws:

(1) It is forbidden to spend more than £2 per present per person.
(2) One is *not* obliged to kiss any woman under the mistletoe.
(3) Christmas cards must be sent only to close relatives.

When I think of the insane, frenzied shopping on the 23rd and 24th – by the 25th, 60 per cent of the nation's shoppers are in a state of collapse and about to be aroused at 0500 hours on the dawn of the 25th. I myself have been woken at three o'clock with the blowing of bugles, beating of drums, squeaking and barking toys. By the night of the 26th I am adding codicils to my will: 'I leave *nothing* to *any* of my family, they've already got enough.'

My list of Christmas cards runs into 600 people – half of them unknown. For instance, about 1959 I received a Christmas card with a snap of a baby, signed 'Merry Christmas from Fred and Family', no address. Next year, the same baby one year older. 'Merry Christmas Fred and family'. Last year the card had six of his kids on – 'Merry Christmas Fred and family'. Every Christmas I want to send him a card but I don't know *who* or where he is, and there are a hundred like him. They sign themselves 'Jim and Mary' as though they were the only Jim and Mary in the world!

I believe it to be the work of one man, who is a sadist, and gloats at my discomfort; his name might even be Tom, Jim or Mary.

And when Christmas morning arrives, that voice says, 'Hurry up dear, the children are waiting to open the presents on the Christmas tree.' Dying of fatigue, you arrive in the front room full of smiling faces, you in that twenty-eight-year-old dressing-gown, with seven-year-old C & A slippers held on with string, unshaven. You force a smile that cripples your face. 'And here's one for Daddy.' You unwrap a plastic battery-operated fish with flashing eyes – Love from Jane. 'Do you like it, Daddy – I saved up and bought it myself,' she says. What can you say but, 'It's lovely, darling.' There's fifty slim cigars; you gave up smoking eight years ago. Two bottles of after-shave; you haven't shaved for five years. Your vagrant son and daughter arrive; more cigars, shaving lotion.

'Oh, lovely,' you say. A late Christmas card arrives: 'A Merry Christmas from the Manager and Staff of Coutts' – the writing is in red. As a vegetarian, something is bothering me – the Turkey dinner.

TURKEY: 'Aren't you ashamed?'

ME: 'Yes. I'm sorry I'm going to eat you.'

TURKEY: '*You're* sorry.'

ME: 'Be reasonable. All my children will be here. If I don't join the festivities they think of me as a Scrooge Father.'

TURKEY: '*I'm* a father. I left behind a wife and six kids!'

ME: 'Look, I promise this will be the *last* Christmas I'll eat you.'

TURKEY: 'Look, mate, this *is* my last Christmas –'

ME: 'You see, turkey, it's a dinner for a Christian occasion.'

TURKEY: 'Christian? I've seen you give bits to your bloody cat, is *he* Christian?'

ME: 'Well, I didn't want any to go to waste . . ?
TURKEY: 'All of me goes to waste, you know. On Boxing Day, when you're slobbed out in the lounge, I'm floating down a London sewer.'

The time of the coming of the God-child is used in most foul ways – there's a perv in Soho who dresses up as Father Christmas, then solicits citizens: 'Merry Christmas – want to see a Christmas porn-film?'

And the unending plague of carol singers. One arrived at 11.30 p.m. on 1 December. I opened the door to a crowd of smiling-faced teenagers with a candle lantern. I couldn't resist it, I gave them a £1. It was only after they'd left I realized they were all Jewish and were collecting for the NSPCC – they had a good sense of timing, that's all. The next choir – I'd teach 'em. It soon came, angel voices. 'What do you bloody well want?' I shouted before I saw they were nuns. You can't win.

Will my father in distant Australia ever forget Christmas 1968 . . . my mother was dangerously ill. A devout Catholic, she asked for Communion every morning. My father (a lapsed Catholic) was told that the priest would arrive at 5.30 a.m. (before first Mass) and my father was to meet him at the door with a lighted candle, a bowl of water, and a towel. Now the priest had never set eyes on my father. Dead on 5.30 the door bell rang. My father, dressed in his best suit, opened the door. It was the local dustman, who eyed my father holding a candle, a bowl of water and a towel, and said, 'Don't worry, Mr Milligan, I've had a few rough nights myself. I dropped by to get the Christmas box.' My father, a bit thrown, said, 'Hold these,' and passed the candle, etc. while he went in to get some loose change, at which moment the priest arrives, sees the dustman (who was absolutely filthy) and says, 'Ah, good morning, Captain – you know, I never knew you were a dustman.' It broke my immaculate father's heart.

My own unforgettable Christmas was in 1956. I was living with my wife and two children in a rented crumbling Victorian home at Highgate. I loved my family, and had built up the children's belief in Father Christmas and how he came down the chimney. Now I was disappointed as a child at having heard my parents say; 'Just missed Father Christmas, he's just gone back up the chimney.' Well, my children wouldn't be denied that.

As fortune would have it, the chimney-breast was huge and still had the inlets for chimney-sweeps' boys to climb up. I decided my children would actually *see* Father Christmas, *and* coming down the chimney. I hired a Father Christmas costume, plus beard and wig. So on Christmas Eve I got up inside the chimney, hammered two nails inside and hung the pillowcase of presents there. On Christmas night it seemed the children would never sleep. Finally at midnight all was clear. I donned the costume wig and beard and, using mortician's wax, changed the shape of my nose. Carefully I climbed up the chimney, while the wife aroused the children with, 'Wake up – Father Christmas is coming,' and led them into the drawing room.

Then disaster. I slipped and crashed with all the presents into the grate, bringing down a rain of soot; the nose bent, the beard came off. I got up in some pain to the children crying, 'Look Mummy, it's Daddy dressed up as Father Christmas.' Sod Christmas.

TRUST

Painful though it was,
    I cut my last winter rose for her.

She turned it inside out
    to see who the manufacturer was.

– from *Open Heart University*

JOURNEY

I think I am going out of my mind
The journey shouldn't take long
Once I get outside I'll be fine
I won't have to worry about thinking
I'll sit on a green bank of Sodium Amytal
　and watch my mind float away
Ah! my mind has a visitor!
A white-washed nurse
　a tray of NHS food
If only it would fit my mind
It's my stomach they're treating
　letting my head starve to death.

January 1981

– from *The Mirror Running*

from Depression and How to Survive It

I have got so low that I have asked to be hospitalized and for deep narcosis [sleep]. I cannot stand being awake. The pain is too much. I have had thoughts of suicide. I get depressed that I am old. Something has happened to me – this vital spark has stopped burning – I go to a dinner table now and I don't say a word, just sit there like a dodo. Normally I am the centre of attention, keep the conversation going – so that is depressing in itself. It's like another person taking over, very strange. The most important thing I say is 'good evening' and then I go quiet and other people will talk. It must be a bit unbalanced at the table with me just sitting there dead-silent.

I love my fellow-man but he's a two-faced bastard. I'm sorry for him principally because he can't change, he's reached the end of the line, and going to the moon smacks of 'I climbed the tree first, so there'. Aren't I in a grim mood.

He [Peter Sellers] didn't understand mental illness. He kept coming to the flat all the time and his phone had broken down and he wanted to use mine. And I couldn't stand the noise. I said, 'Tell him to stop it.' He said, 'Oh, tell him not to be silly.' So I got a potato knife from the kitchen. I had been wanting to get into hospital and I felt, 'Why won't they put me in hospital?' I thought, 'If I get a knife and try and kill him they'll put me somewhere' and I did. I went to attack him with a knife. I didn't mean to kill him, but I thought they will hospitalize me. They took me away to a hospital and put me under deep narcosis.

There are a number of things which go towards my depression. One of them is that I am completely ridden in nostalgia. I get sad when my children aren't children any more. I get depressed that I am old . . . A simple drive through London on my way to the BBC and I see all the sites where I used to be a young man, houses in which my friends used to live, the dance hall where I used to play in the band, the site where I used to work in a launderette, all these reminders non-stop, all the time. And it haunts me, the past, it haunts me. It preys on my mind. I turn on the radio and it suddenly plays a tune, say Glenn Miller's 'Moonlight Serenade', and straight-away it takes me back. Yes it's all gone, Glenn Miller is dead and the band is split up and I am not young any more. It has all come to an end. The nostalgia does that to me.

There is little in this terrible emptiness. I just want to go away, disappear, cover myself up until it goes away. It is like pain yet it is not a physical pain. I cannot describe it. It is like every fibre in your body is screaming for relief yet there is no relief. How can I describe it? I cannot really. I cannot, of course, escape because I have to keep working, which I just about do – though once or twice I have had to stop, had to hide away and wait till I could summon up the energy to keep going.

The last time I cried, really cried, I had gone to a site which used to be my garden and is now full of offices and flats and I went down to a stream and found some of my little girl's toys in the grass and I thought, 'Is this all there is? Is that it?' Yes that made me weep desperately.

I ploughed on without any smile on my face through these *Goon Shows*. I never laughed. I knew 'That's funny, that's a joke,' but I wouldn't laugh at it when I wrote it. I was very grim, very depressed.

TO A VICTORIAN DOLL IN A SHOP WINDOW IN KENSINGTON CHURCH STREET – PRICED £200

Beautiful, porcelain yester-doll,
    still wax fresh
Some little girl all ringlets
    and flounced lace
Loved you, cried on you, slept happy
    in your glass-eyed gaze.
Those long shed safe dreams
    have slipped their moorings.
That great red brick house
    spick-span polished proud
Now hard-boarded uni-rooms reeking
    curry, cabbage and cat's piss.
Polished doors lie Dulux deep,
    with red plastic handles.

So, dear home-less doll in the window
waiting the right price
they've turned you into a whore.

– from *Open Heart University*

BRAVE NEW WORLD

Twinkle Twinkle, little star
How I wonder what you are
Up above the sky so high
Like a diamond in the sky

Twinkle Twinkle, little star
I've just found out what you are
A lump of rusting rocket case
A rubbish tip – in outer space.

– from *The Bedside Milligan*

AGNUS DEI

Behold, behold,
The Lamb of God
As it skips and hops.
I know that soon
The Lamb of God
Will be the Lamb of Chops.

– from *The Mirror Running*

from My Wife and Cancer

In a letter I wrote to *The Sunday Times* I postulated that except in extreme circumstances I see no point in telling a person with terminal illness that they are going to die. *Doctor* magazine asked me to expand on this.

When my wife developed cancer, I of course came face to face with that part of medicine that deals with this incurable disease. It was disturbing to find, in some cases, the totally immature and almost immoral attitude *some* doctors adopted, and in some cases downright inhuman. Likewise the amateur-like biopsy. The latter case I will explain. When a tumour was removed from my wife's breast she phoned me with the joyous news 'Thank God, it's benign.' Half an hour later a second call from my wife, now in an agony of tears and reversed emotion: 'They have made a mistake, it's malignant.' It was unbelievable, especially so as, to avoid conveyor-belt medicine on the National Health, I had had this done privately. I was appalled at this outrageous, amateur, non-professional conduct. The culprit, of course, has gone free and he is possibly still doing it. The breast was removed.

Now comes the waiting. Alas, secondary cancer occurred within two years. This time in the lymphatic system, and so to the expected radiation treatment. After the treatment I had an interview with a view to the doctor explaining exactly the position of my wife's health. I found that the man was incapable of facing up to the consequences of cancer. He gave me an embarrassed, sloppy, mean-ingless talk. 'She will be all right, she will be able to live a perfectly useful life.' It was of course all rubbish. What he should have said was: 'From past evidence in treatment based upon many years during which statistics in carcinoma have emerged, for a woman of your wife's years, with her conditions, we give her chances of survival as slight.' This information is vital to the next of kin. Even I, a layman, knew secondary cancer was round about 95 per cent lethal. So here we have an entire case during which death was never mentioned, nor were those involved willing to give any clue or intimation appertaining to it. (Bear this in mind when we arrive at the 'You must tell them they're dying' brigade.)

So much for the immorality. Now to the cruelty. As the radiation (conventional medicine) had very little effect in regressing the disease, my wife, who had not wished to use medicine that had involved the use of animal experiments, sought help from a homeopathic healer and his wife. Of this form of medicine I have no knowledge, but in my own rationality I didn't think that it would work. However it gave my wife hope, as the homeopath told her that he had cured cancer using homeopathic medicine, one case being himself, though he stipulated at this stage there was no guarantee. With great integrity they applied treatment to my wife. It was quite obvious that these people were of the utmost dedication; likewise they didn't take any payment. However, I could see it was having no effect on the disease. I was stunned then, when in my presence the homeopath said: "The cancer is dead." Of course, in the light of my wife's death I know that statement to be rubbish. I point this particular incident out to show that people with the greatest integrity and intense dedication can go on a 'high' on their own chemistry, i.e. 'a self-induced trip'. Beware.

At this stage my wife did not know she was dying and showed every hope of recovery, therefore she was not in a state of mental anguish. She had a day and a night nurse, a devoted nanny, a bedside phone, a television, books, magazines, plenty of visitors. She received visits from our local Dr Thomas, who in every way was a splendid man with a good sense of humour, and he came regularly despite the fact that she was not taking conventional medicine. He still visited her on humanitarian grounds. My wife looked forward to his visits. At this point I was concerned as to what stage the cancer was at. I wrote to the doctor asking if he could pay a professional visit to her and give me an opinion. He declined to attend. I phoned him and pleaded with him to see her and give me a professional opinion. I was absolutely stunned when he said, in a very spoilt child voice: 'No, I won't see her. She refused my medicine.' I wrote him a letter and I said: 'Some men take the Hippocratic Oath and then hide behind it.' In this case justice was not only blind, but also deaf. And as for his 'medicine' – could somebody name me any 'medicine' that cures cancer?

There are situations in life when a person becomes helpless; this can be divided into mentally and physically, or both. Among homo sapiens very young children present a mental and physical helplessness and this offers an opportunity for applying cruelty, knowing there can be no physical retaliation. I quote the Spartans placing babies on the roof. Child sacrifice among the primitives. Ritual clitorectomy performed on young girls. Child labour in Victorian times. Indeed, once a helpless situation presents itself to the adult world it affords an opportunity for physical or emotional exploitation, a release of sadistic instincts. The removal of hearts from live war prisoners by Aztec priests has its contemporary parallels with cruel experimental operations on war prisoners by Nazi doctors (*not* always Nazis).

Likewise a person who is dying awakes these instincts, and I think it all matures with the 'Tell them they are dying' brigade. In my wife's case it was not an isolated incident. Of the ten nurses that attended her eight were of the 'tell them' brigade. The first nurse:

NURSE: 'Have you told her she is dying?'
SPIKE: 'No.'
NURSE: 'Don't you think you ought to?'

Let's analyse this occasion. The nurse is not a part of my family. She knows nothing about the family. She had no knowledge of my wife's personality, nor of the infra-structure between her and me. She has been employed as a nurse, not as a consultant psychiatrist. Her job is to administer medicine and keep a log of the patient. So what motivates her to ask such a question? Likewise the second nurse:

NURSE: 'Does your wife know?'
SPIKE: 'No. I don't want her to.'
NURSE: 'Isn't that selfish?'
SPIKE: 'What do you mean?'
NURSE: 'Well, you are keeping the knowledge to yourself?'
SPIKE: 'When did you last have sexual intercourse?'

NURSE: 'What?'

SPIKE: 'When did you last have sexual intercourse?'

NURSE: 'That's a private matter.'

SPIKE: 'I see – don't you think it selfish keeping the knowledge to yourself?'

The amazing part of these occasions is the salient fact that the nurse is new and after only, say, thirty minutes in the house, having given no great depth of thought to the matter, makes a statement the ramifications of which are enormous. My family doctor, Dr Thomas, agreed there was no point in informing my wife of her end. Likewise when the homeopathic medicine did not ease the pain, he gave her conventional medicine that did. One day there came a locum. My wife asked him: 'Am I dying?' and he said, 'Yes, you are.'

It shows he obviously had no deep liaison with Dr Thomas and didn't ask a question of paramount importance on entering the house: 'Am I to let your wife know?' This man changed my wife's demeanour to one of depression and a great gloom set in her. There were occasions when, if she saw her daughter, Jane, she cried when she left the room. So, the 'tell them they are dying' brigade eventually got through with devastating emotional results. I still believe that basically the reason is a sadistic one. I remember identical feelings during the war when somebody was killed near to me. I always felt better that it hadn't been me.

I hope doctors and nurses in the light of what I have written will think long and hard about terminal cases when they are tempted to break the news. There might be cases where one has to tell them. Otherwise ignorance is bliss.

[The friendship between Robert Graves and Spike Milligan was an extraordinary one. Two entirely different personalities, yet the friendship lasted from when they met in December 1964 until Robert's death at the age of ninety in 1985. They corresponded frequently.

In 1966 Robert Graves was giving a charity reading at the Mermaid Theatre to help Bernard Miles, its founder, to raise funds for restoration work. Robert wrote to Spike saying he was worried about the concert. Also: 'I am still without funds this twelve months.' Robert was anxious that Spike would appear with him. The concert was a huge success. Paddy Milligan, Spike's wife, sang light opera, Tomás Graves, Robert's son, played guitar and Spike and Robert ad-libbed and read their own poems.]

25 Wed.

Dear Robert,

Your letter arrived. I do hope you aren't worrying about June 19, you ask 'what can I do'. Answer: anything. Talk, read your own verse, sing any song you know or takes your fancy – read excerpts from your books, tell a joke, or if you wish just sit there drinking rose hip cordial '47. It's an evening of mutual enjoyment twix audience and us. Muggeridge, I'm still trying to get him. I'll let you know if I do, really, anybody who wants to appear, let them. Most certainly we won't rehearse, just turn up on the evening and see what happens! Paddy has had a baby girl. Jane Fionella! 10lb 6oz, both doing well. I did want a son but that was primitive ego at work.

You're broke! Everybody's broke. At least you're not taxed on your overdraft. I only need money to buy wine. Must go.

Love to all
from us all
Spike

~⁓

Orme Court
London W2

14 January 1970

My Dear Robert,

It was lovely to get a letter from you at last, especially in the New Year, which it helped to make all the brighter for me.

Sorry that you seem to be having some trouble with your innards. Nervous stomach would appear to be a safe label for a doctor to hang on it. I hope you have taken the precaution to have some X-rays taken.

You're right. Nothing can stop 'progress', especially the destruction of old buildings, that is, nothing except Spike Milligan. I am a pretty old building myself.

I have had some success in the past in Australia. I saved the cottage where Henry Kendall wrote some of his early verse, like 'Bellbirds' and 'Names Upon a Stone'. In England I had success in saving the gas lamps at Constitution Hill. I am giving up two months of my own work to try and organize the various scattered preservation societies into one consolidated unit, which will automatically support one of the members in an attempt to save a building; that is, if the Victorian Society want to save the Town House, they automatically have to support all the societies, like the Georgian Society, and the Holborn Society, etc., etc.

If you would trust me, may I use your name when trying to save something which I think worthwhile?

I was in Dublin last week, to see the Ireland–Springboks match, and was delighted to hear that the canal, which the government wanted to fill in, and build a road over, had been saved. It is now to be a public amenity for barging, sailing, and walks on each side of it. I did my share to save it, so I feel pretty good.

For God's sake, don't stop fighting Robert. Is there anything I can do to help you defend your one unspoilt cove in Majorca, you only have to say. At least seek comfort as a poet. They cannot destroy your skill. Though, most certainly sometimes, they destroy the inspiration.

I have before me, at the moment, the entire tape recording of our evening at the Mermaid Theatre. I have been waiting ever since for the company concerned to get it into a long-playing record, but the fire having gone out of the English personality, the tapes have lain fallow on someone's desk. I have decided to get it together myself, and I will let you know the results.

> *Love, Light and Peace, to all of you, from all of us*
> *Spike*

[Robert wrote to Spike: 'No, I never stop fighting. Congratulations on your saving the canal at least.']

Orme Court
London W2

8 January 1971

My Dear Robert,

To wish you a Happy New Year. Glad you are agin' R.T.Z. Individuals have to take up the sword against these twentieth-century vandals – they exist from local councils up to Company chairman level. I have had two successes. I've saved St Albans – a beautiful 1700–1901 House at Hampton on the Thames – and I think we've saved Wiltons Music Hall (1843) in Whitechapel. Also fighting for John Loudon's house (he was the man who laid out all the great garden squares in London (1790–1850)) – Fight! Fight! Fight!!! If you come to London – see me.

> *Love Light + Peace*
> *Spike*

◠

from Spike Milligan: The Family Album –
An Illustrated Autobiography

1968

16 April – my fiftieth birthday! This has got to stop! Paddy bought me an antique Victorian tie pin. The children bought me a vintage bottle of Château Margaux, 1947. I laid it down. It didn't get up. Years later I drank it at Christmas. It laid me down. I took all the children save Jane to the GPO Tower revolving restaurant. How did the waiters ever remember which table they were serving? Afterwards, we all went to see *Annie Get Your Gun*. What a wonderful score by Irving Berlin, and funny, too.

In May Peter Sellers, having married his dream girl, Britt Ekland, invited Prince Charles to lunch with the Goons at Peter's house. Secombe had a moustache and a goatee beard as he was appearing in *The Four Musketeers*. He was all four of them.

Alas, Peter's marriage didn't last long. I was present one day when she came back from a shopping trip. He eyed her with distaste. She threw a pair of golf cuff links down on his table. The atmosphere was terrible, so I said, 'I've got to leave now, my house is on fire,' and went.

Dick Lester, the bald film director whose films with the Beatles had been a roaring success, wanted me to appear in a film of *The Bed Sitting Room* in June. He wanted it rewritten by his favourite writer, John Woods, who I didn't think was in the same league of comedy writers that John Antrobus and I were. There were some silly, unexplainable jokes where Michael Horden said, 'I've forgotten to put any wooden planks up my back,' before getting into bed. The film won a peace award in Russia. I enjoyed doing it and some bits of the original play were left in, but the stage show had been hilarious and I was sad that the film wasn't. Still, it was a good try by Lester.

In July Laura was voted head girl of St Mary's Abbey School and won the school prize for Senior Art. She also won the drama award!

On Anzac Day in Woy Woy, the veterans paraded in a march past and Captain L. A. Milligan marched with them. After the parade, they all gathered at the Returned Soldiers' Club and proceeded to get blotto, except for the Captain who came home sober. What was wrong with the man?

In August I was back in Australia for my parents' fifty-fourth wedding anniversary. We had dinner in the kitchen. I had bought them a bottle of champagne (master of the obvious).

'Dad, have some,' I said.

'Well, the doctor said I shouldn't,' he said, 'but what the hell!'

So he took a sip, and suddenly his head slumped forward. Suppose the doctor was right? He began to recover a little, but he was still dopey. I took the back of his chair and dragged him to his bedroom. He managed to get his pyjamas on and get into bed.

In the morning he was still dopey. I phoned for an ambulance and Desmond and I got him into it. He kept saying how good it was to have 'two strong sons'. He would never come home again.

I visited him in Gosford Hospital. He was paralysed down his left side. They had rigged up a sling to enable him to try to lift himself up and down.

He spoke quite clearly and asked Mum to buy him some dates. He was worried about his bowel movements. I saw him every day for a week and then I had to get back home for some bloody job. Dad was moved to Newcastle Hospital bloody miles away. Desmond would drive the 120 miles with Mum on weekends. But Dad deteriorated.

My family knew little of this as they were all holidaying in Tobago. They travelled by a banana boat, MV *Golfito*.

1969

In February came a very sad day for me. I received a telegram from my mother:

Father very ill. He may go any time.
Love Mum and Des.

Next day, Dad was dead. At his funeral, a police car led the way. He had been a wonderful father. I shall miss him as long as I live.

It was years since I had written the *Goon Shows*, but it was only after they finished that I received a copy of the newsletter from the Goon Show Preservation Society. Evidently it had been going, as I had been, for years. The Patron was Prince Charles and they were extremely well organized with branches as far distant as Australia, Canada, America and South Africa. The Society is still going strong today. This year also saw the publication of another book, *The Bedside Milligan*. Apparently it didn't reach many bedsides. I had quite a few by my bedside, about a hundred, which I sold for a new bed.

Laura went to her first ball this winter and, therefore, had to have her first ball gown. She looked so grown up!

SPRING SONG, MARCH 18TH 1972

Spring came haunting my garden today –
A song of cold flowers was on the grass.
Tho' I could not see it
I knew the air was coloured
And new songs were
    in the old black bird's throat.
The ground trembled at the thought
    of what was to come!
It was not my garden today,
    it belonged to *itself*.
At the dawn smell of it –
    my children fled the house
And went living in that primitive dimension
    that only they and gardens understand.

My dog too lost his mind
And ran in circle after canine circle
Trying to catch himself –
And do you know what? – He *did*!
It was *that* kind of a day.

> Written in China to
> avoid Income Tax

– from *Small Dreams of a Scorpion*

‿

from Spike Milligan: The Family Album –
An Illustrated Autobiography

1974

I was commissioned by *The Times* to cover a game of backgammon on board the *Queen Mary* sailing to New York and back. My article was entitled 'There and Backgammon'. During the trip I swam in the heated swimming pool and relaxed, so much so that when a young woman came into my cabin and said, 'Would you like a quickie?' I was too stunned to say yes!

In July I did a one-man show, one-man that is, except for the other man, a South African singer called Jeremy Taylor. He sang and played the guitar like a maestro. I liked to end the show with 'San Francisco':

I left my heart in San Francisco
I left my knees back in Peru
I left my little wooden leg
Hanging on a peg

I left my lungs in Dublin Zoo
With you
I left my teeth on Table Mountain
High on a hill they smile at me
When I go back to San Francisco
There won't be much for them to see.

I returned to Australia to finish another volume of War Memoirs – the fourth: *Mussolini, His Part in My Downfall*. Mum looked after me well. She bought beautiful organic vegetables with such variety (Australia – land of plenty) and one evening made a marvellous curry. One evening? She had spent all day on it. We had a civilized dinner with Desmond, sitting on the verandah by oil lamp, talking of Mum and Dad's early days. They had enjoyed such a good lifestyle in India. The disappointments of England could be written off. Here in Australia they had a very happy retirement. I recalled Leo's constant efforts to get money for nothing. He once wrote to his Masonic Lodge Headquarters saying he was down on his luck and could they give him some 'assistance'. Eventually, a letter arrived saying that a member of Sydney Lodge would visit him to establish his circumstances. No date was given. The member arrived on Leo's birthday, for which I had sent him a box of Havana cigars and a case of half a dozen bottles of Heidsieck Dry Monopole Champagne. The Masonic visitor came to see the 'impoverished' Leo sitting on the verandah smoking a cigar and drinking champagne!

The previous year I had written *Badjelly The Witch*. I wrote it longhand in a very good, painstaking, calligraphic style to encourage youngsters to learn how to write. The book did very well and, astoundingly, in far off New Zealand we had several requests to turn it into a school play.

New Zealand was where I was bound next, flying from Sydney to Wellington, where I stayed with Harry Edgington. I took my cornet with me and we relived those years when we were the darlings of Bexhill. We weren't as good as we had been then, but just as enthusiastic.

Back in England there was a property boom. When I arrived

home in September, half the houses in Holden Road had been sold at a huge profit. David White was a speculator who was desperate for me to sell 127. I had bought it for £3,500 and was being offered £30,000 for it. I didn't want to sell. It was the first home I had ever owned and I knew that, if I sold, the house would be pulled down for redevelopment. One day David drove me to Hadley Wood and he pointed to a beautiful Victorian manor. He said, 'I'll give you this for yours.' I couldn't resist it. We moved from 127, sadly, late in September. It broke my heart but what we were getting was a sumptuous property – Monkenhurst. I spent £10,000 restoring it. In the drawing room was a marvellous Adam fireplace and the house was eventually voted one of the beautiful private dwellings of London by the Institute of Architects.

I was proud to live in such a wonderful building. Christmas in Monkenhurst was a fabulous affair. Our Christmas tree was the biggest ever. The ceilings in Monkenhurst were very high, so we had a tree to fit. How do trees have fits?

Right on cue, it snowed and we had a happy Christmas week. Most of my presents were bottles of wine. Paddy bought me a dozen bottles of Orvieto Abbrocado. This is one of my favourites, a wine which I first discovered in Italy during the war. We were in a gun position at Lauro. I was an OP signaller and we were supporting the Hampshire Regiment who were to attack the village of Orvieto. At dawn they took the objective, a typical village with a square and a fountain in the centre. Then we were subjected to a storm of German artillery. We took shelter in the cellars around the square. In these cellars were barrels of wine. We soon filled our water bottles. In fact, we emptied them and refilled them several times. When the shelling ended, the Hampshires lolled about the square, me amongst them. A Jeep arrived with a Colonel Simpson, their commanding officer. He went up to a pissed sergeant, kicked him in the boot.

'You!' he said. 'Do you know who I am?'

The sergeant turned to his buddy and said, 'There's a cunt here doesn't know who he is!'

The wine was Orvieto Abbrocado and now, thirty years later, I had a dozen bottles to drink. I drank a bottle of it with Christmas lunch. Despite everything, over the Christmas period I became very sad. Don't ask me why. Perhaps it was the memory of my own childhood Christmases.

There were certainly worse Christmases ahead. In the very near future Paddy was to develop breast cancer. Eventually she had the breast removed and wore a mould. She was given the all-clear in 1977 but the cancer reappeared in her spine and upper neck. She went to see a naturopath who had 'cured his own cancer'. Amongst other things, he said we must remove all vapour-producing medicines in the house – Vick's, etc. Our usual doctor, Dr Thurman, visited her from time to time to try to persuade her to take a normal anti-cancer treatment but she refused, and gradually she declined. I never told Jane that Paddy was going to die until the day before it happened.

I said, 'Darling, Mummy's dying.'

She said, 'No, she'll be better by Christmas.'

I said, 'No, darling.'

She said, 'But I'm only eleven!'

Oh, God, the pain.

Jane has grown up the double of her mother. She has taken to the stage, sings, dances, plays keyboards and saxophone as well as classical flute. How proud her mother would have been of her.

1975

In February I was taken to Rhodesia to do a commercial for the tourist industry. After I had finished it, I had enough money to fly Paddy, Jane, Laura, Sile, Sean and the nanny out for a tour of the wild places. We travelled overland by Jeep to the Wankie Game Lodge. Venturing forth from the camp early every morning, we went in search of animals. Another wonderful holiday.

For Jane's ninth birthday, there was a big party at Monkenhurst. What a mad house. All her friends were there wearing 'zany' make-up. I had dressed up as Hitler. There was a knock on the front door.

I opened it. It was a policeman. 'Excuse me, sir. There's a car parked in the main road unattended.' I told him I had no knowledge of it. 'Oh, sorry to have bothered you, sir. Good night.' He was totally unmoved by my appearance.

Here the story must draw to a close. Having reached the age of fifty-seven and travelled the world from India and Burma to England, Africa and Australia, I had a great deal to look back on, a great many happy memories and a great deal of sadness. There was a great deal of both still to come . . .

MY DAUGHTER'S HORSE

My daughter has a horse in her head
He gallops thru' fantasies in her mind
She calls him Fury
I can see him thru' her eyes
She rides him thru' her spirit grasses
At night she stables him in her dreams.
He must be beautiful
Her face is alight when she sees him
She feeds him on her soul
He becomes what colour she wishes.
I thought there was no end to him
Until – one day she met
Fred – the butcher's boy.

– from *The Mirror Running*

GROWING UP II

Is that all there is? Goodbye!
After a million hellos
After all those bird-blessed good-mornings,
After the bubbling bathtime laughter,
After so many soul-searching Santa Claus,
After a million wild walks on the moors,
After the swing-swung laughing summers,
After the tear-drenched kiss-better bumped head,
After the new wear-them-in-bed red shoes,
After a tumult of timeless teddy bears,
After a delirium of dolls in prams,
After a rainbow of ice-creams,
After daddy I love you all the world
Goodbye?

17 March 1985

—From *The Mirror Running*

THE BUTTERFLY

This evening in the twilight's gloom
A butterfly flew in my room
Oh what beauty, oh what grace
Who needs visitors from out of space?

Bedroom
Monkenhurst
24 July 1984

—from *The Mirror Running*

6

Final Curtain

No one ever cured me, they just went away like the mist.

– Spike Milligan

The year 1998 saw quite a deterioration in Spike's health but he still wanted to work. His 'One Man Show' by this time had been considerably reduced. It now consisted of reading his poetry, recalling anecdotes, reminiscences and questions from the audience.
On Sunday 20 December he appeared at the London Palladium to a sell-out. That should have been his last performance, as his energy levels were diminished. He performed in Hull and Chichester after that but it was clear to me he could no longer sustain the hour on stage and there were a lot of complaints from the audience.

Throughout his life Spike had collected family photographs dating from 1860 onwards. In 1999 he arranged them in five very large leather-bound albums. In his distinctive calligraphic handwriting he meticulously noted dates, times and places. From this, he had the idea for a book, *An Illustrated Autobiography*, which was published in this year, but work was beginning to be a struggle for him. He found the travelling from Rye to his office in London, even though he had a driver, too arduous. So we agreed I would do the travelling. I went to his home each week and it seemed to work for a while.

In 2000 his last novel was published, *The Murphy*. Certainly not his best work. I encouraged him to write, but it was clear I would never submit any of his future writing to his publisher. The spark had gone.

In 1994, he received a Lifetime Achievement Award at the British Comedy Awards, and in 2001 he received an honorary KBE.

26 October 2001 was Harry Secombe's memorial service in Westminster Abbey. He was too ill to attend. Michael Parkinson read out Spike's last tribute to his friend: 'Harry was the sweetness of Wales.'

26 February 2002: the dynamo went out of my life . . .

from Goodbye Soldier

A Joke Mortician's Shop

ME: I've come to bury a joke.
MORTICIAN: I'm sorry, sir, the graveyard is full. It's been a good year.
ME: What do you suggest?
MORTICIAN: Cremation, sir. You can have the ashes of your favourite joke in an urn. In moments of depression, you can take the lid off and have a good laugh.

If I die in War
You remember me
If I live in Peace
You don't.

– from *Small Dreams of a Scorpion*

I walked along some forgotten shore.
Coming the other way
                a smiling boy.
It was me.
'Who are you old man?' he said
I dare not tell him all I could say was
'Go back!'

Madrid
14 September 1973

– from *Open Heart University*

EASTER 1916

The lights had gone out!
        The sun cannot set!
        The green heart is suppurating!
Heroes' souls are on the English rack
        and the harp's strings are muted.

In the fusillade
        a child is born in blood,
        his heritage will be glory.

Goodnight Padraic Pearse
        and your friends.

February 1975

– from *Open Heart University*

FOR LUCY GATES

Carry me mother – carry me
To where the Romans died,
Take me to the cavern mouth
Where Ariadne cried,
Show me Agamemnon
  and his golden face,
Then show me all the dust of lives
  that lived and left no trace.
Show me, show me Mrs Jones
  who lived in Deptford Town,
  there falling from the sky at night
  the wrath that put her down.
The nameless dustman
  (was it Fred?)
Who found the dying child
  and in the flix-twix
Life and Styx
She looked at him and smiled.
So carry carry carry her
To where the forgotten lie
And on the stones
Above her bones
Carve out the one word
Why.

Monkenhurst
17 March 1982

– From *The Mirror Running*

from Depression and How to Survive It

Isn't it funny, I couldn't imagine her dying. There seemed a permanency, and the shock now of realizing that she's dead is having a depressing effect. I didn't say goodbye to her before she died. I couldn't bear saying, 'Goodbye for ever, Mum' – she was in hospital in a bed and I said, 'I'm going now, Mum, bye bye,' and she said, 'Bye bye, son' and that was it. I feel like that Dylan Thomas poem – 'Do not go gentle into this good night. Rage, rage against the dying of the light.' She died about ten days after I got back to Britain.

How many good-byes?
When I was born
My Mother took me from hospital
The nurses said good-bye
That was my first one
I was too young to hear it
One day I will die
Someone will say good-bye
And I still won't hear it

Monkenhurst
April 28 1987 0100 hrs

How many meals
   did you cook for me mum
No computer can tell me.
You started feeding me
   the day I was born

I can't remember
    when you stopped
But I miss it
    no food has ever tasted the same

January 1990 0200 a.m.
Mum died July 3 1990

TO MY FATHER

Why did you go Dad?
So much left undone.
So much unsaid
You never finished the story.
There was so much wine left
Did you order too much
Or did we drink too little?
Mum had put fresh sheets on the bed.
So why did you go
    in the middle of the song?
The tune was so good
We wanted to hear the end
Why did you go?
There was so much love
The fridge was full of it
If you were coming back
Why did you send your suit to the cleaners?
You know tonight there was *Gunsmoke* on telly
Tomorrow we were going to walk up Blackwall mountain
Why did you go
And what about Mesopotamia
What did happen at the battle of Chaiba.
I've rearranged the muskets in the gun room
So why *did* you go.
We are waiting – waiting.

MY MOTHER

So my mother, my mother
          laid to rest
The fairy dances fade
          but cannot end
The dolls stand
          serious faced
In your empty room
          cast glass eyes
At the Burmese lacquer
I left the piano lid open
So you can play for dad
The Love Lyrics
          The Cubanola Glide
The officers mess glasses
          from Belgium
Have drunk their last
          Regimental toast
You left the house full
          of everything
mostly love.
Good-bye for a while mum.
Remember Rangoon mum
the concerts and the Brigade dance
you made your own dress
          White organdie

And Poona.
     You must have loved Poona
The Governors' Ball
– you singing with the band.
How wonderful it must have been

Heidsiecks Monopole!
    all your life.
I can't say how much
    I love you.
The language wasn't invented
I rang Woy Woy 413662 today
You didn't answer
You must have been out.

> July 8 1990
> G.M.T. 9.30 am

[Marty was a great script-writer and a very funny actor. One of Spike's favourite people. Spike thought he was brilliant. They were great friends. When Marty died Spike wrote a letter to his widow Lauretta. This is an extract: 'He wasn't just a funny man, he was a bloody nice fellow. If life is a game of cards, somebody is cheating.']

Marty Feldman
1600 North Highland Avenue
Hollywood
California 90028

You swine Feldman all these months I've been laying wreaths on a grave in Arlington Cemetery and all the while you weren't there. When you are cremated I am going to package your ashes and sell them as Ready Brek. Will phone you soon.

  Love
    Spike

⌒

Wanker Productions
1600 North Highland Avenue
Hollywood
California 90028

22 July 1981

Dear Spike,

Its been almost a year since I got your very kind letter; just after I went to meet my Maker and He didn't show up.

And I've been meaning to say thank you, but you know how it is and that's how it was and thank you now.

Oddly, I miss you more than England. Perhaps not oddly. After all you're there and most of England seems to be here.

So here I am, full of boozy gush and wishing I could split a bottle or three of cheap plonk with you.

I hear, from time to time, what and how you're doing, and it seems that you're surviving and working and getting laid, so there doesn't seem to be much more to ask does there?

I'm back to what passes for normal around here. Scribbling and acting and as you recommended, reading poems to Lauretta by candlelight – So my status is back to quo and I'm as happy as a Jew can <u>ever</u> be.

Please write, if you have the time, and if you should be looting in Harrod's could you pick up an onyx coffee table for me?

When I <u>do</u> die, I shall ask to be cremated and request that you snort my ashes. Till soon . . .

Fond smiles and manly embraces
Marty Feldman

(Earthman – Naturalized)

~

ODE TO MY MOTHER

If I should die,
Think only this of me,
The swine left owing us
Six pounds eighty p.

– from *Unspun Socks from a Chicken's Laundry*

~

9 Orme Court
Bayswater
London W2 4RL

17 January 1996

Fax to: The Editor
The Times

Dear Sir,

I saw one of your articles headed 'Not enough room for the dead'.
Well let me say if the population goes on swelling there won't be
enough room for the living.

   Yours

   Spike Milligan
   Outraged of Tonbridge

DEATH WISH

Bury me anywhere,
Somewhere near a tree
Some place where a horse will graze
And gallop over me.
Bury me
Somewhere near a stream,
When she floods her banks
I'll give her thanks
For reaching out to me.
So bury me – bury me
In my childhood scene;
But please –
don't burn me
In Golders Green.

Italy 1944

– from *Small Dreams of a Scorpion*

Spike, you got your wish.